What If I Had Taken The Roads Not Traveled

One Woman's Journey of Self Discovery

By
Lillian J. Hunter

Value-Publishing, Inc.
700 Lavaca
Suite 1400
Austin, TX 78701

Email: info@lillianjhunter.com

Manufactured in the United States of America

ISBN 978-0-9884729-1-4

Summary

Regrets. Disappointments. Upon the demise of her marriage, she can no longer ignore the inner voice that chastises her for the many mistakes she has made that have brought her to this unhappy place. She is shadowed by a cloud of dissatisfaction, disappointment and outright unhappiness. She has missed opportunities. She has made bad choices and decisions. She feels like a failure. As she looks around everyone seems to be happier and/or more successful than she is. She is haunted by the "What ifs" of her life and the nagging feeling that she would be happier, more successful, more satisfied if she had only taken a different path somewhere along the way. She desperately wants to enjoy where she is in her life at this moment. So she begins a painful journey down the roads she has traveled in the hope she can "exorcise" the "what ifs" that rob her of her peace of mind.

Her life has been a winding and twisting path of triumph and despair. She has been: married, divorced, widowed, a step parent, financially broke, a single parent to four children, a full time caregiver to a terminally ill husband, a victim of spousal abuse, a parent to two adolescents addicted to alcohol and drugs and a seeker of spirituality. She relives the seminal events of her life searching for some insights, observations and/or "wisdom" she can glean from those experiences. Ultimately she is searching for peace and a good road map for the remainder of her journey. She humbly offers her experiences, insights and perhaps wisdom to the reader in hopes it will spark a "conversation" about her life and start her on her own journey.

The story is narrative non-fiction. It can be read as a whole in the order presented or the chapters or any portions thereof can be read in whatever order interests the reader. May you find serenity and fulfillment at the end of your journey!

Lillian J. Hunter

Table of Contents

Chapter One

"What If?"

I looked across the table over the heads of the two lawyers. Our eyes met and I felt a huge surge of love flowing in both directions and then a wave of despair rolled over me. Wasn't it only yesterday – 8 years ago is like yesterday when you are in your fifties – when we looked across at each other in a very different setting with a huge surge of love. I had just seen our wedding photos. He had introduced them into evidence at the trial. I did not want to cry here in front of him, the judge and the lawyers. It was difficult to hold back the tears as my lawyer began to ask me the questions that are a prerequisite to the granting of a divorce.

The love was still there and at that moment it felt as strong as it had on our wedding day. Why hadn't we – he and I – been able to build on that powerful feeling of love to create a fulfilling and lasting relationship? I wanted to shout to the judge – stop we still love each other – we could still make a go of it. It had to be a mistake if that feeling could last through all of the acrimony of the last two years. What if we just changed a few things – then it would work. I forgot. We, or at least I, had already tried all of those things. Then the reality set in. It was over. The feeling of despair swept over me like the force of a powerful wind. I felt like I swayed from the power of that force. I had to sit down for a moment.

He had already moved onto another relationship. It was eerily similar to what we had shared – at least outwardly. When I heard this I felt a huge emptiness and I was angry with myself for having that feeling. As if feelings can be bad! But I was raised on that. By this time I understood that we can't control feelings only our response to them. But of course that went out of my head in the power of the moment. He was creep, a cad. He had used me. How could I be stupid enough to still have feelings for him? Love – in whatever way shape or form is such a mystery.

I wanted to reconnect even if just for a few moments after the judge announced that we were divorced. We had actually connected briefly a little earlier. I was sitting in a small conference room with my lawyer waiting for the trial to begin. The door opened. "Can I talk to you alone?" he asked but it was his eyes that pleaded with me to let him in. This was probably just another con or so I thought. I hadn't seen him or spoken to him in over 6 months. Any contact was too acrimonious so I stopped communicating. I finally accepted that this marriage would never end in even a remotely amicable fashion. So I was very surprised when he poked his head in the door. I signaled to my lawyer that it was OK. She left the room reluctantly.

His voice and demeanor were so soft and loving that I couldn't help responding. It was such a complete contrast to the anger and animosity of our communications of the past two years. He started talking to me about his new life and business. I wondered to myself why I was listening. What did I care about his new life and why would he think I would care? Still I listened. I found myself listening intently, asking questions, caring if he was happy. He confided in me. But I was better now at distinguishing between his lies and his truth. I needed to engage my brain to remind me that no matter how I felt at this moment – this relationship was over – it was not good for me even though he was right now acting like the person I had fallen in love with. He was at his best but, as in the past, circumstances would call up the worst in him. That is not to say that was not true for me as well but only that this is my story to tell, not his.

Stress was his Achilles heel. Stress brought out the worst in his personality as, I think, it does everyone. Just like pain some people have a lower tolerance to stress. For him stress was created by anything that didn't go his way. He couldn't adapt. That forced me to unconsciously work to create a world for him where everything went his way. It was exhausting and I lost myself in the process. It seems the more I compromised and the harder I tried the less he tried. Could I have forced him to compromise more by being more unyielding myself or would it just have sped up the inevitable demise of the relationship? The seeds of the end were planted at the very beginning. Here we were at the legal end. I so wanted it to be the emotional end as well.

How did I contribute to the demise of the relationship? Did I just make a lousy choice at the beginning and nothing I did or said would have changed the eventual outcome? Or did I make choices along the way that shaped the nature of the relationship and led us to this bitter end? Is it a little of both?

After three marriages and four children you would think I would have something sorted out in the relationship department. I don't. I am a total failure. My Mother never misses an opportunity to remind me that I have been married three times. Her first question after I attended my 25th high school reunion was, "Did you tell them you have been married three times?" I wanted to say, "No but at the next reunion why don't I wear a T shirt that has "I HAVE BEEN MARRIED THREE TIMES" emblazoned on it." You know a more modern version of what Hester Prynne wore.

I held on too long to this marriage because I didn't want to face another failure. Then I realized I was on the downward slope of my life and I started asking myself how many unhappy years are enough or too much? I was acutely aware that I don't know how many I may have left. I didn't want to squander them. I didn't have time to waste. So I filed for the divorce.

He seemed anxious to return to his new relationship and busy life. The new life that was so eerily similar to the life we had shared. I suspect that helped him bury the pain if he felt any. We sat and talked in that small conference room adjacent to the court room in that intimate way married people can and do. It amazed me how easily we slipped back into that mode. He asked about my children. I asked about his. We asked about each other's parents. We had a history of experiences and connections that was unique to the two of us. We relived that connection if only for those few moments. I knew that a part of him was trying to tap into that connection in order to get a good deal in the divorce but it still felt good to connect again.

After a few moments we had nothing else to say to each other. He said what he really came to say – a dollar amount he wanted from me to settle the matter. I nodded and said, "Let me talk to my lawyer." He tried to get me to agree without her but I resisted. He silently left the room. As I waited for my lawyer to return I was struck by the irony of it all. The most intimate relationship in the world was boiling down to a business decision about money.

"Is the marriage irrevocably broken?" my lawyer asked me as I testified from the witness box. I couldn't concentrate on the questions my lawyer was asking me. I was overwhelmed by a sense of failure and emptiness. "Oh God I am in my 50s and I still can't get anything right! I am so tired of it all!" I said to myself. I wanted to scream that this is too painful to bear and that I don't deserve this. Instead I said, "Can you repeat the question please?"

I was struck by the all too familiar realization that we are so very much alone in our times of trouble and with our sorrows. Don't we desperately seek connections as a barrier against the unbearable pain of isolation, loneliness and tragedy? We delude ourselves into thinking those connections will take the pain away. We frantically seek connections with spouses – our soul mates, our children, our friends. The pain may be eased for a time by those connections because the pain is shared but no one can know our pain and so we are still ultimately alone. It is part of the human condition. I believed the person looking at me across the table would be part of my arsenal of pain relievers. Instead he became a source of the pain.

As I testified he continued to look at me with that same loving look he had in the conference room. I was frantically searching for some way to get through this time on the witness stand with some dignity. Tears were welling up in my eyes. "STOP," I wanted to shout. We can make it work. We still love each other. Didn't our meeting in the small conference room prove that?

In an effort to cope, I visualized myself turning around and staring full on into a black hole - the emptiness and loneliness of the broken connection – and saying "I am not afraid. I will get through this." That helped. I have learned that the fear of an event is often much worse than the actual event itself.

"Counsel if you present me with the divorce decree tomorrow I will sign it," the judge pronounced. "You are excused," he said to me in the witness box. The pronouncement felt like an execution – at least of the relationship. We gathered up our papers and left the courtroom. The bailiff locked the courtroom door behind us. The closing of the door and the clicking of the lock resonated with me. It was like the door to our relationship was forever closed and locked but unfortunately not forgotten.

He ran ahead and hurriedly got into the elevator alone. He had many important things to get back to or at least that is the impression he wanted to give me. I walked more slowly discussing and dissecting what had happened that day with my lawyer from a legal standpoint. This settlement had come as a complete surprise to both of us. The halls, along with my soul, echoed with emptiness as the bailiffs shooed away the last few occupants of the building. I was alone when I left the courthouse. This was it. This was the end to a beautiful beginning which had been so full of promise and love that even after all the intense animosity of the past years my composure was shattered thinking of it. I kept telling myself how stupid I was to feel this way but that didn't help me regain my composure or feel less pain. Change is so much our enemy and so much our friend.

He and I had met in the most glamorous of ways. We were both on the same tour of Italy. Is there any place that evokes more of an image of romance than Italy? I was a widow. He was separated with a divorce pending. I was so lonely but then I think I have always been lonely. Accepting that loneliness is a part of the human condition has made me less susceptible to false antidotes.

It was the first night of the tour and we were having one of those obnoxious get acquainted dinners. I wanted to skip it but my Sister, with whom I was traveling, insisted we attend. My Sister and I arrived a little bit late as we were out doing some sightseeing on our own. As we walked down the stairs into the dining room my Sister spied an open table. My Sister nodded to me that we should sit there. He was seated there with his daughter. I can remember that evening – more than 10 years ago- so clearly. Memories are something over which we have no control. So many things I want to remember I can't. So many things I want to forget, like this meeting, I can't. I remember thinking that he was grumpy. The conversation was uneventful and we parted for the evening.

For some reason he struck a nerve with me. I should have known better. Didn't I tell friends when we discussed relationships that if you felt an overpowering attraction for someone you should run the other way? We sat next to each other on the tour bus. We stood together listening to lectures about art and history in magnificent churches and museums. The attraction was palpable. We were always close enough to touch but resisting the urge. Italy is such a romantic country and it prodded and coaxed us into a full blown romance! We sat on a bench, in front of St. Mark's Cathedral, under the magnificent night sky of Venice and kissed. This was a perfect beginning or so I thought.

I was supposed to be on a different tour but due to a mix up at the travel agency I ended up on his tour. We liked the same things. He had the same dream for his future as I did. He was attentive, polite, and solicitous. I remember thinking that a relationship would be easier this time because we were older and more mature. We each knew who we were and what we wanted. We had resolved a lot of our emotional issues we had when we were younger. After all fate had brought us together – hadn't it? We would never have met if I had been on the other tour.

Maybe "fate" does bring people together. What is fate anyway? It is just another term for God or some other spiritual being? When we use that term are we subconsciously ascribing to the theory that God, some spiritual being or some power greater than us has a plan for our life? Do we use it as a way to escape the difficult discussion and decisions regarding the existence of and scope of the power of God, spiritual beings or other forces? Do we simply use it as a way to avoid personal responsibility for our decisions especially when our decisions are failures? Maybe there are forces at work that cause us to be attracted to one person rather than another. I think there are. The problem may be in how we act on or interpret those feelings of attraction. Do certain relationships offer certain lessons and once the lesson is learned the relationship is dissolved. Are we on a journey to constantly grow, learn, mature and connect? Can the outcome of our journey or our fate be changed by the choices we make? Or is there really no rhyme or reason to all of this? Have we just invented God, fate, spiritual beings as a way to deal with the uncertainties and at times chaos of life?

I have been haunted by a nagging compulsion to make sense of my life for the last several years. It became even more intense upon the demise of this, my last marriage. Something is pushing me down this path. I feel agitated every time I put this "project" on hold. I will have no peace until I do. It seems like a silly and useless thing to do. The past can't be changed. I can't change myself much at my age. My life shaping decisions were made long ago when I had absolutely no idea what I was doing. I have passed more than the halfway mark in my life. What is the point? I don't have too many places to go in the future. What could the future possibly have in store for me at this time in my life? Some irrational force is pushing me to sift through my life.

Venice, Rome, Florence, Piso, Orvieto – great food, great sights, great history, great wine, great company, exhilarating romance. It seems to me that that our obsession with a romantic relationship increases in direct proportion to our lack of connectedness and fulfillment in other areas of our life. Is there a better place to fall in love than Italy?   Romance does not always have to lead to commitment except for me. I hadn't learned as much as I thought I guess. I was raised that love and sex could not be separated from commitment. This new generation seems to be at the other end of the spectrum – sex without love or commitment. As a therapist said to me, "You don't have to marry everyone you have sex with." If only I could have internalized that. But perhaps my Sister put it best when she so crudely said, about the trip to Italy, "I thought you just wanted to get laid. You didn't have to turn it into something more".

If only I had listened to my Sisters vulgar words of wisdom. What if I had taken her advice? What would my life look like now? Would I be happier or more content? Did I get anything positive out of my last marriage or was it all just one big terrible mistake? What if I read too much into my chance encounter with Warren? What if "Fate" really had other choices in mind for me other than the one I took?

After fourteen short days it was back to the grinding routine of everyday life for me but now with wonderful memories of romance and Italy. I returned to two teenagers with serious emotional and behavioral issues over the loss of their father, a toddler who would never know his father, a dependable eldest child who was going away to college, a career put on hold – maybe permanently as a result of having been the primary caregiver for a terminally ill spouse, enduring and maybe unending grief over the loss of a much loved husband and nightmares of the ravaging of the body, mind and soul of my husband by a brutal, vicious disease.

The loss of my husband created an aching loneliness and vast emptiness – a black hole, as what I image a black hole in space is, based on the little science I know. It was an inky darkness totally devoid of any light. The loneliness that had been part of my formative childhood years grew to infinite proportions with my husband's death. It was suffocating and omnipresent. This love that blossomed in Italy was to be a light in that black hole. In fact it was going to flood that black hole with light. We often seek relationships, especially marriages, as a bulwark against loneliness. The loneliest I have ever been was in an unhappy marriage.

I had given Warren my phone number before we parted in Italy. I didn't hear from him when I returned home. We were living in different states at the time. I knew he stayed to travel longer in Europe so I was patient – somewhat. Patience in relationships is not one of my virtues. This waiting probably fueled that adolescent feeling that we were meant to be together because we had such chemistry. Surely "Fate" had placed us on the same bus tour and at the same table. About two weeks after my return he called to say he had lost my phone number. A year or so later we married and moved to California. Beautiful California beckoned with the promise of a new life, love and career. The allure was intoxicating. We moved into a beautiful new home. He started a new business.

It all disappeared as magically as it appeared. I don't believe the death of a romance takes longer than the birth of one but certainly the recognition that it has died does. Romance is such a wonderful fantasy and fairytale. For some people it turns into real love or at least a solid relationship. It seems in emotionally unhealthy people that the unhealthy parts are attracted to each other like magnets. It seems like some people just get lucky and their unhealthy parts match up so well. (Lucky if your goal is an enduring relationship not emotional health). I have never been so lucky.

"Everyone has their issues or problems don't they? None of us are perfect. The minute things don't go our way we can't walk away can we?" I would say to myself on a regular basis. I understood the hard times of a relationship but I didn't understand what the "good" times should feel like. I knew romance would fade but what would replace it? My childhood experience observing my parents was of no use. My previous relationships were more about hard times than good times. I had the skills to navigate the hard times but not the good times. What does a good relationship look like for me? Sadly I still have no idea. Is it one of those things you know only when it happens? In that case I may never know because with three strikes I am out.

I called him on his cell phone after I left the courthouse. He answered. We talked more about his life. He talked of including me in his new life with an offer to play some part in one of his new business ventures. I think we both knew that would never happen but we discussed it anyway. We talked for 30 minutes or so and I hung up only when I reached my friend's house where I was to have dinner. He called me back about an hour later while I was still at my friend's house. I didn't answer the phone. My friends wouldn't understand. He didn't leave a message.

My friends wanted to go out and celebrate the granting of the divorce. I couldn't stop crying. You see he and I had loved each other very much once at least I thought we did. We were happy together for a number of years. In spite of the ordeal of the last few years I was sad over the loss of that love.

I am not bitter. I think you can only be bitter if you blame someone other than yourself for a situation. I have acquired at least enough maturity and experience to realize that I am responsible for the present situation. I made the choices that brought me here. I alone am to blame, not him. He could only be who he is. I could not expect him to be otherwise. Sure he could have changed if he wanted to but he didn't want to. His number one priority was getting what he wanted and I was a means to that end. When I stopped serving that purpose the relationship was over.

"Maybe we can celebrate another day" I said to my friends. I stayed home that evening and cried. There seems to be something so wrong about celebrating the end of a beautiful beginning. I couldn't do that. I haven't spoken to for heard from Warren since the day the divorce was granted. I am thankful for that.

I am not writing this to escape any responsibility for the demise or failure of that relationship. In fact the opposite is true. I am not looking to play the blame game that our society so obsesses over. I want to find my mistakes. At times my recounting of the events of my life it may seem I am being unreasonably hard on the people in my life. I don't intend to portray them in a bad light. Maybe it is just that I can see them more clearly than I see myself. It is so very difficult if not impossible to see ourselves as others see us. It is too scary! I can see little bits and pieces of myself but not the whole picture. Perhaps it is in only in seeing the whole picture that we can understand and forgive ourselves. Maybe this writing exercise is an attempt to see the whole picture.

The failure of my recent relationship looms large over my life. How could I have made such a mistake again? A nebulous and infinite array of questions has hung over my life since my divorce from Warren. I can't shake them.

I wonder "what if" I had made this choice instead of that. What if I had decided not to continue a relationship with Warren after the trip? How would my life be now? Would I be any happier or more content? Would I be more successful? Would I have more and better connections to friends? Would I feel less lonely? Would I have made less costly emotional and financial mistakes? Would I have experienced less stress and heartache? I am haunted by those roads not travelled. They keep tugging me backwards to the past and I so want to live in the present.

I can't seem to shake it no matter how hard I try. It even overshadows my state of contentment in my new city and with my new life. I am haunted by this feeling that somehow my life would have turned out better or at least been easier if I had chosen a different path(s) than the one I did choose. Of course "choice" may be the wrong word. I tell myself everything turned out as it should be but that doesn't stop the pull from the past. So I have embarked on this intellectual journey. Did I make the "right" choices? Is there a "right" choice? How did I get to where I am? What were the forces that lead me to choose the roads I did? Where would I be if I had chosen differently or taken the roads not travelled?

I know I cannot change the past but I want to make better choices in my remaining years. I want to actually make a choice. I am not sure I did that before. I felt more buffeted around by forces and emotions that I didn't understand and by misperceptions about myself and others. I convinced myself that none of my decisions were impulsive because I took a lot of time to analyze and think about them. I dissected the consequences, pluses and minuses in my mind of each proposed course of action, sometimes for a year or more. But I realize now that I was just rationalizing my impulsive decision. I see now that I often dismissed the voice of reason or prudence. In my loneliness over the loss of my husband, I overlooked the warning signs that this most recent relationship would never work.

What if I had decided not to marry early? What if I had decided not to marry my ex-husband? What if I had married instead my first serious boyfriend? What if I had decided to seriously pursue a career? What if I decided to delay or not have children? You see what I have been doing to myself these last few years. I can't live in the present as I am continually dragged back to the past. Sometimes I feel paralyzed to act because I recognize that I have made so many "bad" choices in my life. How do I move forward? I think I can only do that by coming to terms with my past.

I don't have any idea if I can answer all or even any of those questions. The" what ifs" are infinite. I know that I have to try if I am going to find any peace. And above all I want to make peace with my life and my choices. Only then will I make peace with where I am right now and begin to live more in the moment. I will keep my eye on the future –where I am going but with more of a sense of trust that I am making choices and those "choices" are taking me where I want to go.

I have tried but I can't find peace in superficial answers or in busy activities. So I have to venture down this difficult path that is strewn and overgrown with "what ifs". I reluctantly look down the roads not travelled. I try to imagine my life if I had made another choice. I imagine I would be happier, more successful or in a better place. But I don't really know that. That is all fantasy and I don't want to base my journey on fantasy and imaginings. I only really know the outcome of the roads I have travelled. And so I decide to embark on a journey to review the roads I have travelled in hopes I may come to terms and make peace with the roads I didn't travel.

This is not meant to be a comprehensive or chronological recounting of my life. This is the story of an emotional journey, not a physical one. Emotions or should I say emotional memories don't lend themselves to any kind of order. They perhaps are better told as they are remembered, that is, as a series of unconnected vignettes. Their formation and experience is a process and not a very orderly one at that. Emotions surface at inopportune times. Emotional growth does not progress in any chronological order. Oftentimes an experience will have an impact on us only many years after it has happened.

As I look into the mirror I see the face of a middle aged women staring back at me. The image reminds me so of the passage of all the years. It frightens me that so much of my life is now behind me. Why did I do the things I did? If I understand that will it make any difference in my life as I look toward the future? In the end will my life have any meaning?

I started on my life journey with no roadmap. It might be more accurate to say I had small bits and pieces of a roadmap that were unconnected and huge pieces were missing. In some of my darkest hours I would sustain myself by saying if my children learned from and were able to avoid even some of the mistakes of my life it would all be worth it. I hope in my life and with this journal I have provided them with at least a rudimentary roadmap for their journey. It would give my life some meaning.

The following chapters contain some of the experiences, observations and insights I have acquired in living my life. The chapters are in no particular order. The events related in each chapter are in no particular order. The chapters are not really connected except for the fact that they relate my personal experiences and observations. This is not a novel. The chapters don't build on each other. You can read as few or as many chapters in any order you wish.

I hope you, the reader, can find at least one thing of value for your own life in the pages of this book. Perhaps you will start thinking about the choices you have made in your own life and about the roads you have travelled. Perhaps it will help you to understand why you made the choices you did or help you to recognize what you have learned along the way. It may help you abandon the fantasy of the roads not travelled. Perhaps it will open the door to discussions between you and your family or friends that can lead to a closer connection with them. It may help you make peace with where and who you are or help you to be more open to the spiritual side of life. Perhaps you will come to know what roads you do want to travel in the remaining years of your life. I humbly offer my own personal experiences and insights to you in hopes they may help you on your own journey wherever it may lead you.

CHAPTER TWO
Love and Death Together

Why do we have such a fear of the unknown? Why do we torture ourselves with wild imaginings of what lies ahead? Have you ever noticed that our anxiety or dread of a future event is almost always worse than the actual event? In my experience the fear surrounding the end of a relationship is usually much worse than the reality after it ends. I have discovered that there is one exception to that general rule.

We met through work. We didn't work at the same company. Our paths just randomly crossed and we were thrown together working toward what eventually became a common goal. Brian is the one who transformed an adversarial situation into a cooperative business venture from which we could both benefit. He had a real knack for or intuition for bringing people together in a business setting. It was so sad that the exact opposite was true in his personal life. From my observations it seems that it is exactly those qualities that make people successful in the business world that make them unsuccessful in their personal life. Brian was, to put it mildly, a very intense and demanding person. He was also very charismatic and charming. I was a little put off by his intensity. If he wanted something it was no holds barred and for some reason he wanted to have a relationship with me. It was a little scary but also very flattering.

Brian and I knew each other for four or five years before we married. We were able to evaluate, somewhat rationally, all the baggage that came along with the other person. He could readily see that I had three very young children. He had one young child. It was not so easy to identify our respective emotional and relationship issues. Still, during that time we were able to see each other with all our warts. There was something between us that made us want to connect in spite of our issues. That desire made us willing to work on connecting with each other. Why we were both so willing to do such hard work is still a mystery to me. There was something that brought us and held us together. Was that something a genuine and enduring love for each other?

It was wonderful to finally have some adult companionship and support. It was a relief to have someone to share the responsibilities and stresses of life. Brian genuinely loved my children. His love seemed to flow naturally – not contrived at all. Maybe when you really love the other person you love what they love or all that comes with them. That is not to say we didn't have issues between us regarding the children just that they didn't derail our relationship permanently as they had the potential to do.

I think the fact that we saw and acknowledged each other's warts made us love each other more. We didn't have to be expending all our energy trying to be, pretending to be perfect or protecting our perfect image. We were slowly tearing away our respective protective shrouds to reveal our true selves to each other. Romance, infatuation and all the baggage we bring to relationship can be transformed into real love. It is of course a process. Brian and I were working on that.

"I don't want any more children. If that is important to you we should stop seeing each other," I said to Brian one day as we were driving to attend a business event. I am not sure why I brought the subject up at that moment. We had been seeing each other for a while by this time but we had not yet discussed marriage. Brian never said anything directly about that subject but we continued to see each other. I think he understood how much I had struggled as a single parent of three young children.

Isn't it odd how life's most routine events end up, later, having the biggest impact on our lives. This was one of those situations. I made my annual visit to the gynecologist. There was a problem. The doctor asked me to return. It was described to me as potentially very serious so I asked Brian to come with me. We had been married a few years by this time. That is how we both came to be seated in the doctor's office on this particular day.

"You have a condition that will require the removal of your uterus – a hysterectomy. I know that you mentioned to me that you might want to have more children. If you do want another child you should do it now," the doctor said to Brian and me. Brian and I were seated next to each other. We turned, looked at each other and said "yes" to each other with our eyes. We seemed to have an ability to communicate without speaking – at least regarding some issues. We never had an actual verbal conversation ever about having a child together. We instinctively knew it was the right thing to do.

I was 37 years old at that time. Brian was older. Good Lord! That would make 7 children between us with the new one being 9 ½ years younger than its next closest sibling. I figured that, by making this decision, I added 10 years to my full time parenting years. In the ensuing months of my pregnancy when I would become anxious or question the soundness of my decision I would remind myself that I would not be doing it all alone this time. I know Brian sensed my fears. He had a knack for reassuring me in a very real way without words. I can't explain it any better than that. Brian was a very involved husband and father. I knew he would share the burdens, responsibilities and joys with me. I so wanted to share the experience of parenting a child. In addition to shouldering the financial and physical burdens alone, life as a single parent it is a very lonely experience emotionally.

"What's wrong with your arm?" I asked Brian. He had been moving his right arm in circles and rubbing it for several minutes. "It feels a little numb. I think it might be a pinched nerve," he replied. We had just completed our morning swim together. Brian and I carved out certain times to be alone together as a couple. That was something of a challenge as we had my three young children full time and regular visits with his daughter. We both worked at demanding jobs. In the summer time we would wake up early in the morning and swim laps together. We had a beautiful backyard and after swimming we would sit together for a brief time and talk over a cup of coffee. "It will probably go away on its own," Brian said to me. "If it doesn't I will make an appointment with the doctor after the baby is born. It is probably a pinched nerve in my neck. I have already been through this once before with my back," Brian continued.

"Are you still grieving?" she asked. I was taken aback. After all 14 years had passed. I had just answered a question regarding why Gary's father wasn't attending the swim meet to watch Gary. I felt a few tears on my cheeks. "Some part of me will always grieve for what I lost," I replied.

A couple of weeks after Brian first complained about his arm our son, Gary, was born. Brian was ecstatic. He had always wanted a son. He was a rather macho guy. I didn't hold that against him. Being a mother again was exhilarating and I was pleasantly surprised by that. For the past three years we had been working hard to blend our families. This baby accomplished in a moment what we had been unable to do in years. We all finally had a common bond or connection– a baby that we all loved and adored. I pinched myself to see if I was awake. Life was so great it had to be a dream.

"Samuel, Jessica, Ellen, Bridget can you all please come into the family room," I yelled. Several different voices chimed in asking why we wanted them all right then or asking if they could come in a few minutes. "No we need everyone here right now," I said firmly. There was the sound of pounding feet or was maybe it just the pounding of my heart as Brian and I waited for everyone to arrive. Brian was seated in the middle of the sectional sofa. Samuel sat down right next to him. I don't remember where the girls sat. I was holding Gary in my arms. They were all looking at Brian eagerly waiting for him to announce plans for our next family vacation.

"I am going to die," Brian said. No one moved. No one made a sound. Even Gary was quiet in my arms. "I have a terminal illness. There is no treatment or cure. I don't know how long I have to live," Brian continued. Samuel's head was bowed and he was quietly crying. I could see the tears dropping onto his shirt. I felt the tears on my face as I hugged Gary close to me. Should I let the children see me cry I wondered? They are already losing one parent. If they see me cry will they be afraid they are losing both parents? I didn't want them to think I didn't love Brian. On the other hand I didn't want to make life more traumatic than it already was for them.

It was surreal how the routines of life pushed the illness into the background. They acted like a salve. But the knowledge of illness and death was always there – like a dark specter following you and haunting you everywhere you went. The only relief was sleep at least some of the time.

You see Brian had gone to visit the doctor as he promised. That night, as our two week old infant slept in his crib next to our bed, Brian told me the doctor thought he had ALS. They wanted to do more tests to be certain. I had never heard of ALS before. Brian gently explained to me what it was and told me that there was no treatment or cure. I was numb. Somehow I was able to sleep.

"How do you live with this pain every day? How do you get up every day and do the things that need to be done knowing that one of the persons you love most in the world is dying a little more each day that passes?" I asked Walt. He was a marriage counselor Brian and I had been going to see, on and off, for several years. I didn't really expect him to have an answer although I secretly hoped he might have even some small insight. Walt just looked at me with eyes that mirrored the despair in mine. He had no answers, not even any insights.

This was unchartered territory. There were no road maps and no guideposts to be found. There were no instruction manuals. Doctors provide the information regarding the physical progression of the disease but they have absolutely no information regarding the emotional aspect. I felt like I was falling off a cliff with no safety net. There was no hope that Brian would survive and I was starting to think there was no hope that I would survive either.

The demands of daily living came to my rescue. They numbed me to the pain. I felt like a zombie. I was physically present and functioning but emotionally I was absent. My physical body or shell performed the daily tasks but there was nothing inside.

Many years have passed yet I still get overcome with emotion as I write this. I am both sad and angry and everything in between. My emotions run the gauntlet. The past still has a powerful hold over me. Is that true for everyone or am I just weird?

I believe that some wounds are so deep they never completely heal. It is as if a piece has been ripped out of your heart leaving a huge gaping hole. In the beginning the edges of the wound are shredded, torn, raw and bleeding. The pain is excruciating and constant. Over time the wound begins to heal but the hole remains. If you touch the hole you no longer experience a sharp, stabbing pain as you did when the wound was new. But the wound is still tender enough that a touch can bring tears to your eyes. For me certain memories "touch" the wound.

My wound has remained tender for many, many years and I expect it will remain in this condition for the remainder of my days. I have come to accept that this wound will never completely heal. In some ways that is a good thing as it reminds me of some of the important lessons I learned from that horrendous experience. I learned to be grateful for what I do have and not to get distracted by less important things. It also has its dark side. If I am not careful, I can find myself travelling down that dark and well trod path of anger and bitterness.

"Get your affairs in order and prepare to die," the doctor said to Brian when he gave us the final diagnosis. "There is no treatment or cure. The average life span after the onset of symptoms is 3 years," the doctor continued. Brian asked some specific questions. Why is it that we often find comfort in knowledge? It is as if we believe a bunch of facts can change the outcome or ease the pain. I didn't really listen to the conversation between Brian and the doctor. I listened to the sound of Brian's voice thinking that I wouldn't be hearing that for much longer. I was startled back to what was happening when the doctor spoke the word "coffin". "It is often called the coffin disease because you are trapped in a dead and lifeless body. The brain is never affected by the disease," the doctor continued.

Brian and I didn't explain all of this to the children when we returned from the doctor's office. I am not sure I ever really explained it to them. They were still in shock from the initial announcement. The children weren't interested in details. I think it would have made things worse for them. They would have something else, in addition to death, to dread.

For the previous six months our life had been a series of highs and lows as we lived through a myriad of medical tests that would confirm or maybe even reject that diagnosis. ALS is a cruel disease. The emotional devastation begins long before the physical deterioration manifests itself. It started as we waited for the confirmation of the initial diagnosis. The only way to diagnosis ALS is by a process of elimination. If it doesn't fit the pattern for other diseases then it must, by default, be ALS. I think we were given the final diagnosis at Christmas.

The disease ate away at and ravaged our emotions just as it ate away at and ravaged Brian's body. Brian first lost total use of his left arm. It just kind of hung on his body like a dead tree limb hangs from the trunk of a tree. When he walked it would flap around like a dead tree limb does in the wind. Brian developed the habit, whenever he moved, of using his right arm to hold his left arm close to his body. His left arm would still hang loosely at his side when he held Gary with his right arm pressing him close to his chest. That left arm was a gruesome and constant reminder of the disease that was eating away at his body.

Physically his body deteriorated in increments. Brian started to shuffle when he walked. He couldn't stand for long periods of time. His right arm deteriorated. He couldn't hold our baby son in his arms anymore. After 18 months he was in a wheelchair on a full time basis. The damage was irreversible. The doctors had informed us that there are just about as many variations in the way the disease progresses as there are individuals that have it. We had no information regarding the emotional deterioration.

I do believe some people experience or feel things more deeply than others. I believe I am one of those. Oh I wished many times that I wasn't.

Right after the diagnosis the best time for me was early in the morning when I was half awake. Initially, when I was waking up, I would have this ominous feeling in the pit of my stomach that something bad was going to happen. In my half awake state, I could convince myself that the foreboding feeling was just the remnant of a very bad nightmare. I would sigh with relief. But when I was fully awakened I could no longer delude myself. As time went on I could no longer be comforted by the delusion that this was all a nightmare. I would bolt awake with the feeling that I was going to throw up. It was a nightmare - just not the kind you have when you are asleep. Fortunately whatever I was feeling could not be front and center for very long. There were many things to attend to including a crying baby. However, this evil was never forgotten for long. It had taken up permanent residence in my psyche. It was like a black blot in my consciousness comprised of every horrible feeling you can imagine – pain, desperation, loneliness, rage, fear, anxiety. That black blot grew in size and shape as the disease progressed until at the end it swallowed me.

Tears would have been such a relief. I couldn't do it. I couldn't cry except on a very few occasions. And I wouldn't describe what I did then as crying. I emitted some kind of a primitive sound deep from within my body. It scared the hell out of me. I couldn't believe that sound came from me. It was a primordial sound. The first time it happened I was in the bathroom of our house. It was shortly after Brian told me about the disease. The last time was when I first saw Brian's lifeless body. I have no idea what brought it on the first time. I was alone in the house except for the baby who was sleeping. I collapsed onto the bathroom floor, screaming, crying, sobbing, heaving, writhing and emitting that sound. I must have looked like some primitive animal that had been fatally shot and was slow to die. Words were not coming out of my mouth only that weird, non human sound. After several minutes I was exhausted. I lay on the floor quietly for a while, more exhausted than I had ever felt. I heard the baby cry. I slowly pulled myself up off the bathroom floor. It was time to get back to the demands of the living.

Adversity by its nature is unique. We each define it differently and we each cope with it in our own way. Hearing the stories of other widows and widowers gave me hope that I could survive but it really didn't give me the tools to get through each and every day. I didn't want to go about my business as usual pretending everything was "fine." Yet what was the alternative? I had to find my own way to live with the pain just like I would eventually have to find my own way to heal. I felt like I was slowing sinking into a quicksand of despair. No one seemed to be able to throw me a lifeline. Certainly Brian could not.

We seek and crave connections especially in our darkest hours but we really are alone. No one is experiencing what we are experiencing. We are isolated in our despair. Only those who are also experiencing it can understand it and share the burden and pain. Brian was the one person who shared the experience with me. But he was enveloped in his own dark world of fear and despair. Physically Lou Gehrig's disease deprived Brian of the ability to reach out and touch me. Emotionally it rendered him incapable of reaching out and connecting with me. I lost him the minute the diagnosis was given. Our emotional connection was severed when the death sentence was pronounced. I didn't realize that at the time. I so wanted to connect with him – to grow even closer to him for whatever time he had left. But wishing doesn't make it so. What is that old expression? "If wishes were horses beggars would ride." Brian was entirely wrapped up in his own world – a maze of fear, anxiety, regrets, physical pain, anger, remorse, hatred. And I was angry with him for pushing me away.

All that remained was the memory of our great love. That memory would have to sustain us for the few remaining years. I was reminded of a car rambling down the last distance of road on the fumes from its once full gas tank. Our lives were reduced to waiting for the end to come and trying to manage the final journey as gracefully as possible. It was about wheelchairs, bedpans, feeding tubes, bedsores, insomnia, assisted showers, assisted trips to the bathroom and containing the rage and fear. His pain was my pain and so we traveled down that long, dark road to death together but apart.

We were separated by a wall of silence and anger – his and mine. I tried to talk to Brian about how I felt. I often asked how he felt. He was silent. He would look at me with eyes filled with anger and hatred. I suppose he thought it should have been obvious to me how he felt.

Eventually I stopped trying to connect with him. I think Brian remained angry until the day he died. I recently read that a person dies in the same way that he lived. Brian was, in many ways, always a person filled with anger. I couldn't control how he chose to die. I could only control how I chose to react to him and the situation. My anger over his refusal or inability to connect faded. I realized I had no right to judge him. The answer for me was found by asking myself the question, "How do I know how I would be if I was the one dying a horrible and agonizing death?" I had no right to presume I would handle it any differently or any better than Brian was handling it. There was no right way to handle this – at least none that I know of. How arrogant of me to presume that there was. When I would become exasperated or impatient or angry with him I would ask myself that question.

When I first met him, one of the things I found attractive about Brian was the way he dressed. I am not referring to the type of clothes that he wore. They were not expensive. But he was always neatly dressed. Perhaps the best way I can explain it was that Brian was in the military and he continued many of those habits into his later life. His clothes were always neatly pressed and he was always very well groomed. He had beautiful hair. I know that is a strange thing to say about a man but he did. One of the nurses even commented on it when he spent some time in hospice care. She described it as "U.S. Senator Hair." It was a beautiful gray color and very fine and soft.

Brian would wash and dry his hair each morning, comb it into place and then apply some hairspray. Well the time inevitably came when Brian could no longer fix his own hair. This happened early on in the disease or as soon as he could no longer use his left arm. He had use of only one arm and you needed two to manage the hair dryer and the comb. He was still going to the office at that time. Brian was very particular about his appearance, especially his hair. It became my task to style his hair every morning. It was a huge process for me to try to get his hair to look like he did it. I could never do it right. He was usually disgusted with me because I never did it the way he did. Disgusted may be too tame an adjective but I will leave it at that.

After I dried and styled Brian's hair I would dress him. That was a bit easier at least at that point in time. Brian's balance was impaired but he was still able to steady himself on a counter or wall while standing. Once he was fairly steady he would lift each leg and I would put his pant leg over his foot. Unfortunately each day brought many more and new aggravations and limitations.

"You b****. You whore. You are so stupid. How can anyone be as stupid as you are? F*** you! You are a piece of s***," Brian shrieked at me. Brian was staring at me and his entire face was contorted with rage and hatred. "Get the f*** out of here," he screamed at me. I had just raised my head up from the floor where I had been putting on Brian's slacks. My hands are trembling as I write this.

I had felt something brush against my head after I bent down. I realized that Brian had taken a swing at me with the fist of his good arm. He missed me because I had ducked down to put on his pants. It took me a minute to sort all this out. I was stunned. The look on Brian's face was terrifying. It was beyond rage. "Get the f*** out of here," he kept screaming at me.

I was shaking as I left the room. "Close the f****** door on your way out you b****!" he screamed at me. I left the bedroom and closed the door. My whole body was shaking. I felt like I was going to throw up. I waited a little while and then I knocked on the door. "Get away from that f****** door," Brian screamed from inside the room. I ran to the telephone and called one of his friends.

"Richard I don't know what to do. Brian is in the bedroom and refuses to come out. He is acting irrationally? Can you come over?" I asked. I didn't tell Richard about anything that had happened. To his credit Richard came right over to the house. Richard knocked at the bedroom door and announced his presence. I heard Brian tell him to come in. I have no idea what was said between them that morning. Richard left after about an hour. I went in and helped Brian get dressed. He left for the office shortly thereafter. After Brian left for the office I asked myself, "How do I know how I would act if I was the one dying a horrible and agonizing death?" Brian and I never spoke about the events of that day.

Brian's walk became increasingly unsteady. He would teeter and totter when he walked and I was terrified he would fall down. He started using a cane to steady himself. He couldn't use that for very long because he couldn't hold it when he lost the use of his right arm. I bought a wheelchair and put it in the family room hoping he would use it. It sat there empty for quite a while. Brian was having difficulty standing for any extended period of time. He was becoming fatigued very easily. One night we had a few of his high school friends over. He grabbed the wheelchair and sat in it. He was able to move around to talk to everyone that way. It still sat there empty for a while after that.

"Do you want to rent a wheelchair for the day?" I asked Brian. He just ignored me and my request. I didn't say anything else because I knew it was useless to do so. We started walking through the zoo. Brian started to get very tired. He found a bench to sit down. Without asking him I went back to the entrance and rented a wheelchair for the day. I arrived back at the bench with the wheelchair. Brian didn't say anything. He just got into the wheelchair. He looked haggard and defeated. Brian refused to look at me for the remainder of our day at the zoo. He seemed to feel a little better when Gary asked to ride on his lap. At two years old Gary thought it was great fun.

The phone rang. I picked it up. "This is Officer Smith of the Police Department. We would like you to come to the police station tomorrow at 10am to talk to us about your son, Samuel." "OK" I responded. I hung up the phone. "Who is it?" Brian asked." I lied. "It was nothing important," I said. Brian accepted that answer. If he weren't sick he would have known I was lying.

"I have to go to the bathroom," Brian said. He wasn't able to physically shake me at this point in time. "OK," I said. "Just give me a minute to wake up," I replied. "I have to go right now!" Brian said desperately. Patience was never one of Brian's virtues but, in his defense, who knows for how long he had been trying to wake me. His voice was not very strong at this point in time. I walked to his side of the bed. I wrapped my arms around his waist and hoisted him to his feet. He steadied himself for a minute. "OK" he said to me. We started to walk very slowly to the bathroom. Brian held onto my arm as he shuffled his feet. I lowered him onto the toilet seat. After he was done I leaned him against my body as I reached around to wipe him. I pulled his bottoms back up. (We had actually done this in an airplane bathroom on several occasions). We proceeded slowly back to the bed. Just before we reached the bed Brian lost his balance and fell to the floor with a thundering thud.

"Help, help," Brian was pleading. I was frantically pulling and tugging to try to get him on his feet. It was the middle of the night. Last time this happened my Father had been around to help. He wasn't here now. "I'm going to have to wake up Samuel," I said to Brian. ""Please don't," he pleaded. "I have to. I can't get you off the floor," I said. I rolled Brian over onto his back and put a pillow under his head. I went to get Samuel. Samuel and I managed to pull Brian off the floor in increments using a vanity stool and to get him back into the bed. Brian would fall a few more times before he finally agreed to use the wheelchair all the time.

"I really need a break," I said one morning to Brian. "I would like someone to come and help for 4 hours a day a couple of times a week." "No" Brian responded and by the look in his eyes I knew he meant it. That was not the first time I had said this or the first time

Brian rejected my request. Brian would not allow anyone but me to do anything for him. That is not to say that there were a lot of offers of help but there were a few. He would stay alone with his daughter, Bridget, but that was awfully hard on her. She was 12 years old. If I did leave them to take the other children someplace or go to the grocery store I would be sure to take Brian to the bathroom before I left and to arrive back before he had to make another trip. Usually he and his daughter sat in the family room and watched TV while I was gone. That was the extent of the help he would accept. Brian refused to allow his sister, Nancy, to stay with him so I could go to the store. I understood his reasons and I honored his wishes for as long as I could.

I really didn't want any of the children to have to do any unpleasant things for Brian. Sometimes Brian couldn't wait for me to finish doing something so one of the children would feed him. They had such a look of distress on their face when they were doing that. They occasionally helped before Brian had difficulty swallowing when he ate. We stopped eating dinner together after he almost choked at the dinner table a couple of times. We had some type of a suction apparatus to use when he got something stuck in his throat.

"Brian this is Susan. She is going to stay with you while I go to the grocery store," I said. I was surprised that Susan agreed to stay after seeing the look of hatred and rage Brian gave both of us. After the nurses' aide left Brian would complain about her for hours.

"You know she is going to drop me. She isn't strong enough. I am going to get really hurt when she drops me," Brian said when I arrived home. Brian insisted on getting a shower every morning. That didn't fit with the hospice schedule. Hospice would send someone to shower him but it would have to be in the afternoon. Brian wouldn't agree to wait so I showered him every morning. I tried to turn that duty over to the nurse's aide one day of the week. It was worth it to put up with Brain's complaining and looks of hatred to have a brief respite. Eventually Brian would have worn me down and I would have stopped using the nurse's aide. It never came to that because not long thereafter Brian ended up at a hospice in patient facility.

After Brian was unable to drive himself one of the employees at the company, Clark, would come to pick him up every day. Clark would put Brian and the wheelchair in the car. When they arrived at the office Clark would put Brian in the wheelchair and arrange his arms on his lap. If he didn't do this carefully the arms would dangle and flap around and get caught in the wheels. Brian would sit in the wheelchair in his office. He didn't have the ability to move the wheelchair. What a blessing the day I discovered that we could get him an electric wheel chair. For a while, he had enough use of his right thumb that he could push the lever to control the chair. But by the time he lost the use of this thumb he had already stopped going into the office.

You need to be civil to me," I said angrily. "I am not going to do anything else for you until you agree to be civil to me!" I exclaimed. "I can't take being called names, struck at or cursed at any longer!" Brian's outbursts had become much more frequent. I knew from the few ALS support group meetings that I attended that this behavior was not unique to Brian but that didn't make it much easier to bear. When I said this to him Brian was sitting in his lift chair in the family room watching TV. He ignored me. I returned to the kitchen where Gary was helping me with dinner. A little while later I heard Brian call my name several times. His voice was getting weaker at this point and I think, at first, he wasn't sure if I had actually heard him. By this time Gary was hanging out with one of his siblings in their room. "I am not going to help you with anything until you tell me you are going to stop calling me names and cursing at me!" I repeated. "I have to go to the bathroom," he demanded. I walked into the family room. "I'm not going to take you to the bathroom." I already told you that I am not going to do anything else for you unless you agree to start treating me better. I will be happy to call someone else to help you if you want me to," I said firmly. Brian just stared at me again with a look of rage and hatred. I imagine the need to urinate was becoming urgent and he finally realized that I was going to let him piss in his pants unless he agreed to stop trying to hit me and stopped cursing at me and calling me names. I was at my wits end with him. "Call James for me," Brian demanded.

I dialed the phone and held it up to Brian's ear. "Can you come and pick me up?" I heard him ask James. A short time later the doorbell rang. I answered the door and escorted James into the family room where Brian was seated. James looked very confused. "If Brian wants to say right now that he will stop mistreating me I will be glad to help him go to the bathroom," I said to James in front of Brian. "Let's go," Brian said to James. James looked pretty scared. James had some experience with helping Brian. He would assist Brian to go to the bathroom on occasion at the office. James didn't say anything. He had known and worked with Brian for many, many years. They left to go to James' house.

"Brian wants to come home," James said to me over the phone an hour or so later. "OK, as long as he knows the conditions under which I will take care of him," I replied. "He does," James said. Brian arrived home. He and I never discussed anything about that day. Brian never apologized or even acknowledged that he mistreated me. Brian was still difficult, to say the least, but the (attempted) hitting and cursing stopped "How do I know how I would act if I was the one dying a horrible and agonizing death?" I asked myself. I didn't want to judge him. I just wanted the abuse to stop. It took me a while to realize that I had a right to set some standards for acceptable behavior from Brian. Typically I would only set limits when the situation affected my ability to function in the other parts of my life. With Brian I had passed that point a while ago.

The fuel tank was empty but the fumes of love were propelling me forward. Somewhere along the way in dealing with this disease my deep love for Brian had turned into devotion and compassion. Even the fumes would become scarce as time went on.

Before the illness, Brian was one of the most energetic people I ever knew. He reminded me of the energizer bunny in that old TV commercial. He ran a business. He attended sporting events, social events, and business events. He did all kinds of projects around the house. After we were married he cooked, cleaned and spent time with the children at home and with them at their extracurricular activities. He had his regular visits with his own daughter – driving to pick her up and take her home several times a week. He was always moving. I rarely saw him sit down and relax.

"What do you want to watch today? " I asked Brian. He turned to me with a look of disgust on his face. I tried to find something that would interest him. It was daytime TV after all and this was before the proliferation of cable networks. The pickings were slim. I settled him into his lift chair located in the corner of the family room. He would sit there and watch TV until it was time to go to bed. Occasionally we had an outing but it was very rare. He was not really interested in going anywhere. I think it was physically tiring for him but it was also embarrassing for him as people stared at him.

"What do you mean you are out of mini vans!" I shrieked at the poor man at the rental car counter. "I made this reservation over a month ago. I have to have a minivan. My husband is handicapped and I can't get him in and out of any other vehicle. I am begging you to please find us a minivan," I continued. As I said this I waved in the direction of the family seated on the floor to the right of the rental counter. Brian was sitting in his wheelchair and the four older children were seated in the midst of our luggage for six people and a baby, port a crib, car seat, electric wheelchair battery and stroller. One year old Gary was seated on Samuel's lap. Needless to say we looked like a group of displaced persons.

"Samuel and Jessica you are in charge of the luggage, port a crib and electric wheelchair battery. Bridget you are in charge of Gary. Ellen you will take and set up the stroller for Gary. We can leave the car seat in the minivan. I will set up the electric wheelchair and get Brian into it. Does everyone know what to do?" I asked. Everyone said they did. I will never forget the look of amazement on the face of the valet parking attendant at the hotel as we unloaded ourselves, the luggage and equipment from the minivan. We must have looked like a "Chinese fire drill". We were going back to visit Brian's hometown. This was the last trip we ever took together.

"Can you come downstairs and scratch my nose?" I vaguely heard Brian say over the baby monitor. To this day I can't hear the static of a baby monitor without feeling depressed. After a prolonged period of sleepless nights I started going upstairs to the bedroom to lie down when Gary was taking his nap. I would turn on the baby monitor that I had set up next to Brian's lift chair and the one I had next to me in the bedroom. I rarely got a chance to rest, much less sleep. As soon as my head would touch the pillow I would hear Brian's voice over the monitor. "Can you come downstairs I need you to scratch my nose." or "Can you come downstairs I need you to rearrange my arm" or "Can you come downstairs I need you to change the TV station." or "Can you come downstairs I need you to ...." Sometimes I would simply turn off the monitor and open the bedroom door so I could hear if anything serious happened. I couldn't sleep but at least I could rest. Brian's voice was soft but I could still hear him call me. "Why didn't you come downstairs when I called you?" Brian would ask on the days I turned the monitor off. "I didn't hear you," I would lie. Of course he knew I was lying.

Insomnia is a by-product of this disease. So Brian didn't sleep and that meant I didn't sleep. He would sleep a little. As the months went by the nights and days blurred. It is impossible to describe the level of exhaustion – physically, spiritually and emotionally. Numbness was my friend. Brian would sleep in fits and starts. I would be jolted awake by, "I need you to turn me over." or "I need you to scratch my leg" or "I need you to rearrange my arms." I didn't have the energy to put him in the wheelchair at night to take him to the bathroom so we used a urinal in the bed. Often after Brian would use the urinal I would find myself lying in a wet spot. I didn't care. I just wanted to get a few minutes of sleep.

I cry as I write this. It has been more than 10 since Brian's death and yet the wound still seeps and oozes. Am I still grieving? Maybe. It is more likely that the memories of intense emotional pain live on in our psyche like memories of intense physical pain. Something touches the wound and it begins to ooze and seep. The specific cause of the oozing and seeping is a mystery. I fully expected that birthdays, anniversaries and special events would trigger that reaction. I got through those days fine. It was the unexpected little events that triggered it. In the beginning the phone would ring and I would run to it expecting to hear, "Hi Honey." Now it usually happens when I see our son, a young man now, doing something I am so proud of and I want to share it with Brian.

His face was contorted, his eyes were wide and he was flailing, at least with his eyes. Funny how Brian's body language was so limited but I could read just about everything in his face and his eyes. His eyes were moving rapidly in all directions – imitating the flailing of limbs. I had come into the room in response to some commotion I had heard. "Take me outside; take me outside NOW!", Brian kept saying. I put him in the wheelchair and took him outside. I called for my oldest daughter, Jessica, to sit with him while I called the doctor's office to see if I needed to take him to the emergency room. I didn't want Brian to hear me discussing him with the doctor. "I will call in a prescription," the nurse said to me. "What is the prescription for?" I asked. "The prescription is for anxiety," she said compassionately. "Should I take him to the emergency room?" I asked the nurse. "No there is nothing physically wrong with him. This should be all he needs," she replied. I went back outside to see how my daughter and Brian were doing. "I am going to die," I heard Brian say to my oldest daughter. That was the first and last time I ever heard him say that. I wheeled him back into the house after a little while. Anti- anxiety drugs became a daily part of his life.

Brian unexpectedly recovered enough to return home from hospice. He was totally bedridden. He was able to come home because his company generously agreed to pay for caregivers. "Thank you so much for your generosity," I said to John one day. He was Brian's business partner. "I am glad to do it even though if the roles were reversed I don't believe Brian would do it for me," John replied. I understood what John said and there was an element of truth to it for both John and I. John made it possible for us to have two caregivers - one person for 12 hours during the day and another for a 12 hour night shift. The hospice nurse was also coming on a regular basis after Brian returned home.

"Brian is still in a lot of pain. We need to check his urine. He shouldn't be experiencing that much pain with the amount of morphine he is taking," the hospice nurse told us during one of her regular visits. This disease is a particularly cruel one, I remember thinking. The afflicted person can't move his/her limbs but he/she has full sensations or feeling in his/her body. They are in a great deal of pain.

Tony, our day time caregiver, threw a fit. Brian had a catheter so it wouldn't be difficult to obtain the urine for testing. I couldn't understand Tony's resistance to the request. Tony and I got into a heated argument. "I will quit if I have to do that!" Tony finally shouted. "Then quit," I said. "The nurse says we need to do this for Brian so we will!" I shouted. The hospice nurse was silent during this exchange but she never followed up on the request. Maybe she knew what Nancy, Brian's sister, apparently already knew. Tony was stealing Brian's morphine. He was a drug addict. I was apparently the only one who didn't know this.

After Brian died Nancy told me about Tony. "We didn't want to add to your burdens," Nancy explained when I asked why she hadn't told me earlier. That would explain a lot of things like the disappearance of items of value from the house and the fact that Tony was often late for work. Our night person, Sela, was a saint. She would wait patiently for Tony to arrive even though it made her children late for school. I told her I could manage for a while without any help. Maybe she didn't believe me.

Would it have been better to have known about Tony earlier? Maybe it would have helped me recognize the signs of drug use in my children. I had no idea what the signs of drug use were. Maybe I could have prevented the loss of some of those sentimental items. "Tony took good care of Brian," Nancy said. She was right and that is really what mattered at the time.

For a while I think Brian believed he was going to defeat the disease by sheer willpower. He was going to will himself to live. He had so much to live for. He had always wanted a son. Now he had one. He had always wanted a family. Now he had one.

Against his doctor's wishes, or without his knowledge, we tried all types of alternative therapies. I know that one of the therapies actually stopped the progression of the disease. But Brian wanted more. He wanted to be cured. I guess this is greed of a different sort. I argued with him to continue the treatment. But he never went back for that alternative treatment. I accepted his decision. I think part of dealing with a terminally ill person is letting them have control over those aspects of their life they can still control. The disease had not affected his brain.

"Could you do it?" Brian asked me long before the final diagnosis was made. He never said what "it" was but I knew what he meant or at least I thought I did. I said I didn't know but I was going to expect the best from myself. You see I was referring to being able to take care of a terminally ill spouse. Brian was referring to assisted suicide. "Please don't ask me to do that," I begged. He never mentioned it to me again. Instead he summoned one of his closest friends to the house. They talked behind closed doors. I knew Brian asked him if he would do it. I know his friend said "yes" only because I saw the look of relief in Brian's eyes after his friend left.

This friend never came to visit Brian the entire time he was sick. But somehow the commitment his friend made that day comforted Brian throughout this ordeal. Maybe he just wanted to feel he still had some control over his life or maybe he wanted to know the suffering could be ended when he couldn't bear it anymore. He knew he would be physically incapable of doing it himself. I often wondered if I let him down. But how do you kill someone that you love? That is not a decision I wanted to be faced with. After that conversation Brian and I never again spoke about his death. We never shared our feelings of what we were going through. Brian was a pretty macho guy. I guess I can be macho too. We just soldiered on.

If only if it played out like it did in the old movies. The sick person becomes immersed in love and wants only to connect with and ease the inevitable loss and suffering of his loved ones. I can't remember any of the names of those movies but there were many such heroines who were in wheelchairs or dying. They thought only of the suffering of their loved ones. We viewers wanted to be like them and of course we inevitably failed. Today we have reality TV. We measure ourselves by the lowest common denominator of human behavior now. I wonder if this reality stuff is any better for us than the creation of a perfect image. It seems to have given us permission to stop striving to be a better person or to act nobly. Of course Brian didn't emulate the "perfect" behavior of the terminally ill heroes of the old movies and neither did I. We didn't celebrate our basest behavior either. I strived to meet the ideal of the ever patient, attentive and loving caregiver even though I knew I would fail. Isn't that the way it should be?

Brian was totally bedridden for the last five months of his life. He stayed in another part of the house. His caregiver would wheel him into the family room but that happened less and less. Later, the caregiver would open the blinds in Brian's bedroom so he could watch Gary and I play in the back yard. I would pop into Brian's room often during the day. At night Brian and I would watch a TV program together. The misery and suffering dragged on, seeming at times to be endless. Brian elected to get a feeding tube but he remained steadfast in his decision not to use a respirator. I have to admit I was thankful for that.

"It is 10 am and Brian is still asleep. What should I do?" asked the weekend caregiver. I went into Brian's room to check on him again. He was sleeping peacefully. I checked to make sure he was breathing. He was. "Let him sleep a while longer," I said. "He was awake unusually late last night and must be very tired. Remember that I am going out for a few hours this afternoon", I told the caregiver. I was taking an outing other than my usual trip to the grocery store or to attend the children's activities. The Russian ballet was in town performing Swan Lake. I was so looking forward to the performance.

I am not particularly knowledgeable about ballet. I just enjoy it. I have always loved the scene in Swan Lake called "Dance of the Swans". I have always found the music, the imagery and gracefulness beautiful and peaceful. This performance was no exception. I was totally immersed in the scene. On the stage, the ballerinas fluttered their arms gracefully upward. I "saw" their entire bodies floating upward, not just their arms. They were angels ascending into heaven. As I watched I had a feeling of intense peacefulness and contentment. I was totally drawn into the image on the stage. I became part of it. I was disconnected from time and place.

The curtain fell for intermission. I always wondered what the dire circumstances were that necessitated someone being paged over the PA system at a large venue. Doctors had pagers in those days to be summoned in the event of an emergency. I heard my name announced over the PA system. The feeling of peace and contentment vanished with the sound of my name. I already knew. As I rushed home I felt scared, apprehensive, relieved, and guilty but mostly I just felt numb.

The room was exactly as I had left it just an hour or so earlier. Brian was resting peacefully on the bed. It was only on very close examination you could detect that Brian's chest was not moving. I had known for three years that this day would come. It was inevitable. The day the doctor gave that diagnosis almost three years ago was the same day Brian and I received our death sentence. We knew that his life – our relationship, our life together, our job as

co-parents and our world would end much sooner than we expected. On this beautiful sunny Sunday afternoon Brian had simply stopped breathing.

I reached out and touched Brian's hand. It felt like a stone on a cold winter night. I felt my body shudder. I remember being amazed that life could depart so quickly. I dropped to my knees and laid my head on my knees. Then I heard a horrible sound. It sounded like a primitive wailing- like something an animal in pain would make. It definitely was not human. I looked up. I looked around the room. I was alone. I realized it was coming from me! I continued to wail while I rocked back and forth on my knees. I remember thinking it was strange that I wasn't shedding any tears. I have no idea how much time I passed like that. When I was spent I got up, kissed Brian and left the room.

My remorse at not being at his side when he stopped breathing was short lived. We had been together at the moment of his death. Brian died during the "Dance of the Swans" or maybe it was angels. As I left the room I again felt the peace that I had experienced during the ballet performance. I must tell the children I said to myself.

I can hear you the reader saying to yourself "this stuff is crazy and stupid." You wonder if it was not the incredible strain that was causing me to be delusional. After all I am talking about "knowing" when Brian died even though I wasn't in the room with him, about ballerinas dressed like swans floating up to heaven like angels when he died, communicating with another human being without words, knowing what another person is thinking without being told. Perhaps it is just something you cannot understand unless you open yourself up to it and experience it for yourself. Ten years earlier I would have thought someone was crazy who related this to me. Living through something like this opened my eyes. I realize that we limit ourselves and our experience of living by closing ourselves off to spiritual matters and by not trusting our intuition. I believe there are things that cannot be explained, described, understood, and judged by scientific or rational standards. The events of this time in my life certainly fit that description. But that doesn't make them any less real nor does it make me doubt that they actually happened.

One of my goals throughout the trauma of Brian's illness was to have no regrets. I promised him we would care for him at home until the end. I was able to do that with a lot of help. I wanted to take care of and treat Brian they way I would want to be treated if I was in his shoes so to speak. Of course I had times when I was definitely not always kind, loving or patient. Sometimes I was angry that he just wouldn't die and get this over with. I blamed him for taking so long to die as if he had any control over it. Other times I just didn't want to let him go. I am surprised that I haven't beat myself up, mercilessly, over those failings these past many years. It is probably because I believe I did the best I could. I could have done better but I can't change that now. I think Brian knew that I loved him and that I did the best I could for him. Maybe I am finally learning to forgive myself for not "being perfect" or always doing the right thing.

In my quest to give Brian the best that I could and to make his time as comfortable as possible I inadvertently thwarted my other goal of sparing the children as much pain and suffering as possible. I put Brian's needs above everyone else's including the children. I shielded the children from the physical demands of caring for a terminally ill father. I made a point of not asking them for much help in that area. What I failed to see was that Brian's presence in the house made it impossible to shield the older children from the brutal reality of watching someone you love die a horrible, agonizing death. It wasn't a real problem where Gary was concerned because he was so young. With Gary I tried to maintain a "normal" routine for him, to shield him as much as possible from the stress and anger and to surround him with love.

If I had realized the scope of the damage to the children I may have made other choices. I kept my promise to Brian but at what a price to my children? The first hand witnesses to this nightmare, the children, may have suffered the most. I was focused on doing what was best for the dying. Should I have been focused on doing what was best for the living? As I evaluate my choices in retrospect I think that sending Brian to a nursing home might have sent the wrong message to the children regarding how we care for terminally ill loved ones. But, I didn't think about that at the time.

I have struggled with whether I did the right thing by my children for many, many years. Occasionally I beat myself up over my treatment of Brian. When I find myself starting down that path of inconsolable recrimination I stop and remind myself that I really did the best I could. I gave all that I had and then some. Can we ask anything else of ourselves?

"My mother in law is coming for a visit. She and I don't really get along. She wants to take over the house when she visits...," the woman related. She went on to complain and complain about her mother in law. I sat quietly and listened but I wanted to scream at her and others like her saying "Your problems are stupid and ridiculous". They all seemed like cartoon characters. I knew it was wrong to take my anger out on them. They couldn't know what it was like to have your life be only about pain, suffering and death. So I withdrew from the world while Brian was sick. I couldn't sit around and discuss food, movies, and issues regarding toddlers when my reality was about watching my husband deteriorate, physically and emotionally, on a daily basis and matching my care to his increasing needs? The little bit of me that was left over after caring for Brian I gave to my children, especially Gary. I had no desire, time or energy for other people. In part, I was angry and bitter because they weren't suffering like I was.

It would be a long time before I could rejoin the world. For a long time after Brian died everything and everyone seemed so petty, meaningless and stupid. I used to wonder how they could get upset over such stupid, insignificant things. I still feel very different as a result of my experiences with Brian but it doesn't separate me from the world now. I have come to really understand how precious life and loved ones are. It isn't just some platitude that I read on a plaque. I really know it. I can't be hard on others because they have not suffered as I have. They can't know what I have learned. They can't understand the preciousness of life. Maybe it is part of the human condition that certain knowledge is acquired only through experience. The terrifying part for me is when I forget what I have learned.

The phrase "pearls of wisdom" is a bit corny but it has helped me to remember what I have learned so I hope you will indulge me. When pearls are first discovered they are shiny and fresh. We treasure them. We place them on top of the heap called life. There we can see them often and remember the lesson they represent. As time goes on the demands of daily life – earning a living, paying the mortgage, raising children, etc. causes the pearl to become buried in the heap where it becomes tarnished. The burial is not a sudden, traumatic event. It is a slow insidious burial and dulling of the pearls. Eventually the pearls will move completely out of our consciousness and into oblivion if we are not vigilant. We have to purposefully keep these pearls of wisdom at the top of the pile of stuff – in our immediate consciousness. If left at the bottom of the pile long enough the luster dulls, fades and eventually is chipped off until the pearl is permanently damaged or lost

I have found it is an even better practice to regularly polish the pearl to bring it to a bright luster. As we hold and softly rub the pearl we can't help but slowly turn it over and over, all the while examining it carefully. As we look at it and touch it we focus on the pearl and we can't help but be reminded of its meaning. Through his process we learn to treasure it over and over again and again.

I do this with my memories of my experiences with Brian. When I find myself focusing on and getting worried or anxious over insignificant daily matters, judging and blaming others or being vindictive or angry, I stop myself. I take out those memories and examine them like I would a precious pearl. I close my eyes and imagine I am examining and softly polishing a precious pearl. I touch it and feel it. The pearl represents my "knowledge" of the preciousness of life, love and the importance of compassion and connections. I am reminded that these daily trials and tribulations are minor and will pass. Often I call upon my litmus test. I ask myself, "Is someone I love sick or dying?" If I answer "No" then whatever is troubling me can be resolved. I am prevented from taking myself or events too seriously. I am able to keep things in perspective. . I am reminded that we are all connected in this life and world and we must show compassion and care for each other. I am able to remember to be compassionate and forgiving of myself and others.

How often have we looked back on events in our life and wondered why we were so upset at the time? How often have we had a huge fight with someone and later wondered what we were even fighting about? The importance of these events is fleeting. The "pearl" and the "litmus test" clear my mind of the clutter and bring me back to what is most important. They help me remember the lessons I learned through so much suffering. For each person the "pearl" and the "litmus test" may be different. Whatever it is for you, it will hopefully remind you of what is really important in your life – what you need to treasure. Once you know that the actions will follow.

CHAPTER THREE

Marriage – And Sometimes Even a Love Story

I won't make it to 50 years with anyone I thought. I did the math in my head. Yeah there is no way I will make it to 50 years with anyone. I don't have enough years left. Does it really matter? I won't be missing out on a gold medal or anything. I don't even think I will be missing out on having a close connection with another person. I will miss out on having a shared history but that requires too much living in the past and I have sworn off doing that.

I still remember the 50th wedding anniversary party held for my Grandparents. It was quite an event – like planning and executing a wedding. My Grandmother wore a beautiful lace dress. There was a huge cake. It was held at a beautiful hotel. Guests brought gifts. I remember my Grandparents standing side by side in front of the gift table for a photo. They weren't standing close enough to touch each other. What I remember most, because it struck me as so odd at the time, was the triumphant look on my Grandmother's face. I didn't understand that look back then. I was in high school at the time. She had triumphed. To her I think it was equivalent to winning an Olympic gold medal. She had made it. She crossed the finish line into the marriage longevity hall of fame. I realize, now that I am older, what an accomplishment that was and why she looked so triumphant. I, on the other hand, have failed. I respect my Grandparents for working to achieve something that was very important to them and their generation. I just don't know if I place as much value on it. Maybe that is just a defensive attitude because I couldn't do it but I don't think so. My Grandfather died a few years after that celebration. I never saw my Grandmother cry over his death. I was jolted back to the present.

"Take the stand please m 'am," I heard someone say in my direction. I walked slowly up to the witness box. "Please raise your right hand and be sworn," the bailiff said. I did. I was. I sat down. I looked around the courtroom. It was almost empty. He didn't even bother to show up. I didn't really expect him to. I was relieved he hadn't fought the matter in the courts. The judge asked me a few questions. "You may step down now. If you wait the clerk will give you a copy of the divorce decree," the judge said. That was it. Legally it was over. If only the emotional connection could be severed as quickly and simply as the legal one I thought. I didn't "feel" anything. That drama – the emotional end -was playing out on a different stage. I moved on to the next task at hand. I had to get back to the office.

Have you ever noticed that unhappiness just kind of creeps up on you like vines growing on a trellis? A vine starts with gentle tendrils. The tendrils grow large and strong and become vines. If left alone, without any pruning or tending, these vines will warp and eventually break the trellis. So it is that little tendrils of unhappiness ever so surreptitiously start clinging to our soul. Some unhappiness is good as it helps us to grow and mature. However those tendrils of unhappiness can grow and grow until, if left unattended, they choke your soul. This is not sorrow. Sorrow is palpable and real. It makes itself known. This is not real depression. Depression has you totally in its grip.

Unhappiness is insidious. It is so easily disguised or explained as a momentary response to a temporary, unfortunate situation. It can be so easily ignored. It is so very dangerous because we can become accustomed to that emotional state and we stop being able to recognize when momentary unhappiness grows and becomes something more. We must always keep our finger on the pulse of our happiness or the tendrils of unhappiness will become vines and choke us. We must prune and tend. I let my unhappiness go for far too long. By the time I realized how unhappy I was it had much too strong a hold on me. Pruning and tending were ineffective. I had to tear the vine out by its roots and in the process my soul was irrevocably damaged.

"Mom, mom," Jessica greeted me at the door when I arrived home from the office. It was about 7 pm. I had left for the office around 7 a.m. It was the day after Christmas. Usually the children came to greet me at the door when I arrived home. Today they didn't. There was an eerie silence in the house. "Where are Ellen and Samuel?" Where is your Dad? "I asked Jessica. She was clinging to me silently with her head buried in my stomach. "David, Ellen, Samuel," I called out. No one answered. "Jessica you have to let go of me," I said. Jessica finally looked up at me and said, "Mom, Dad broke all of Samuel's toys with a baseball bat. He smashed them to pieces!" I started up the stairs to Samuel's bedroom. I could see that the door to his room was closed. Jessica was still clinging to my waist. I felt like I was going to throw up. I pushed open the door to Samuel's bedroom. Broken pieces of toys covered the floor. The ramp to the hot wheels garage he had just excitedly opened yesterday was in pieces on the floor in the middle of the room. I recognized other pieces of toys he had received for Christmas just yesterday. I was now calling frantically for Ellen and Samuel. David was nowhere to be found or so it seemed. I walked next door into Ellen's room. She and Samuel were seated together on the floor playing with some of her toys. None of her toys were broken. I hugged and kissed them and then I went looking for David. He was in our bedroom. "How could you do that? You need to get out of the house right now!" I shouted at him. He said nothing. I think I shouted at him a while longer. He still said and did nothing.

In true WASP fashion and emulating my upbringing I went downstairs and fixed dinner. At dinner I talked a little bit but, for the most part, we ate in silence. We didn't discuss what happened. I had Jessica do her homework. I bathed the younger two and put them to bed. Samuel slept in Ellen's room that night as I was too exhausted to clean his room. I would do it tomorrow night I said to myself. I closed the door to his room and told the children to stay out of there. I fell into bed exhausted. I convinced myself that it was better to maintain some order and predictably after such an ordeal. It was as if David had smashed our marriage to pieces that night along with the toys. I closed the door on the relationship that night as I closed the door to Samuel's room with the broken toys in it. I knew then that I would file for divorce. The marriage had been broken for a long time.

"Let's watch this movie together tonight," I had suggested to David a few weeks before this event. I remember distinctly watching the movie "Ordinary People". "That was exactly what it was like for me growing up," I said to David. "You're just stupid," he retorted angrily. He got up and left the room. How does the person in whom you could confide your deepest secrets become the last person in the world you can or would confide in?

"Get out," I told David again the day after he had smashed the toys. I said it every day for weeks after that. He simply ignored me. He pretended nothing out of the ordinary had happened. How can he do that? It made me feel like I was crazy. Was I imagining what happened? I knew Jessica had seen it and that gave me comfort and strength. I couldn't afford to move anywhere with the children. I didn't have the money for the deposits needed to move into an apartment. I didn't have money to go to a hotel. I didn't have money to hire a lawyer and I am not sure that would have helped if I did. The next several months passed without any further incidents of violence. Then the violence returned with even more force. It was now directed at me. I am not sure the children really knew the difference.

"You are out of control. You are crazy!" I yelled at him. "You make me do the things I do because you are such a lousy wife!" David shouted as he hurled something at me. I ran in the direction of one of the bedrooms. He followed me. I turned to face him in the doorway of the bedroom. He punched me and I fell down. Samuel was standing behind me and he fell too. I landed on top of Samuel. He was five years old.

"You are not going anywhere," David said to me. He stood between me and the door. He wouldn't let me leave the room much less the house. Every time I tried to leave he pushed me back into the room. I tried not to scare the kids more than they already were scared. I heard the kids in the next room playing together. They came in and said good night to me.

The next day David got Samuel and Jessica off to school. Ellen went next door to the sitter's house. Eventually David dragged me into the car with him on some errands. He stopped for a red light. I jumped out of the car. I was fortunately only a few blocks from the office. I can't really remember what I said or did at the office. I know I really didn't tell anyone what had happened. I was too embarrassed. Somehow I got a ride back to the house. I called the police. David didn't come back to the house that night.

"We can't do anything m 'am since your husband isn't at home. If he comes back give us a call," the police officer said to me.

I went to work the next day. The children went to school and the sitter. The children were understandably acting out at home. I was feeling totally overwhelmed. I called a few family lawyers but I didn't have the money to hire one. That night David came home again. The next time David became violent and tried to keep me in the house I was able to run out the front door and get to my neighbors. My neighbor called the police. I ran back home immediately to see David pulling out of the driveway with Samuel in the back seat of the car. My heart sank.

"Do you have someplace you can go for the night?" the officer asked me. Finally I was talking to a compassionate officer who didn't look at me like I had horns. Domestic violence wasn't taken very seriously by police officers or even the courts back then. I frantically searched in my mind for someone to call. We had just moved to this city several months ago. This isn't exactly something you want to talk to good friends about much less new acquaintances. "You need to call someone," he insisted. Since David had fled before the officer arrived there was nothing that could be done to him right then.

"He is your son's father and there is no custody order so I can't do anything about him taking the boy," the officer said. Very reluctantly I picked up the phone and dialed the person I knew the best in my new city. "Eva can the kids and I stay at your house tonight?" I heard myself ask. I felt like I was outside my body – like I was watching this happen to someone else. I knew Eva was going to ask why and I dreaded that. She did and I responded, "David has hit me and tried to keep me from leaving the house. The police officer does not want the children and me to stay here tonight. " Eva hung up the phone without saying anything. "We will be all right here," I told the officer. I spent the better part of the evening in a panic wondering where Samuel was and if he was OK. David dropped Samuel off at the house later that night and left. Maybe things are going to get better I thought.

I had a restraining order issued but I could never get David served with it so it was of no use. During that time I think he would have simply ignored it anyway. I filed for divorce. By some miracle David simply stopped coming back to stay at the house. That didn't mean he disappeared from our lives entirely.

I was afraid if I told people at the office I would get fired maybe not right then but eventually. I kept everything a secret for a while in true WASP fashion. I must have made some excuses for leaving the office on occasion but I don't remember anything about that. I know that I never told anyone about the violence. We never spoke about it with the children but I know that the children kept everything a secret as well. We were an isolated island of misery and despair surrounded by and functioning in a huge ocean of normalcy at least for others. I went to work. The children went to school. We carried on as if our life was not all about fear and violence. I felt disconnected as if I lived in two separate worlds. I had no idea how to help the children cope.

"I am going to kill you, cut your body up into little pieces and bury it in the desert so no one will find you. I am going to kidnap the kids and take them to Mexico," David spewed this venom. He had barged his way into the house on the pretense of picking up the children for a visit. Suddenly he stopped. Jessica had entered the room. It had become a pattern that was repeated over and over again. He would say these things every time I had contact with him.

Each time Jessica would enter the room David would stop. I know Jessica heard what he said. My poor Jessica! I was afraid David would really carry out his threats. I think Jessica was too. He was crazy enough, at that time, to do it.

The phone was ringing again. I looked at the clock. It was 2 am. "Who are you sleeping with tonight you whore?" I heard David scream. I hung up the phone. I double checked to make sure all the windows and doors were locked. I lay awake all night. I was afraid if I didn't answer the phone he would come over to the house and do something worse.

David picked up my mail from the mailbox and read it. He broke into the house, answered my phone and ransacked my things. He stole my car. He called me at the office and at home accusing me of having affairs with every man I came into contact with. He would come to pick up the kids for a visit and punch me in the face when I opened the door.

How does one respond to all of this? Should I fight back? Should I be passive in hopes of placating him? Would it really matter what I did? Is my response really going to affect his behavior to any significant degree? It seemed no matter what I did he was hell bent on abusing me. Nothing could stop that. Any change that could have affected his behavior would have to have been done long before he first raised his fist to punch me. I knew he was in a rage and wanted to destroy everything. Things like courts and police have no power over such a person. That was perhaps the scariest thing of all.

I apologize to the reader if this all seems out of order or makes little sense. As I write this I am overcome by potent remnants of the fear and anger. I feel confused. It is as if my defenses kick in and my mind becomes foggy to protect me from too many bad memories. I have tried so hard to forget the details of what happened. I don't even want to remember them here.

These events went on regularly for at least nine months during which David engaged in all of the above and more on a weekly basis. The children and I lived constantly, every minute of every day, with the fear generated by his actions. I was trying, perhaps mistakenly, to keep things as normal as possible for the children.

I don't recall why I did not get more help from the courts or police. Was I right to feel bad about myself because I didn't fight back? Or should I just judge myself as a victim who is helpless to change, at that particular moment, the course of events? I tried not to judge myself too harshly. In some way I sensed that if I fought David too much and involved the courts and police he would fight harder and maybe carry out one of his threats. I hoped David's rage would eventually be spent and he would simply go away.

It is difficult to imagine that attitudes were so different in the mid eighties regarding domestic violence but they were. The police were not sympathetic. They would come to my door after a 911 call. They would look at me in a totally disgusted manner. When I said David had fled they would simply turn and walk away. They never examined me for bruises or marks. They never even made a report. They never gave me any information about any domestic violence shelters or court remedies. The procedures to have emergency court hearings were not in place as they are now or if they were they didn't tell me about them. I stopped calling the police because they made me feel like the scum of the earth.

The process of obtaining the restraining order was humiliating. The courts and judges were not particularly sympathetic to domestic violence victims especially well educated ones. The fact that I was well educated made it even more embarrassing. I didn't have any police reports to corroborate my story. I sensed that they thought I was making it all up – a hysterical woman. There was no self help available through the courts like they have now where you can obtain forms and instructions on how to do everything yourself. I was totally on my own.

Why did I marry him – David? It was obviously a poor choice but of course I didn't recognize that at the time. The violence didn't start until the very end when the marriage was falling apart. There may have been warning signs that he was disposed to such violence but it wouldn't have mattered to me. I would simply have ignored them. I was "in love". I wanted to "save" David. He has his problems but the power of my love would change him or so I thought. It is hard to believe that I could be that stupid but I was. I have since learned that it is OK to want to "save" the world or help people but it probably isn't something you should do when choosing a mate. It is better to choose a mate with whom you can form a solid relationship so that relationship can provide the support you need to go out and help others and "save" the world. Crippled partners make for crippled relationships which in my experience can have disastrous consequences.

I was special because only I could understand David and see his good qualities. I would make excuses for his behavior based on his motivation and character that only I could "see". This motivation and character didn't exist anywhere but in my mind. "You know how people feel about you by how they treat you," my friend told me. That was, sadly, not obvious to me.

I thought we had the right feeling for each other. My Grandmother said something to me once. She said what held her and my Grandfather together for 50+ years was the knowledge that they had the right feeling in the beginning. Well sometimes I wish she hadn't said that to me. Even before there was a media obsession with romantic love I had imbibed enough literature and personal lore to know that I had the "right feeling" for David.

I had absolutely no idea how to discern infatuation from love. I didn't even know there was a difference. One of my friends told me he was lucky because his infatuation turned into love. I was not so lucky. If I was not so impatient I might have discovered the difference or at least been able to see David rationally. I was impatient to find love or get married or something else.

I was just about to finish college. I had no sense of direction other than getting married. I am embarrassed to admit that but it is true. When the voice of prudence did once or twice whisper in my ear about marrying David I dismissed it. I had convinced myself this was not an impulsive decision because I had analyzed and dissected the pluses, minuses and consequences of such a marriage. I managed to convince myself this marriage was not the result of impulse. But it was.

"I like you a lot," one of the regular customers at the health food store where I worked in high school said to me one day. I didn't know quite what to say. Richard had graduated from an Ivy League school and was working in my hometown. He seemed much too old at the time – 5 years older than I. I really can't recall how it was that we starting dating. Over the next four years we spent a lot of time together. We broke up after he moved away. He came by my parents' house several years later to hear from my Sister that I was married and having a baby. I only appreciate now, almost 30 years later, what a great guy he was. You see I wanted to fall in love like Jennifer Jones and William Holden did in "Love is a Many Splendored Thing." I wanted some adventure or something different from my middle class upbringing. As to the latter, I got my wish!

I wasn't "in love" with Richard as I understood that phrase with all of my 19 year old wisdom. I didn't have that burning feeling in the pit of my stomach that told me he was the right person for me. When he wasn't around I didn't feel agitated and anxious like something was missing. I had that feeling for David so I had to be "in love".

Why am I lately so filled with regrets over lost loves? Have I really missed opportunities for love or am I just experiencing some middle age pangs of regret for my youthful choices? It is one of the principal ironies of life that we make the most important decisions of our life when we have absolutely no idea what we are doing – like choosing a spouse and a career. I found myself continually daydreaming along the lines of "What if?" What if I had married Richard was a question that was haunting me.

Do I really believe that certain relationships are meant to be or conversely not be? Do I believe in fate? Did I make the right decision or a grievous mistake? It was so long ago who really cares and why does it matter? As I passed the halfway point in my life I seem haunted by a need to find answers to those questions or somehow to put the inquiries to rest- permanently. That question was pressing in on me as I had just ended another marriage – my third. How did I end up here I wondered. I have experienced so much adversity and my life has been such a struggle. How do I make sense of it all? Sifting through my past relationships seemed like as good a starting point as any.

Brian had pursued me vigorously. I had been pursued before. That is not to say that I am so great. It is only that I am part of the generation where men pursued us and the women protested or played hard to get. In this case I wasn't playing hard to get. I really didn't want another relationship at least not with Brian. After my experiences with David I was not the least bit interested in having another relationship. Brian and I ended up getting married. But this time I spent a number of years getting to know Brian before we decided to get married.

"It is your husband on the phone," the receptionist at my office said over the intercom. I picked up the phone. "My Dad is back in the hospital. It doesn't look good. Can you come to the hospital right now?" Brian asked. I went to the hospital. I called the sitter from there, "Can you stay late today? I will be at the hospital until visiting hours about 8 pm." "OK," she said. "Let me talk to the children, "I said. I talked about how their day went. I reviewed whether homework was done and preparations made for the next day. I kissed them all good night over the phone of course. I went back to the vigil by the bedside.

The bedside vigil went on for at least two weeks. It was grueling. Brian and I had been back and forth to the hospital almost every day. During the course of those two weeks, I had received multiple urgent messages at the office advising me to come as soon as possible as the end was imminent. This all took place just a month before our wedding. In that same month I sold my house and moved out. The children and I had moved into Brian's house. Brian and I were making the final preparations for the wedding. I moved out of Brian's house when we had a huge blowout and we called the wedding off I was in court everyday as lead counsel in a huge trial that was expected to last at least 6 weeks. Brian and I were both physically and emotionally exhausted.

"Get your stuff together right now. We are leaving!" I shouted as I opened each of the doors to my children's respective bedrooms. They didn't question me. While they gathered up their stuff I gathered up some of my clothing. We threw our stuff into the minivan and we drove to a hotel where we would spend the first of several nights. I drove the children to school the next morning and then I went to court. In a few days we would move into a rental house. As I pulled away from Brian's house that night I looked in the rear view mirror. I saw Brian standing at the front door. He was still very angry but also incredulous.

I remember it so clearly. Brian and I were sitting on the couch in the TV room of the first house we lived in together. The children were in their bedrooms getting ready for bed. I have no recollection of what was said. Brian and I exchanged angry words. I decided I couldn't marry him. I decided to leave. I had no idea, at that time, what drove me to do that. I am sure I convinced myself it was something Brian said or did. As I look back on it I think I was driven by fear. I wanted the security and comfort of marriage but I was afraid of what that would mean to my independence and identity. Brian had very traditional ideas about marriage. What price would I have to pay to be married? A huge conflict was raging in me. It drove me to leave Brian's house that night. I was so selfish I didn't even think about the price my children would pay for my erratic behavior.

"You don't need to do that," Nancy, Brian's sister said to the young respiratory technician. She had just placed an oxygen mask over their Father's mouth to start some treatment. We were all standing in the hospital room around their Father's bed, Brian, me, Nancy and her husband, Bob. The last year had been a roller coaster of ups and downs regarding his health. Brian was very close to his Father. "He's dying," Nancy continued. The poor young girl looked like a fawn that had just looked into the headlights of an oncoming car. She took her machine and slithered out of the room. "How could Nancy know that?" I asked myself.

A moment or so later I heard a gruesome sound. It reminded me of the sound I have heard mortally wounded animals make in TV documentaries. It was emanating from Brian. He was face down on the bed next to his Father's lifeless body. I wanted to go over and comfort Brian but I couldn't seem to move. That sound went on for what seemed like an eternity. After a few minutes Brian pulled himself together. He and Nancy went out into the hall where they made arrangements for the body. Our wedding was to take place in less than two weeks but for now we had to plan a funeral.

Brian and I didn't talk on the ride home from the hospital. I so wanted to comfort him at least one part of me did. I had come into this relationship as a strong, independent single mother of three children who was competing in a very intense business environment. I had just recently learned to be tough. Instinctively I was afraid of getting sucked into the traditional female role. Sadly I thought it would demean me. I did not yet know how to be tough and tender.

I felt terrible for a long time that I had failed Brian because I didn't hug him or make any overt act to comfort him. Emotions were very scary to me back then. I couldn't let my guard down. I literally felt paralyzed from reaching out to Brian. If only I had some time and energy to really think about all of this back then! It might have spared Brian and I a lot of agony.

Women instinctively know how to do that stuff except for me or so I thought. I berated myself. I wasn't a good wife or mother because I lacked that gene. I wondered if I was born that way or whether the demands of the workplace and life eradicated that part of me. I always felt inadequate especially back then so I just added this to my list of inadequacies.

"Are you sure you want to marry her?" Brian's friend Paul asked him a week or so before the wedding. "She is awfully independent," Paul said with some trepidation. Brian told me this much later. I think Brian liked my independence and admired it but he wanted a traditional wife as well. He wasn't the only one who was confused or had competing ideas about the role of a wife and mother. I was too. I wanted to be a strong, independent working woman and a good wife – serving my family, always putting everyone else's needs first, always being available to comfort and support my husband and children. I just couldn't seem to reconcile the two. Maybe Brian couldn't either.

"We are having our annual company barbecue. It is a lot of fun. I would like you to come. "Brian said over the phone. "I will be busy barbecuing the meat and entertaining customers and other guests but you could meet a lot of people." Brian and I were seeing each other very casually at the time. I accepted the invitation. As I was standing at the event in the middle of a huge group of people I heard a familiar voice say my name. I turned to see who it was. Before I could say hello to that person Brian swooped down, grabbed me by the hand and whisked me away. I have no idea where Brian came from. "That was your old boyfriend wasn't it? " Brian asked me as he propelled me away. How did he know that I wondered?

Brian had an uncanny ability to "read me." It was quite irritating at times and also a relief at times. I was relieved because I know Brian knew the depth of my desire to comfort him when his father died even if I couldn't show it. This ability to communicate non verbally served to connect us through the many hard times that lie ahead for us. Maybe there was no mystery to it. Maybe Brian just cared enough to look and notice what was going on with me.

I have often wondered why some marriages dissolve in times of crisis like the loss of a child. I would think that is a time when you need each other the most. Sure blame and recrimination can poison the relationship but that can be overcome. Is it that in times of crisis we come to fully realize that we don't really love the other? A foundation of genuine love might be a prerequisite to the survival of the relationship in times of acute crisis. And so the relationship breaks under the strain without love to bind the parties together. Conversely if the parties love each the crisis can be a catalyst for a deepening of their love.

Brian and I were together 4 years before we married and during that period of time we broke up and got back together several times. We worked some things out before we married. But I don't believe you can work everything out. Marriage creates so many secret expectations. You can't really deal with all of that until you are married because most of it isn't triggered until that time.

I think my main criteria in choosing Brian was that he was a good provider and would make a good father and husband. I wasn't imaginative enough or equipped to find another way to raise my children outside the confines of a traditional marriage. I did not want to go it alone forever. The truth is that I had no conscious idea as to what I wanted my life to look like at that time in my life. I was making choices based on the image of a traditional wife and mother of my childhood. I had no conscious idea that the role didn't suit me.

I felt as if was being forced into a certain mold called "traditional wife and mother" –like one of those cooking molds. In my marriage to Brian I had to add corporate wife to that "mold". The mold was comprised of all the expectations, code of conduct and "have tos" that I was required to comply with on a daily basis. The expectations were rarely verbalized. I just seemed to understand what they were. I complied for the most part but inside the mold I was banging against the walls. I didn't want to be confined. I felt like I had no control over my own life. It was all determined for me by someone else. Sometimes I even "bloodied" myself and Brian in the process of rebelling. It is only as I look back on that time in my life that I realize I didn't like the role I was playing or maybe was forced to play. I would have had no idea what to replace it with even if I had realized the reason I was so unhappy.

I would occasionally experience a vague dissatisfaction with my life. I would tick off the list of things in my life and they all seemed to be running smoothly. I didn't look beneath the surface. I thought I should be happy because I had financial security and all the material perks that went along with that, a good husband and children, health and a job. How could I ask for more?

"I don't want to do that! I am not going to go!" I shrieked at Brian. Why is it that he didn't hear me or didn't listen to me until I got angry? I was really angry at him because 99% of the time I went along with what was expected of me whether I really wanted to or not. I rarely said "no". I didn't understand why he couldn't see that. I would only draw the line with Brian where my children were concerned. This was one of those times.

Brian wanted to attend every business event, sporting event, etc. That meant being away from home most nights. Since I was working full time that I meant I would rarely have time at home with the children. It took some time but I finally rebelled.

Why did it take me so long to say something? The simple reason is that Brian did not take "No" easily. Any "No" meant there would be a huge fight. I didn't always have the energy for that so I had to pick and choose my fights.

On a deeper level I traded control over my life for financial security and help with the responsibilities of daily living and raising my children. I abdicated responsibility for my life to Brian. I think implicitly we agreed that I owed him because of what he was doing for my children and I. The unspoken attitude I bought into was that I should appreciate what he was doing for my children and me. I could show that appreciation by doing and being what Brian wanted me to do and be. My job was to make my sure my family was happy and had everything they needed and wanted starting first with Brian. I was about to break our agreement. As a result there would be a great deal of conflict between Brian and I.

As I look back I realize that I sought out, unconsciously, relationships with a lot of adversity and conflict. After all that is what I knew from my relationship with my Mother. It was one of the behavior patterns I was doomed to repeat multiple times. I think my penchant for adversity was one of my attractions to the practice of law.

I am amazed that Brian and I did as well as we did. We brought into this relationship a lot of baggage. In addition to the competing, unspoken and misunderstood expectations of our respective upbringings we each had a prior failed marriage and children of prior failed marriages. The first few years of our marriage were overshadowed by conflict and adversity. We stuck it out because we both wanted the relationship to work. Maybe neither of us wanted another divorce. But it was more than that.

I really loved Brian. I didn't come to fully realize that until he was terminally ill. I often wonder if it is human nature to only appreciate things when we are about to lose them or have lost them. Surely there must be another way. I knew that Brian really loved me early on. I just didn't know how much I really loved him. Maybe he didn't know that either.

Maybe the depth of my love for Brian was stifled by the expectations placed on me in that relationship and in my life at that time. My life was an endless series of "have tos". I don't blame Brian for all of the expectations. It was a joint effort. I did it, in part, to myself. He and I were products of our upbringing. I was trying to be a traditional wife and mother like my mother as well as a working wife and mother. I had no role model for the working mother. I functioned in that role on a trial and error basis. Was it any wonder that these competing roles and expectations created huge conflicts between Brian and me? I was totally conflicted over it myself.

At the end of the day the love we had for each other held us together through all the adversity and trials. Sometimes it felt as if that love didn't exist or had disappeared but if we were patient it would always resurface. I didn't recognize it as love at that time because it didn't look like the infatuation that I had come to understand was love. It is only as I look back on my life that I see it was always there binding us together. I was too focused on the petty conflicts we engaged in at the time to recognize it.

"I really love you and I want us to stay married," Brian said. After he said that Brian bent over in his chair and sobbed uncontrollably. I froze. George, the marriage counselor, waited a moment and then started to talk. I was thankful that I didn't have to say or do anything. This was the first time I had seen or spoken to

Brian in over a month. He had moved out of the house and filed for divorce. Shortly after he filed the divorce petition Brian sent me a note asking me to go to counseling with him. I reluctantly agreed. We had tried counseling before we split up but it hadn't helped. Why would this be any different I wondered. Then I saw this tough, macho guy sobbing and I knew this time it would be different.

I think that, for my generation and those that came before, men were expected to keep all of their emotions bottled up – stuffed down. They were permitted to express only one emotion – anger. I think that is why in all of our more intimate conversations Brian's response was always to get angry. We really couldn't communicate with each other on important issues without one of us getting angry. Brian seemed to only be able to express tenderness and love in our most intimate physical moments together. Those were moments of unparalleled love and connection.

"You don't have to marry everyone you have sex with," my therapist aptly said when I was exploring dating after my divorce from David. I didn't realize I was operating under that rule. It was great to recognize that I was operating under that false assumption even if I could not change my behavior. I had no clue what to think about sex when I was young. I was told it was reserved for marriage. That was about it. The unwritten message was that good men don't marry loose women. So I functioned that way for most of my adult life. Sex was reserved for serious relationships and ideally it was a product of love between two people. In my generation men did lose respect for you if you had too many partners. That was in the back of my mind but that wasn't the primary reason I followed the rule. I am glad this next generation has escaped the notion that you have to marry or at least believe you are going to marry everyone you have sex with.

I understand that now people engage in sex on the first date or just for the heck of it. That saddens me. Isn't the sexual act the physical joining of two persons who are emotionally connected? Isn't that what makes sex so wonderful above and beyond the physical pleasure? The emotional connection enriches the sexual experience.   The sexual experience enriches the emotional connection.   How can the two be separated without losing the essence of the experience? Don't we elevate romantic relationships to a level above all others because the act of physical intimacy engenders unparalleled emotional intimacy that cannot be achieved in any other relationship? Are we cheating ourselves by rushing to have sex before there is any genuine emotional connection?

I have found sex to be the best barometer regarding the emotional health of a relationship. Our attitude toward sex tells us so much about our attitude toward our partner and our relationship. If only we could read and understand the barometer better!

"Why buy the cow if you can get the milk for free?" was all my Mother said on the subject of premarital sex.   She had this perfunctory discussion with me because I had started to menstruate. "Do you have any questions?" she asked. I didn't. I had already learned the mechanics from the older kids in the neighborhood. My parents never said nor allowed us to even say the word "sex". If we did we were told in a certain tone of voice to "hush". The tone of voice and look of disgust said it all. Sex was dirty and disgusting. There was no other possible interpretation.   As a young, busy working mother it was something you wanted to get over with so you could finally go to sleep.

"When Brian is really angry I want you to go up and hug him. It is impossible to stay angry at someone when they are touching or hugging you," George, our marriage counselor said. "There is absolutely no way I can do that. Have you heard me when I told you the incredibly cruel things he says to me when he is angry?" I shot back. "Look at Brian and say to yourself that this is my best friend who is in terrible pain. Don't get caught up in what Brian is saying," George replied. I stared at George incredulously. "You know it takes two to fight," George said to me. "What the hell does that mean? Do you really think I should just silently by and take all the insults and cruelties without saying anything –without defending myself?" I shrieked. "Yes," George replied. "Just remember that Brian's anger is usually fueled by something other than what you have done or what you two have discussed. Please try this," George said calmly.

Why should I do all of that I thought to myself. It is Brian's problem and he should deal with it, not me. Brian was verbally abusive, not me. George should just tell Brian to stop verbally bashing me I arrogantly said to myself. I wanted to be able to blame Brian for the struggles in our relationship. I didn't want to take any responsibility for them. I was playing my own "blame game." I could be arrogant because my bad behaviors were not so easily recognizable. I didn't get angry and say cruel things but I got the message across in other ways. Brian and I both had much to work on although my progress would be delayed by my refusal to give up the higher moral ground.

If only we could see others, especially those closest to us, the way George wanted me to see Brian. Why is it so difficult for us to see the anger being expressed by the person we love as an expression of his /her pain? We take it all so personally and react accordingly. I would remember and nurse old hurts and wounds over the mean things Brian had said to me in the past. I wish instead I could have remembered his acts of kindness and love as he vented his anger. I know that would have diffused his anger and the situation. Nursing old hurts and becoming defensive only served to fuel his anger and escalated almost every disagreement to epic proportions. I know this because slowly I was able to do what George asked. Oh I can't say I always did it kindly. In the beginning I think it made me feel superior to Brian and more in control. But eventually that faded as well.

Brian and I were two very dysfunctional people who were trying to form a healthy relationship. We were making progress. You see, in part, that is how I knew Brian loved me. He was working hard at making changes in himself for the good of our relationship. I hope he saw the same in me. We were transforming ourselves, each other and our relationship. Unfortunately all progress came to a screeching halt when Brian was diagnosed with Lou Gehrig's disease. All of our old habits resurfaced.

"We don't have to earn love. My grandmother told me that I was loved just because I was born. I didn't have to do anything else," Melissa said to me one day. Strangely I hadn't heard that before. It seems rather stupid that this concept struck me as so profound. I had been operating under the premise that I earned love by being a good girl. Conversely I would no longer be loved if I stopped being a good girl or failed to be a good girl. Being a good girl meant doing everything that everyone else wanted me to do and putting all of their needs and wants ahead of mine. I was selfish if I wanted anything just for me. My Mother would tell me regularly that I was very selfish.

This is a lesson I started to learn in my relationship with Brian. When I was able to be honest with myself I knew that there was no way I had earned Brian's love. My behavior had been, on more occasions than I cared to remember, absolutely atrocious. I couldn't delude myself that I was a "good girl" all the time.

We women were expected to do and be everything to everyone and do nothing for ourselves. Even if we wanted to do something for ourselves there was usually nothing left over. We raced through life trying to fulfill everyone else' needs or make everyone else happy. A good wife and mother could do all this effortlessly, without any help and with a smile on her face. Was it any wonder I was always exhausted and yes depressed? We didn't know how to temper our expectations for ourselves or to ask for help from our mates or children. I think our daughters have learned that lesson. For my generation that may not be possible. The old messages have too strong a hold on us.

"After I cleaned the dinner dishes, got the children to bed and spent some time with my husband I started sewing the costumes for my daughter's school play. I was up until after midnight sewing. If I work every night I should be able to finish them by the end of next week. Of course I have a big deadline at work as well but I think I should be able to do it all," one of my neighbors said to me. I nodded in complete understanding as she related this to me. She wasn't complaining. She said this all very proudly.

We were all trying to be "superwoman". We were going to prove to the world that our children were not suffering or were not neglected because we worked. We were engaged in a competition regarding who did the most in a day, a week or a month. We would each try to top the other's list of activities or accomplishments so we could claim the prize of being "super woman". The image of "superwoman" still lingers in me. It rears its ugly head on occasion.

"I am doing what a good spouse does. I am working in the business Warren started and giving up or postponing some things I want to do so we can build this business and life together. We are supposed to support each other through tough times aren't we?" I asked my friend. "Well I can't argue with the concept," was all she said.

I was doing it again. Despite my "maturity" and all my good intentions, the old messages had taken over. I was doing way too much for Warren. How do you stop? How do you know where or when to draw the line and say "no more"? I know I definitely waited too long to say "No". By the time I did the marriage was already over.

I was a victim of the Old Protestant work ethic. We think working harder or working more will correct any situation. When things started not going so well in the business I did more and more. I didn't focus on whether Warren was doing the same. As the business started to fail the marriage started to fail. It is amazing how they tracked each other maybe because as the business failed Warren also stopped functioning.

Warren never noticed what or how much I did or if he did he didn't say anything to me. I worked full time at a law firm, worked in Warren's business, handled some active litigation for his business, managed everything in the house and parented my young son. Before I knew it my brief stint at pitching in to do more resulted in me doing everything and Warren doing almost nothing in the business and in our relationship. I was, in part, driven by the mantra that "if you fail it is only because you didn't work or try hard enough."

"The doctor says I have a rare liver disease. It is terminal," Warren said one night. "I have to go see a liver specialist next week," I felt terrible. I had doubted his claims of illness for months. "I will go to the doctor with you next week," I said. "You don't have to," he replied. "I think I should so I can know what to do and how to help," I replied. I spent hours researching the disease before we visited the doctor so I could ask intelligent questions about it.

"We will need you to go to the lab for this test," the doctor said to Warren. I piped in, "Will that lead to any possible treatments for the disease?" "No" the doctor said. "Your husband doesn't have that disease. I am ordering a routine test related to another health issue. But this is a minor health issue. It is nothing serious". When the doctor left to get the paperwork for Warren I left, without saying a word, and went back to the office.

When Warren first told me he had this terminal illness I immediately offered to do whatever I needed to do in order to help him. Secretly, I panicked over the thought that I would have to take care of Warren. I can't adequately express my feelings of anger and revulsion over the prospect of taking care of him. I had been down this road before and I knew that the situation required more of us than we could possibly do – physically and emotionally. My anger and revulsion were not a result of my past experience with Brian. When I found out Brian was ill I was devastated, not resentful and angry. I realized that I felt an enormous sense of panic because I didn't love Warren. I was relieved to find out that Warren wasn't sick. Now I wouldn't have to face a moral dilemma.

I have witnessed two marriages that were also great love stories. Brian's sister and her husband, Nancy and Bob, and my friends, Martha and Mark were in marriages where you could literally feel their love for each other when you were in their presence. In both of those one of the partners was very, very ill. The illnesses went on for many years. The healthy spouse had to physically care for the ill spouse. With each passing year their love seemed to grow and deepen. I have often wondered if the possibility of losing the other person is a prerequisite to creating a great love or at least a prerequisite to recognizing and appreciating it.

I have heard of marriages where the partners share a great passion and that shared passion has fueled their love. I have never witnessed such a relationship. Maybe that is because people hide the best parts of their relationships from others. We don't seem to have trouble complaining to our friends when things go wrong in our relationships. I don't see us talking much about what is right with our relationships.

"I am too sick to work or do anything," Warren said. "I can't handle any stress at all. I need time to get my health back. The stress of the lawsuit and failure of the business took a huge toll on me." For a while, before I accompanied Warren to the doctor's office that day, I thought Warren might really be sick. But as he visited more and more doctors without a firm diagnosis I suspected he was a hypochondriac. I guess that is why Warren made that outrageous claim that he had a terminal illness. Now I knew his "illness" was an excuse to avoid the realities of a failing or failed business and failing marriage. Warren simply checked out of life and left me to handle everything. Still for a while I hung in there hoping that Warren would get back on his feet and we could go on with our relationship and our lives.

How did my resolve to maintain limits and make this relationship work for me evolve into me as the caregiver again? I know I had limits in the beginning. How did they slip away so quietly like a thief in the night? I thought that couldn't happen to me again. How do you know when being a good mate - helpful, supportive, compromising for the greater good, accepting things that aren't exactly the way you would like them to be crosses the line into being taken advantage of, used and/or abused? How do you know when you are being asked to do too much – more than your share of work and sacrifice to make the relationship work?

If I had been happy to take care of and do almost everything for Warren we could still have a "working relationship." But I wasn't. Just because a relationship is working doesn't necessarily mean it is healthy for the partners. My goal was to have a healthy relationship. Maybe that was the problem. I have seen many marriages that function or work. Each partner seemed to like who they were in the relationship and what they were doing. Their role and their partner's role met their expectations and needs. The relationship validated their self image. Of course I am only an outsider but those relationships did not always appear to be healthy for one or both of the partners.

My self image was one of the self sacrificing wife and mother or as a survivor of difficult circumstances. I created difficult circumstances for myself to overcome. I thought I had "cured" myself of that self image. I know I didn't start out that way in this relationship with Warren but I definitely ended up there. As I look back I think Warren intuitively knew I would become that person. I wanted to discard, not validate, those self images. I didn't see any way I could retract what I had done. Warren had firmly entrenched himself in the role of the victim of life, me and poor health.

Don't you just get married and live happily ever after like "Father Knows Best" or Ozzie and Harriet Nelson or the Clevers on "Leave it to Beaver"? Isn't that the image we learned from watching TV and our parents? Unfortunately we weren't given even the most rudimentary instructions regarding how to achieve "happily ever after".

Warren and I were very happy for five years. What happened? Did I just pick the wrong person? Did I miss or ignore signs early on that this wouldn't work? Was Warren only pretending to be a loving husband for that period of time? Did I want the "security" (albeit false) of a relationship at any price? How could he change so dramatically? Did I contribute to that? I started to think of all the things I should have or could have done differently that might have changed the outcome. I call these the "what ifs". I don't know why I felt compelled to torture myself with "what ifs". It was too late to change anything about the relationship. I knew that by indulging my compulsion to relive this marriage I was not going to make sense of it all. I know that can't really be done. Still I couldn't stop myself.

It seems the more I did the less Warren did in every aspect of our life together. It seems the more I compromised the less he compromised. Could I have forced him to compromise by being more unyielding myself or would that have simply sped up the inevitable demise of the relationship? Could anything have helped when I finally saw that he was unable to deal with any adversity? Should I have been willing to accept a partner who fakes illness to avoid all the responsibilities of life? Would Warren have stopped coping in that fashion if I had changed some of my behaviors?

I think the seeds of the failure were planted in the beginning of the relationship because we were each who we were. You have to really love the other person to make any substantial changes in yourself. Warren and I didn't have that kind of love for each other although, in the beginning, we thought we did. We confused infatuation with love.

Can you know if you have that kind of love at the beginning or is it only revealed as we face the trials and tribulations and joys of life? We can't really know what another's response to the challenges of life will be until we have to face those challenges. That is one of the risks of a relationship.

There are so many false "loves." Love is a master at disguise. For Warren and I the worst parts of our personalities connected to each other. We felt like we had met our other half or our soul mate. The unhealthiest parts of our personalities were a perfect match. Warren's need to be taken care of matched up with my need to take care of someone. His need just became too great and my drive to take care of someone had diminished. I was no longer willing to give up my whole self or everything I wanted for a relationship and that is what Warren was asking. Warren was a master manipulator and I was a willing victim. The list goes on and on.

I know Warren and I didn't genuinely love each other because I know Brian and I did. I knew Brian really loved me, in part, because he worked so hard on himself and at the relationship. That effort made me love him more and work harder on myself.

Warren wasn't going to make any changes for the relationship. That was apparent pretty early on but I missed it. If I had waited longer to make a commitment I am sure I would have "seen" it. I did too much compromising in the beginning. We moved to the part of the country where he wanted to live. We started the business he wanted to start. I worked in the business with him because that is what he wanted. I thought it was right to give a lot to make a relationship work. The more you give the better the relationship will be I thought. It wasn't like Warren was asking me to do something I didn't want to do at least in the beginning. The only thing I felt very strongly about was our relationship. I was going to adjust almost everything to accommodate that. It wasn't a sacrifice.

But it is like the relationship with your children. If one person does everything in the relationship it becomes unhealthy for everyone. It might be better to say you become the only participant in the relationship. Is keeping your guard up to prevent being taken advantage of part of all relationships? Maybe that is just the wrong way to look at it. Maybe you have to feel good enough about yourself to set limits and stick to them. I still don't trust myself to do that. I am fortunate in that my children have set limits on what they will allow me to do for them.

"We knew you were so unhappy. On our drive to your house Jay and I would talk about how difficult it was to see you like that," Doris said to me after I told her about the breakup of our marriage. I kept waiting for Warren to recognize my unhappiness and stop taking advantage of me. Surely it was as obvious to him as it was to Doris. Apparently it wasn't or he didn't care that I was unhappy. How could I have fallen into that old trap of waiting for him to do something about my unhappiness? I think I did, for a while, point out my unhappiness. At some point I just gave up saying anything because when I had nothing had changed.

In the end I realized Warren never really loved me or he loved himself much more. In the end it seems to have boiled down to the fact that he wanted to have his own way more than he wanted to have a relationship with me. I just couldn't compromise any more without totally losing myself.

"How can he expect me to give up my whole life and move to Africa with him?" Lee Remick said to the group of women. I can't remember the name of the movie. "He wants me to have another child. I don't want to do that. I am done having children. He doesn't understand why I won't do these things," she continued telling her friends. At the time, as a very young adult, I didn't understand why she wouldn't do those things either. How could you choose to be alone or choose to give up love? He wasn't asking so much was he? I thought she was crazy. I see it so very differently now. If only I had understood that back then!

"How long have you two been together?" the flight attendant asked Brian. We were seated next to each other on a plane traveling to a business meeting for Brian's company. Brian looked down sheepishly and replied, "Three years". The flight attendant didn't say anything but I saw her response in her eyes. She was touched that Brian's love for me could be so strong and so obvious after three years. I was touched as well. Don't women, for the most part, fall in love with a man who loves them? When men stop loving or showing the love all is lost. For me distinguishing between manipulation and love has always been difficult.

For most of my life I have felt starved for love and affection like I imagine a starving child must be for food. My appetite for love and affection was insatiable. It caused me to ignore all the warnings about the object of my love. I realize now that I equated craving with love or I should say craving was love. It was, for me, like a drug addiction. My craving increased as the other party withdrew the love or at least stopped being romantic. I would wait for some little act or crumb of "love". The anticipation was exhilarating. There was such a high when some small act of love was dispensed. Getting the other person to show that love was my mission – my challenge. Writing this it is easy to recognize what I did and maybe still do. The hard part is when I am caught up in that all consuming feeling of "love." My brain seems to shut off or disengage.

"Are you and Brian back together again? Is the wedding still going to take place as planned?" Walter asked me. I answered affirmatively. "Glad to hear that. You two have been together for what five years now. That is a pretty long time," Walter replied. "See you at the wedding," he said. Relationships take time. They have a rhythm. If you push too fast or too hard you can destroy it. It is a mystery to me why Brian and I were so patient. Neither of us were patient people in other areas of our lives or in our past relationships.

"I am not one of your employees," I used to say to Brian. "You can't order me around and tell me what to do all the time." Brian was a very successful businessman. But it seemed to me that it was exactly those qualities that made him successful at business that made it difficult for him to be successful at home. He was forceful. He would push to get things done. I admired those qualities most of the time. Sometimes he would push too hard. Sometimes he just didn't know when I really knew what I wanted or what I didn't want. Most of the time I didn't know either.

"Counsel what is it that you want from me?" the judge said to me from the bench with a look of disgust on his face. Isn't it obvious I wanted to say to him. Apparently it wasn't since he asked me again with even more of a total look of disgust. Knowing and expressing what I wanted wasn't just a problem in my personal life. It invaded my professional life as well. Now I can understand the judge's frustration with me. This issue was a little easier to resolve professionally because I knew what my goal was. I just needed to express it.

In personal relationships I didn't know what I wanted or expected. If I did know I was afraid to express my expectations for fear they would not be honored. Or I just felt guilty or selfish for expressing what I wanted. I didn't want to appear too demanding or unfeminine. That attitude wrecked a lot of havoc for me at home and in the business world. It was difficult for me to navigate those waters. I can't imagine how difficult it must have been for Brian.

"Can you stop and get me a cup of coffee when you go out this morning?" I asked Warren on Saturday morning. I was working for Warren's business on the weekends after a full week at the law firm. Warren complained but he did it. I took a sip of the coffee Warren brought for me. "We have been married six years and you still have no idea what kind of coffee I like," I said to him. He shrugged his shoulders, turned and walked away. I might have forgiven his ignorance if he had gone to get the coffee without me asking.

It is usually not any one event that causes the final break. It is the little things that make or break a relationship. The little thoughtful daily acts sustain the love. Oh sure the great birthday or anniversary present and celebration are wonderful. But unloading the dishwasher, taking out the trash, putting the kids to bed, helping them with their homework, putting a load of wet clothes in the dryer mean so much more. The words of appreciation for all we do accompanied by those acts seals the deal. We women can accept we will do more in a relationship as long as we know that the "more" that we do is recognized and sincerely appreciated by acts and deeds. Brian understood that. We were a team regarding our home life especially in raising the children.

"You have six months to find a job or I am filing for divorce," I told Warren after I found out he had lied about having a terminal illness. The humiliation of getting divorced for a second time impeded my resolve to end the relationship. In the end I couldn't stand being gut wrenchingly unhappy any longer. I had been in that state for three years. I didn't have that many years left and I wasn't going to squander them. I had finally given up hope that anything would change. I guess I have made some progress. Once I would have stayed until there was nothing left of me.

I see a successful marriage as two concentric circles that overlap but never completely rest on top of each other. We are individuals and we are a couple. They must intersect but never completely overlap. When we first meet we have our individual interests. As we become a couple we abandon those interests our partner doesn't share in order to pursue joint interests or to devote more time to our partner. But it is those interests that attracted us to each other. It is our separateness that helps to keep the relationship vital, invigorated and growing. Without individual experiences we bring nothing unique to the relationship and it becomes stale. We must share those experiences and our individuality. If we don't share ourselves our connection withers and we drift apart. It is typically not a conscious decision. The relationship just simply atrophies over time.

As we mature individually, and as a couple, we seem to be faced with a choice as to whether we will embrace or reject the changing world. Couples can decided to shut out the parts of the world that don't fit their joint "reality" or aren't to their liking. Change and individual differences become their enemy. They are eliminated or "contained". What is the price for these long term marriages? Challenging ourselves to move outside our comfort zone is the catalyst for growth. Without change, relationships and the people in them become stale like bread that has been kept too long. Over time way pieces may break off. Finally the entire remaining piece is hard and unyielding.

Over the course of my life I know that I have changed substantially. In the process I have become someone that I like. I honestly don't believe this would not have been possible if I were in a long term monogamous relationship. Change is difficult to navigate alone but the resistance of a partner to the change could be a death knell especially for someone like me.

I am discovering that I can have a fulfilling life without a romantic relationship. The nine to five work routine makes finding a fulfilling life without a monogamous relationship difficult as that schedule leaves little time or energy for pursuing it. It seems society is still based on the married couple model. Still it is a wonderful process of discovery. The loneliest I have ever been was in an unhappy marriage.

"Mom I need help today with the baby. Can you come over?" Jessica asked.

"Mom can I drop over for dinner tonight?" Ellen asked. "I have something I want to talk to you about".

"Mom can you go to the dog park today with me?" Samuel asked.

Having adult children is the most wonderful experience in the world. I am so fortunate. It is because of them that I feel "complete" without a romantic relationship. The connections I have with them fill me up. Having satisfying connections in my life has brought many changes. I don't "crave" a connection to that romantic partner who will change my life or make me "complete".

Oh I admit that some part of me still hangs onto that idealistic image of the perfect mate. They myth of the "soul mate" won't die. Isn't the romantic and sometimes adolescent notion of love constantly perpetuated and encouraged by our culture? These romantic notions are best stored in a box in my brain marked "romance- to be removed only under controlled circumstances" or "Open at your own risk". Entering into a relationship is akin to opening Pandora's Box, at least for me.

I know I am still conflicted over what to expect of a partner and a relationship. I carry around stale expectations from my childhood and youth. I would expect him to be strong, confident, decisive, supportive, and protective in that old Sleeping Beauty and Cinderella model. I also expect him to be the new age male – soul mate, best friend, compassionate, loving, sympathetic, romantic, and thoughtful. I have stale expectations for myself as well. I find myself falling into the traditional role of wife and mother and becoming a caregiver, putting all of his needs and wants first. I don't want to have that type of relationship but I found myself playing exactly that role in my last marriage except that in addition I was the only financial support. It crept upon on me. I went, automatically, into that role. I don't know how to prevent myself from doing that.

I have made some progress though. At least I can now identify most of my unrealistic expectations. Maybe that will make a difference if there is a next time. Still I sincerely doubt that I can engage in a monogamous relationship without imposing the confining expectations upon it that would, at the very least, create a lot of conflict for me, internally, and in the relationship and might inevitably destroy it.

I am at a time in my life when I no longer have to seek a mate who is a good provider or a good father. My children are all grown now. I can find someone who enriches my life. I shouldn't say someone as that implies he alone has that responsibility. The relationship that enriches my life is created by he and I together. Our parts make up the whole but it is separate and distinct from either of us alone. It is the interaction of those two individual parts not just the parts themselves. I cannot passively sit by and expect him to enrich my life. I must be an integral part of the formation and maintenance of such a relationship. Underneath this idea of the "perfect" relationship the basic questions still haunt me and the answers still elude me?

It is a given that Cinderella living happily ever after with Prince Charming is a romantic myth. But what do we replace it with? What are realistic or unrealistic expectations in the context of the daily ritual of marriage? Can we only discover this through trial and error? How do we make it all work? How do we sustain and nurture our love for each other? What brings us together? How do we develop bonds with another? When have we compromised too much? When do we lose ourselves in the process of making the relationship work? Where do we draw the line? Is there a way to know and avoid giving up too much of ourselves before we throw up our hands in disgust and end the relationship? When is the work required in a relationship too much?

Part of what binds us together is the struggle to remove our baggage so we can connect to each other. The connection initially appears only in rare moments. We build on those rare moments. Connections are forged through sharing the joys and trials of life. The connections that bound Brian and I together were forged from sharing events like the death of his mother, the illness and death of his father, the challenges and joys of raising four children, the birth of our son, enjoying trips together and with friends, sharing the burdens of the physical demands of daily living and facing a terminal illness and death. Those individual, separate connections eventually formed an unbroken chain. The chain grew stronger with the addition of each new link. It grew so strong it could be broken only by death. The connection could never even begin to form without love – the type of love that caused us to commit to each other. By commit I don't mean marriage. I mean commit to change ourselves and our lives to make the relationship work and flourish. Setting limits and demanding some change from our partners is part of the commitment we make to ourselves.

Love can't be rushed or maybe I should say the recognition of love takes time. We have to allow the time to eliminate the many false loves that seek to deceive us. A relationship has to be a give and take.   We can't be so desperate for a relationship that we compromise what we want and who we are. If genuine love is at its core the give and take will flow although not always steadily or consistently but it will always resurface at some point.

Let's go on a trip," I said to my youngest son shortly after my divorce from Warren. From the moment I said that I had a queasy, uneasy feeling in the pit of my stomach. I couldn't shake it. I recognized this feeling. It had been my constant companion in my childhood and most of my adult life. It was present from the moment I decided to go on this trip. It would just be my son and I on this trip. We had gone of trips with Warren while we were married. When we had traveled with Warren I bore all the responsibility for the trips.

That is why the feeling of anxiety struck me as so odd. Why did Warren's absence so profoundly affect my emotional state? Why did 1 I feel more secure when Warren was around? I had been doing it all by myself before he left. What is it about a male presence that gives me such comfort? Is the comfort of a male presence, any male presence, a vestige of the notion that men are our protectors or that women need a man to take care of them? Whatever its origin I have successfully been chipping away at its hold over me.

"Gary you are such a self sufficient young man," I said one day to him. "You get your homework done. You manage your time well. You follow the household and school rules. You are pretty much on auto pilot," I said. As I said that I felt the same anxiety that I felt when Gary and I went on our first trip alone together. By this time I had been a parent and in various marriages for almost 30 years. Now with no husband and a very self sufficient child I had no one to focus my energies on other than myself.

I realized that when the family would go on trips or daily outings I would focus on whether everyone else was having a good time. If they were having a good time then I was happy. If things were going well in my children's lives then I was happy. If it wasn't I would work at "fixing" it. The same was true for husbands. Making them happy was my "job". Now I had no one to focus on. I could enjoy things for myself – plan things that I would enjoy. You would think I would be elated. I wasn't. I didn't know what I enjoyed or how to enjoy it. Without someone else to focus my attention on I was very anxious and fearful.

I am a veteran of many failed relationships. I have learned what not to do and what makes a relationship fail but I am not as certain regarding how to or what makes a really good relationship. I didn't have any advice or answers for my friend Lisa who is really struggling with a new relationship. They constantly break up and get back together. She would try again with Bill I know that. Each of us has to work it out in our own way. There is no magic formula for creating a fulfilling relationship. Love is the key ingredient but it is a mystery what creates and sustains that love. It is not a mystery what can destroy that love.

I get exhausted just thinking about all the work I would have to do in order to have another relationship. I see it all as entailing much more work than benefit. I certainly understand myself better these days but that doesn't always translate into avoiding bad behaviors. It seems that as the relationship progresses my new forged self flows away like the ocean tide and the old me flows back in. It happens as predictably as the flow of the tides.

I had seen Brian at his worst. He had seen me at my worst. We had said and done terrible things to each other. Sometimes it seems like it was almost a contest to see who could be crueler. Brian punished with words. I punished with silence. We brought out the worst and the best in each other. We experienced together every day events and catastrophic events. We shared a history. We shared our lives. Through it all I still loved Brian. Through it all he still loved me. We knew each other with all our warts and yet we still loved each other. That is a true love story isn't it?

"Can you come over tomorrow and help me clean out the garage and Brian's bedroom?" I asked Tony, Brian's former caregiver a few weeks after Brian died. Tony agreed to help.

Brian was something of a pack rat so the garage and bedroom were filled with boxes and boxes of paper, documents and other stuff. Brian had closed out a storage unit and put everything in the garage and the extra bedroom he eventually occupied. He never got a chance to sort through it.

Tony started in the garage and I started in the bedroom. Some of the boxes in the bedroom were ones that had been delivered to us from Brian's office after he stopped going there. Brian didn't seem interested in looking through them so I had simply put them into the closet. They sat there unopened for many, many months.

I pulled the first box out. It contained all sorts of outdated papers from Brian's business. I went and got a huge trash bin and started throwing things away. After sifting through three or four boxes I came to one that contained some photographs. I set them aside to look at later after I had gone through all the boxes.

I decided to take a break. I grabbed the photos and went into the kitchen to get a cup of coffee. I would browse through the photos leisurely. I was concerned that the photos would bring up some painful memories and I wanted to be prepared when they did. I steeled myself and opened the first envelope. It contained photos of Brian and Bridget on a trip. It looked like a trip to Disneyland. Yes I could see Cinderella's castle in the background of the photo.

I didn't remember going to Disneyland with the children and Brian. I looked at the date stamped on the photos. We were definitely married and had been for several years at that time. I looked through a few more photos before I saw it. I recognized her right away. She and Brian had their arms wrapped around each other. She was the former girlfriend of one of our mutual friends. There were several envelopes full of photos of Brian and Kendra together with their arms wrapped around each other. In some they were embracing and kissing each other.

Forgiveness may be the key ingredient in a marriage. It is ever so much easier to punish the other person who has wronged us especially where the wrong is so egregious. I am not advocating that all mistakes can or should be forgiven. Doesn't the act of forgiveness start with recognition that we too could have easily made the same mistake?

Would my marriage to Brian have become a love story like Nancy and Bob or Martha and Mark? Would it have become a love story worth the sacrifice of certain parts of myself? I like to think so but our time together was cut so short – only six years, half of which Brian was sick. We were on the right track. I felt a bond with Brian that I can't describe. I don't know if we would have made it work for 50 or 60 years. I do know that we had much to forgive each other for.

Chapter Four

Childhood Hauntings

I was acutely aware of how embarrassed and humiliated I felt. I was sitting with my head bowed, tears streaming, snot running, shoulders shaking, sobbing uncontrollably in front of another person – a complete stranger! It was the mid 80s. My first marriage was crumbling. (Yes there has been more than one much to my mother's chagrin!) Through my gasps for air, I heard this other person in the room say that I had stuffed down all the hurts and emotions for so long I couldn't stuff anymore. Weird what we think of at such a time of crisis. I pictured my head as the top of an erupting volcano. I envisioned the top of my head with gross stuff oozing and spurting out of it and me trying to push "the stuff" back down and close the lid but the stuff wouldn't stop spurting out.

I don't have any recollection of what said to that psychologist. Mostly what I remember is promising myself not to go back and humiliate myself a second time. But I did! For the first few months I repeated that "grotesque" conduct once a week. I had absolutely no idea what I was crying about. I guess I was lucky I could cry. Normally I simply couldn't or wouldn't let myself cry especially in front of other people. After all we WASPS control our emotions at all times and we never, ever cry in front of anyone else. A display of any emotion is, after all, a sign of weakness. I had broken one of our cardinal rules and the humiliation was palpable. The worst part was that after making a complete fool of myself I didn't feel even slightly better. In fact I felt worse. I felt totally alone, abandoned, empty. I had that same feeling as a child. I realize now that these feelings have waxed and waned all my life but they have never totally gone away.

And yes I have a confession to make. I am a WASP. I feel like I should be standing in front of a group like AA, beating on my chest, agreeing to atone for my shortcomings and failings and to make changes in my life. We are the evildoers vis a vis the rest of America. We are the majority and we are the present and the past oppressors of everyone else. I have this amorphous bad feeling because I am a WASP. This feeling of guilt just kind of floats around in my psyche. All this animosity just because I happened to born a WASP? I don't feel like a bad person just because I am a WASP but I am told that I am. Perhaps it is cyclical that the oppressor becomes the oppressed because I feel oppressed. Oh not in the economic sense but in the moral arena. I, for one, am tired of apologizing or being embarrassed for being born a WASP. This attitude may make a lot of readers angry. But ask yourself do you want to be blamed ad infinitum for conduct that your ancestors engaged in or other persons beyond your control currently engage in. I think not. Certainly we and our ancestors have done some good, haven't we? Well enough of that digression. The fact that I am a WASP is important as, believe it or not, there is a WASP culture. At least I think there is.

"Tell me about your childhood – what was it like?" I heard the psychologist ask me. A wave of panic passed over me. Did she really want to open that can of worms I thought to myself. It might be more accurate to describe it as a plunge into a black, foreboding abyss. She must have sensed that I couldn't or didn't want to discuss my childhood. She narrowed her inquiry, "tell me about an event you remember." Another wave of panic passed over me and my mind went blank. "I don't have many memories of events from my childhood," I told her. She paused one of those long scary pauses when you, as the patient, think she is saying to herself – this patient is really screwed up. "Well how did you 'feel' as a child"? The wall holding back those emotions must have burst. The tears exploded. I didn't know if I had the strength or stamina to go down that road.

"NOOOO. I don't want too...," someone was screaming. I looked over to see where that horrible noise was coming from. I saw my Sister crumpled in a ball on the floor crying and writing as if she were in pain. She was about 8 years old at the time. We were getting ready to go to school. My Sister had neglected to put on the right outfit.

It wasn't so much what she said to my Sister as how she said. They were harmless words really but the tone of voice, the facial expressions and body language said it all. She didn't need to use hurtful words. Her eyes were bulging out. Her face was contorted and her body seemed poised to strike at any moment. "You are stupid, worthless and I hate you," she said with her eyes, voice and her body. Her interaction with my Sister and I was always adversarial. I felt like she was my enemy – my adversary. She was, in fact, my Mother. This lack of hurtful words was particularly difficult to deal with because when I would review events later in my head I couldn't find fault with what my Mother actually said. Had I imagined that my Mother looked at my Sister in evil ways? After all she really didn't say anything evil. In going over what happened in my mind there was a disconnect between what objectively happened and my reaction to it. I reacted as if my Mother was verbally and emotionally abusive. But, she wasn't overtly or objectively abusive. This was all part of the dishonesty that shrouded everything my Mother did and said. I learned not to trust my instincts. I would berate myself for thinking ill of my Mother. After all she really didn't say anything mean or strike my Sister. I would decide that I imagined the meanness because I had to give my Mother the benefit of the doubt. After all she was my Mother and she loved us didn't she?

Going to therapy was a daunting task. If I had not met a psychologist in the course of my work I don't know if I would have ever gone. I certainly would not have gone at that time in my life. After all, I come from a long line of stoics that believe we solve all of our own problems by ourselves without any help.

If we just persevere and try harder things will get better. If they don't get better it is because you didn't try hard enough. In other words it is our fault. We are weak if we seek psychological help or really any help. We don't talk about our problems. We muscle through them. In fact I am not sure we were ever allowed to admit we even had problems or emotions for that matter. We certainly don't discuss our problems or emotions with anyone, not even, or especially not our family. We had a very limited range of emotions we could express and any expression had to be temperate and moderate. We have to suffer in order to earn the right to go to "heaven." Life is about survival, not enjoyment. We women do not express anger. For men that is the only emotion they are permitted to express and if their expression is not moderate or temperate that is a failing but one that can be tolerated and explained away. These are some of the unwritten rules or teachings of our WASP culture. They shaped my world and me. I really wasn't conscious of them until I started going to therapy. They were deeply buried.

"Do I really have to talk about my childhood?" I later asked the therapist. "Isn't that all behind me.? I survived it and I am here. That is all that the needs to be said about it. I can't change any of it so why bother with all of this. Anyway I just don't think I have the energy to retell and relive all of that or even a portion of it," I ranted. But there was no escaping the journey into the past. As I understood it childhood was a hot topic in psychotherapy at least when I first starting going in the mid 80s. The theory was, I think, that discussion and recognition of childhood experiences and hurts could lead to the healing of old wounds and changes in adult behavior patterns. That is a huge oversimplification but this is not a psychological treatise but merely the recounting of my perspective, observations and experiences. This psychologist started me on the journey that saved my life.

"I have to leave early today. I have a doctor's appointment," I said to one of the partners at the firm. "Is everything all right?" he kindly asked. "Sure," I replied. I wasn't going to tell him I was going to see a psychologist! I was embarrassed to seek help and I have kept it a secret pretty much until now. My self image, at that time, was that of the self reliant, strong person who can handle everything and has her life together. I couldn't maintain that image if I confessed my fears and problems to someone. I couldn't let anyone see the real me —only the image.

I was definitely in acute crisis mode at that point in my life. It was the mid 80s. I think I have always functioned in some kind of crisis mode. It is one of the legacies of my childhood. During that time in my life I had great difficulty restraining my tears while I was in the presence of others. That was absolutely terrifying. It was perhaps, for me, the most terrifying part of all of this and what finally drove me to get help. I couldn't cry in front of others! They would ask me what was wrong and maybe even feel sorry for me!

"What do you remember about your childhood?" the psychologist firmly asked again. I was quiet for a time thinking I guess. "Mostly I felt afraid – always afraid," I whispered out loud. "You felt afraid," she repeated. "Yes," I said. "I felt totally alone," I continued. She didn't say anything else. I hated the sympathetic look she gave me when I said that. I felt the fear and loneliness welling up in me right then. It could do that – just appear at any time. Even as an adult I felt paralyzed by it. As I got older I learned to talk myself through it but I couldn't do that when I was a child.

By all outward appearances I had an idyllic childhood. After all it was the 1950s and 60s in a small Midwestern city. The 1950s and 1960s have been so overdone that it has become tiresome to even think about it much less write about it. It has been glorified and vilified and everything in between. It is hard to escape from all the generalizations and romanticism hoisted onto that era. What really happened is of little significance. It is our memory or perception of what happened that is most significant. The romantic veneer is dangerous as it can taint our memory of our own experiences of those times. I find myself remembering this era in terms of "Happy Days" or "Leave it to Beaver" or "Lassie". This makes it all the more difficult to see my own childhood reality. Each of us experiences and remembers things differently and each perception of that time is as different as there are people who lived through it. Others may not recognize the 50s and 60s that I describe. This writing is the story of my journey and the 50s and 60s as seen through my eyes.

"Where are your shoes?" my Mother screamed at my sister. My sister was crying. My sister didn't want to wear her (ugly) orthopedic shoes that day. In fact she never wanted to wear those ugly saddle shoes and this was a fairly typical morning scene at our house. Usually my Dad had already left for work. We were supposed to be leaving to get on the school bus. My Sister had a whole physical writhing act that went along with the screams and tears. It wasn't really a temper tantrum. It reminded me of the scene in "The Wizard of Oz" where the wicked witch melts after Dorothy pours water on her. My sister would just dissolve into tears and start writing on the floor as my Mother heaped her abuse on her. My Mother was exceptionally hard on my sister that morning maybe because we were going to miss the school bus. Something my Mother said even triggered some tears in my eyes. I can remember clenching my teeth and my fists and saying to myself, "She will never make me cry". To this day I have kept my promise. No one else has made me cry much either. My poor sister just didn't have the ability to withstand the abuse. As you would expect our respective coping mechanisms have taken a toll on each of us.

We lived in the middle class suburbs in a very small cape cod and later in a somewhat larger ranch style brick house. Both houses were very small by today's standards. We had one bathroom for five people in our first house. My sister and I shared a bedroom until I was 13 years old. We had a large yard – not fenced. (It was and maybe still is un-friendly and

un-neighborly to fence in your yard in that part of the country). They were both basic houses with no perks. Our first house was part of a small row of about 8 houses all of which were exactly the same. My family consisted of my parents, my older brother and younger sister. We had a dog. My Mother didn't work but devoted herself to the family and community. She was actively involved in church and school committees and organizations.

My Father went to work each day at the company where he would spend almost his entire working career. My Mother cooked dinner every night. It was basic Midwestern fare – meat, potato or rice and an overcooked vegetable. We rarely had fish and if we did it was terrible. My Dad coached little league for my brother. We – the girls- didn't have any sports until high school. We did have the Girl Scouts. My parents never fought, at least not in front of us. I had no experience with any type of illness or death as a child. With a few minor variations everyone else's outward or physical life was the same. By outward appearances it was an idyllic childhood.

"I am quitting Girl Scouts," I blurted out with my eyes shut tightly. It took weeks for me to get up the courage to tell my Mother but I finally did. I knew the consequence would be severe but I had to do it. My Mother had been looking in the other direction when I said it. Her head whirled around so fast it now reminds me of the scene in the Exorcist. She started spewing similar venom as well. "You, WHAT!" she screeched in my direction. Now in all fairness I have to say that my Mother was very involved in the Girl Scouts. I took a deep breath and repeated the statement, "I am quitting Girl Scouts. Beth, (my Sister) is still a scout". I hoped this would diffuse some of the anger.

My Mother screamed at me for a while as I stood silently looking at the floor. I think she told me all the things she did for me and how ungrateful, unappreciative and selfish I was. That was the usual fare anyway. My Mother liked to play the martyr. She picked a few objects up and threw them in my direction. She didn't hit me. Her anger spent, for the time being, she turned and left the room. All disobedience and/or disagreements were followed by a long period of stony silence and being ignored at least when it came to me. I knew this outburst was only the beginning. There would be more. She didn't usually act this way when my Father was home. I don't know if it would have mattered if she did. My Father had a real ability to live in his own reality. In his world my Mother didn't act like this or do these things.

"Mother I need you to sign the permission slip and give me a check for the field trip next week," I said. She didn't look at me or acknowledge what I said. I left the field trip information on the table and left the room. If I spoke to her again who knows what might happen. You see only a few days had passed since I told my Mother that I was quitting Girl Scouts. It would be several months before she would talk to me or even look at me. I simply didn't exist for a few months as far as she was concerned. I knew this would be the price I would pay for going against something that she wanted. To me, at the time, it was worth the battle. Sometimes she would give me hateful looks when I walked into the room. My Father never noticed. This was all part of the battle with her. My Mother expected or demanded everything go her way and if it didn't there was a price to pay.

We went to school and church with our neighbors. Our neighbors were all WASPS. I grew up in a very ethnic city but all ethnic groups were segregated at that time. The Greeks, the Poles, Italians, Lithuanians each had their own section of the city in which they lived. It wasn't exclusionary or we didn't think so. We all lived with our own kind. That contributed to the predictability of our lives. I can't judge whether it was a good thing. It was just that way. All I can say is that later, as an adult, when I lived in a large ethnically mixed city, life could be very stressful. We didn't know what to expect from each other and other people did not behave in a manner I was used to. The stress was, at times, exhausting. Every daily interaction had to be negotiated and renegotiated just like in my marriages.

"She's here," I heard one of the other mothers whisper to my Mother. All of the mothers were seated at a couple of tables talking together. They all turned their heads to look in the direction of the entrance. We were all spending the day at the community swim club. That is what we did in the summers. There were no day camps and very few sleep away camps. Usually those were too expensive to attend anyway. The woman they were all staring at didn't come and sit at the table with all the other mothers. She sat on the other side of the pool with her two children. I noticed that no one talked to her at all during the time she was there. The women never discussed why she didn't sit with them, at least in my presence. I picked up on the reason over time. She was divorced. There was no such thing as divorces in the 50s and 60s. To put it mildly differences were not appreciated in the 50s and 60s. Conformity was the buzzword although no one would ever overtly admit that. She was ostracized because she was divorced. I guess her children probably were as well.

Family vacations were typically road trips. Our family vacations consisted of visits by car to all the historical spots within several days driving distance of where we lived. We had three channels on TV. Television went off the air at 10 pm. Cartoons were only aired on Saturday mornings. Tampons and ED were not advertised on TV. Black people did not appear in TV commercials until much later. Birthdays were celebrated by inviting the neighborhood kids over for cake and ice cream. Gifts were a rarity. We played sports or hung out with the other kids in the neighborhood. Sex was a total mystery and was never ever mentioned. In my house you couldn't even say the word "sex". Only the routine events of the day were ever discussed. They were typically discussed at the nightly dinner table.

Families on TV behaved perfectly. They were all WASPS of course. They always got along. They always behaved "nicely". They never argued or fought with each other or their friends. Any mistakes they made were minor and easily fixed. We were expected to be like these families. We were doomed to failure. Now, on TV, we primarily see people that behave abominably. I think it has lowered the standards for behavior in our own everyday life. I hope we can find a middle ground.

As a child and young adult, I so admired those people who didn't seem to have many emotions or who seemed to be able to remain calm and control their emotions at all times. I tried very hard to be like them. I wanted to be like them. There had to be something wrong with me since I had to struggle so to control my emotions.

"Dad, Mother refuses to put the money I need for college into my bank account. I can't even buy any food until she does that. I have been asking her for several weeks. Now she just hangs up on me when I call," I said as I started to cry. "Now dear .... ..," my Dad said. He always said the same things, "I was imaging it. My mother had been busy and was going to do it right away. I could wait a little longer." I am not sure why I even talked to him about it on this particular occasion. Usually I just muscled through it.

I'm not sure why I asked my Mother about the money. I learned long ago not to ask her for things. If I asked for something I would be sure I wouldn't get it or it wouldn't happen. You would think I would have learned that lesson well by the time I was in college. "When you graduate from college you are on your own. Don't ask us for anything else," my Mother constantly told me. I worked very hard to comply with that request.

My childhood, outwardly, resembled one of the current movie scripts. I am referring to the formula stories that are repeated, ad nauseum, by Hollywood. These stories all have the same beginning, middle and end. The only thing that changes is the actors and maybe the physical location. It amazes me that those are such hits. To me they are so boring. My generation followed the "script" or "formula" in our childhoods and youth. Maybe this generation loves those movies precisely because their childhoods and even adult lives have been far from predictable. In fact we were guaranteed that if we followed the script we would have a good life. That happened for some people. But it did fail miserably in preparing us for the world some of us would inhabit as adults, that is, worlds that deviated drastically from the script.

Our childhood days and years had a distinct rhythm to them. The sameness of our daily events and the uniformity of our lives were comforting. It connected us into a community. But in that world of intense physical connectedness, I felt totally emotionally disconnected and isolated. The predictable rhythm of the days, years and events served as an anchor and also as a prison. The rhythm and sameness of our lives was our savior and a source of our comfort but also of pain. I had no idea how far my life would deviate from the script and what a sense of failure that deviation would create.

"I have been betrayed!" I said through clenched teeth to the psychologist. It wasn't really said in anger – at least not at first. I was relieved that I was finally able to identify the source of some of the present pain. I continued, "I did everything I was supposed to do. I was a "good girl". I got an education. I was supportive of my husband. I love and spend time with my children. I devote myself to my family. I put them first. I go to work every day and work very hard." "How have you been betrayed by doing all of that?" she asked me. "I should have had a "good life". I earned it! I don't deserve this life!" I said.

There had to be something wrong with me because really bad things don't happen to "good girls" or good people. What had I done wrong? Did I really deserve to be broke with three small children to raise on my own? Did I deserve a lousy husband and did my children deserve a lousy father? Did I really deserve to be abused by my husband? Of course I kept the part of the domestic violence a secret even to this day. There was no way I could hide the fact that I was divorced even though I wished I could. How could this happen to me? I felt utterly betrayed by life and by God. I was full of rage.

It woke me up – the screaming. I looked at the clock on my nightstand. It was 2 o'clock in the morning. I could hear my parents screaming at each other. In all of my 16 years I had never heard them even raise their voices at each other. I listened for a while. They were saying something about my younger Sister and hospital. I was afraid. I pulled the covers up over my head waiting for this to be over. More time passed and the screaming continued. I don't know why but I ventured out to the living room. As I passed my Sister's room I didn't hear anything and the door was closed tightly. Both of my parents were in their pajamas standing in the middle of the living room. My Sister was nowhere in sight. My Mother was crying - not uncontrollable sobs just tears in her eyes. I had never seen that before or since. My Father was shrieking, "I am sick to death of her. I don't care what happens to her. Just let her die!" He stormed out of the living room into the bedroom and slammed the door. Between the stomping and the door slamming the whole house shook. I had quietly taken a seat in one of the chairs in the corner of the living room. My Mother didn't say a word to me or even look at me. She got up and went to the kitchen to make a phone call. "Can you send an ambulance to 642 Mulberry Lane right away? My daughter has swallowed an entire bottle of some type of pills – aspirin I think".

I was dumbfounded. Why had she done it? Had there been warning signs? My Sister was and always had been, you know, (it was whispered) "emotional". My parents in their typical fashion explained away her behavior – behavior she exhibited her entire life – as a phase, a stage. As a last resort they would explain that she was just an "emotional person."   Being an emotional person in WASPdom is akin to having a terrible disease. Emotional persons were the lepers of the WASP world. There wasn't much worse you could say about a person back then. I did occasionally hear some veiled expressions of sympathy expressed to my parents regarding my Sister being "emotional". Things were whispered or looks were given as if her condition was a curse from God. My parents had a real ability to ignore or explain away abnormal behavior. They never wanted to deal with a problem head on. Those things were never discussed. My Sister was just "that way" or so my parents believed. They hoped she would grow out of it. She never did.

"Janet," my Grandmother called out desperately to my Mother. "I can't believe it. I just can't believe your Father is gone". My Grandmother started to cry and reached out to hug my Mother. It had only been a week since my Grandfather's funeral. My Grandmother was able to catch herself before she fell. You see my Mother had turned her back on my Grandmother and simply walked away. "He's gone Mother," is all my Mother said as she left the room. My Mother always called my Grandmother "mother." My Grandmother "got a hold of herself" in true WASP fashion. I never saw my Grandmother cry or grieve again.

My Mother didn't like her own mother much. I suspect there were good reasons for that. I intuitively knew early on that my Mother never liked me. It took a lot longer for me to formally acknowledge it. When I did it was a relief. My Mother has never told me she loved me even when I said it to her. That seems like quite a record even for her stoic generation.

"Oh she decided not to continue with Girl Scouts. She has a lot of other things she needs to do. She is a straight A student you know," my Mother said to our neighbor. I would hear my Mother tell people calmly and almost proudly that I had made a decision not to continue with Girl Scouts.

I never heard my Mother mention or even allude to my Sister's attempted suicide. My Sister and I talked about it a little bit when she came home from the psychiatric hospital. But except as between the two of us, my Sister's behavior and this "episode" were another secret we carried around with us like the secret of my Mother's verbal abuse. To this day, almost 40 years later, no one in our family has ever even tried to discuss the "episode". After this many years that is probably best.

My Mother always had a cheery tone of voice when she would discuss her wonderful family at bridge club, church or school. Everything was always wonderful or so she told her friends. Who knows maybe she really believed what she said. I was confused. My experience of things at home was not as my Mother described it to other people. I can remember thinking I must be wrong or confused about what was happening at home. I learned not to trust my perceptions.

I passed through my childhood with a constant feeling in the pit of my stomach like something bad was going to happen. I was always anxious, tense and afraid. I was terrified I would do something "wrong". My emotions raged out of control but I never let on how I was feeling. I was able to control them for the most part. To the world and my parents my inner life appeared as calm and predictable and controlled as our outer life. We children intuitively knew never to discuss the inner workings of our family with anyone. To this day I have not discussed any of this with anyone not even my Sister. Well that is not exactly true I may have told my therapist, I don't really recall.

You see WASPS do not discuss things like thoughts, feeling and especially not "bad things." It is one of the unwritten rules. They were swept under the rug forever. Only mundane, pleasant things -

the banalities of life were discussed like the events of the day from a factual standpoint. I don't know how I learned these were the rules. It was just always so. The price for breaking these rules was too scary. We would be ostracized or avoided in our family and in the larger community. We would be labeled "emotional". Our outward appearance was one of calm, contentment even happiness. My inner life was exactly the opposite.

I felt as if I had been kicked in the stomach when I watched the movie "Ordinary People" as a young adult. It was perhaps the scariest movie I have seen. I have never been able to watch it again. It expressed the reality of my childhood better than I can. When I saw it, it stirred up all the feelings of emptiness, loneliness and fear of my childhood – the black hole opened up. I can remember when I tried to tell my ex-husband, David, about how it made me feel he told me I was stupid and walked away. In that movie the father believed the son and left his wife. That would never happen in my family.

I heard a clanking like the sound of something metal striking an object. I turned to look at my Father. My Father was seated at the head of the dinner table. But he wasn't serving the dinner plates to each person as was his custom. Instead, his face contorted with rage, he was throwing pieces of silverware in the direction of my Mother although I don't know that he was aiming for her. I froze. I heard a few more clanking sounds and then my Father stormed off to his bedroom, slamming the door behind him. Let's eat," my Mother said cheerfully without batting an eye. "The food is getting cold," she complained. My Mother didn't smile much but she had a smile plastered on her face as she said this. My brother, sister and I were all seated in our respective places at the dinner table. My Mother went around to the head of the table and began serving the plates. We ate our dinner in silence. Fortunately my Father hadn't hit anyone. My Father never emerged from his room that night. He was already at work when we left for school the next morning. Everything was back to normal the next night at the dinner table.

My Dad is a very kind and gentle man who also has a fierce temper that rarely flares up. He was interested in you and what you were doing as long as it was something he was interested in. That pretty much limited the sphere of interaction with him to books and reading. Anytime he wanted to go somewhere or do something, even if I was not interested in it, I went with him. When he wanted to talk to me I was always available. This was true even as a teenager and into adulthood. I am not complaining mind you. I learned a lot and I acquired a lifelong interest in books, reading, history, etc as a result of my relationship with my Dad. I have good memories and good feelings when I think of my Dad. I love my Father. He was one of the bright spots in an otherwise bleak childhood. As a child I felt like I had to take care of my Dad and my sister. I had to protect them from my Mother. I had to be my Dad's emotional support or so I thought.

"Your Grandfather has passed away," my Mother told me over the phone. I was in my first year of college. I was devastated. He was the only outwardly loving, fun member of our family. He always made me laugh and feel happy. Everyone he met loved him. It is funny but my oldest son resembles him in a little in character and interestingly is named after him. By today's standards he did not live long enough. He was only 73. Just that past summer I had stayed with my Grandparents and helped out for a few weeks. I felt so connected to him while I was there. He even told me some things about his life I doubt he had shared with anyone else in the family. I don't know that I was special to him. I was just physically present when he knew he was dying.

My Mother, by her own accounts, adored my Grandfather. She had always been a daddy's girl or so the family lore goes. I never saw her shed even one tear for him when he died. I never saw either of my parents cry or grieve when any of their parents died. Did they love their parents? I know my Mother claimed to love my Grandfather very much. "Do you love me?" I asked each of my parents on a very rare occasion. "That is a silly question," each of them responded. Was it?

My world had come tumbling down. The catalyst was my first divorce but the crisis was of more epic proportions. The WASP prescription for happiness hadn't worked at least for me. Maintaining uniformity and predictability in my outward life did not create uniformity and predictability in my emotional or inner life. I followed the script but I didn't get the right result. In fact for me the exact opposite was true. My emotions got repressed to the point where they screamed to be let out. The outward pressure to control or even deny my emotions created and fostered an inner turmoil for me. I guess everything came spilling out as I sat on that couch in the psychologist's office. I can't even describe the level of betrayal I felt. Is it any wonder that I actually felt worse for quite some time after I started therapy?

"It is OK to have emotions. Emotions aren't bad. It is how we express those emotions that can be inappropriate," my therapist said. Until that time I thought certain emotions were bad and if you experienced those emotions you must be a "bad" person. In my rush to free my children from that type of thinking I confused having emotions and expressing emotions. I let them express their emotions however they wanted because I didn't want to them to repress them as I had done. Naturally I discovered that was a mistake. I confused those two concepts in my own emotional life as well for a time. The rage took a long time to dissipate. Even small incidents could release the rage.

Finally for me small incidents no longer generate a huge eruption of emotion that is all out of proportion to the actual event. Maybe it is just a function of aging. My emotions don't overwhelm me so as I get older. Their intensity and strength are definitely tempered. I no longer have to fight to control them or hold them in. My outward and inner lives are more in tune with each other now. My emotions seem to ebb and flow in sync with or in relation to the events of my life. How refreshing! I have given myself permission to express my emotions. I can cry, laugh, be disappointed, be excited, etc. I no longer express everything as anger and rage.

The legacy of my childhood is a mixed bag of fear, anxiety, doubts in my abilities and perceptions, lack of self worth, feeling of being unloved or unlovable, pessimism, strength and perseverance in the face of adversity, honesty, appreciation for what I do have, faith in God and the goodness of humans and life. Sometimes I think the majority of my adult life has been devoted to undoing the damage of my childhood. I don't blame my parents. I eventually arrived at a place in my life where I realized that this is my journey. I am solely responsible for who I become and what I do with my past, present and future. I refuse to blame my present issues or problems on my childhood.

"I want to come home. Can you send me some money to buy a ticket?" I said to my Mother from a payphone. We, my first husband and I, could not afford a phone. My parents never asked why I didn't have a phone. They never asked anything about my life at all then or ever. My Mother wired the money. In the meantime I changed my mind. I can't remember why. Maybe I couldn't decide which was less welcoming – my old home with my Mother or my new one with my then husband. If only I had possessed the wherewithal to strike out on my own. I can't even remember entertaining that as an option. As I look back on it that was such an obvious choice. This was the late 70s after all. Emotionally I was not prepared for doing that. "Don't ever do that to us again," my Mother reprimanded me when I called later to say I wasn't going to come home.

"I really need you to come spend this holiday season with us. Things are a little rough right now. Gary could use your company and I could use the help with him while he is on vacation and I am at work," I said to my parents. This was a few years ago when I hoped we could change our relationship. Maybe we could even talk about things and ask each other for help. I was going to make an effort anyway. "We have made other plans this Christmas and we can't change them. We are going to spend Christmas with your sister," my Mother said and promptly handed the phone to my Dad. My Dad listened to me and then said the same thing in a nicer way. They always spent Christmas with my family as my sister works on the holiday and doesn't have any children. Sometimes she would come to my house as well. My parents would always visit her for a few weeks after Christmas. That is the way things worked for at least the last 10 years. I guess this year they were going to break tradition. My Mother always abhors breaking any tradition. I made the mistake of asking for something. I had forgotten that if I wanted something from my Mother or asked for something it would never happen. I had to not want it or pretend to not want it in order to get her to do it. I should have known any request would be denied. She never changed her plans once they were decided. My parents never asked what was going on that I wanted them to come. I guess it really didn't matter. Some things will never change.

"I'm leaving tomorrow," my Dad said to me. "But you are not scheduled to leave for another week," I replied. "I'm leaving tomorrow," he repeated angrily. "Why are you going now?" I asked. My Dad simply turned and walked away. Brian was about half way through his battle with Lou Gehrig's disease. I think my Dad was angry with Brian over something he had said or done to Samuel. Samuel has always been my Dad's favorite grandchild. He never saw Brian again.

"She is really tense. She is getting angry and upset over everything. I wonder if it would have been better if we had stayed home for Christmas this year," my Father said to my Mother. I could hear them talking downstairs in the kitchen. "Well I am here for the sake of the children," my Mother replied. I had actually tiptoed down the stairs so I could hear what they were whispering to each other. I had suggested that my parents spend Christmas with my sister instead of me, this year, because I was under a tremendous amount of stress. My divorce trial was scheduled for the week after Christmas and I had a lot of preparation to do. They ignored my request. This year of course they insisted on spending Christmas with me. They usually stayed two or three weeks. This year was no exception.

If only my parents could have reached out, hugged me and asked if everything was OK or if I needed help at any time in my life. I should have initiated something during this last holiday visit. Maybe I should have told them about my stress. I simply had never had much success explaining my adverse circumstances to my parents. Maybe the realm of divorce, death, terminal illness and other such matters were too much for them to handle. I had no reason to think anything would be different now. Still I probably should have tried to reach out to them. I couldn't. Stress is my enemy. The stress of their visit and the stress of the impending divorce trial were too much for me. I was as they described me as they whispered to each other in the kitchen. That is not the first time I had heard them whispering about such things. I was spurned by them during that visit when I needed some love and support. Some things never change. I really didn't expect it.

Something an acquaintance said to me kept running through my head. "You know how people fell about you by how they treat you," he said to me many years ago. That should have been obvious to me but it wasn't. As I look back over the relationships in my life I think he was right.

She has done it probably for the past 25 years. Every time she comes to visit my Mother insists on cooking and baking. What a great way to help you might say. It could have been but it wasn't. My Mother would cook and then leave the kitchen a huge mess for me to clean up when I came home from the office. It would take me several hours to clean it. That is not an exaggeration. My Mother can destroy a kitchen in ways you could not imagine. After many years I have concluded it was one of her passive ways of expressing her anger at me or getting back at me.

After 50 years I finally realized that I had an image of my parents that was mostly fictional. That realization was strangely liberating. I imagined them loving, kind, and concerned for me. Perhaps it is just that – pure imagination. They have never called me much at any time in my life. They didn't call or come to visit when Brian was sick or even afterwards except for their annual holiday visit. In their defense they didn't know how to deal with divorce or Brian's illness or much of anything else. Neither did I. I have never talked about anything other than mundane events with my Mother and books with my Father. Usually I can talk to my Dad about my children and that has been wonderful. My parents know nothing about my life except for the basic facts. I am partly to blame. Maybe I expect too much of them. I tend to do that with people. After a few attempts in my younger years to talk to my Dad about my life and my feelings I stopped. My parents came to visit me mostly to see the children. I heard my Dad say that a few times to my Mother and my sister.

"She can't stay here," my Mother yelled. "I can't believe we had to pay for her ticket and she wants to stay with us too," my Mother said in a very loud voice. My Mother was talking to my Father about my aunt – my Father's Sister. They were talking in the other room but we could all hear what they were saying. The hatred was palpable. Of course my Aunt overheard it. She was meant to.

My Aunt's crime was that she had come to my parents' 50th wedding anniversary party. She had travelled by bus for more than 24 hours while she was recovering from foot surgery. My Mother followed up her outburst by giving my Aunt hostile stares and the silent treatment. We all apologized profusely to my Aunt for my Mother's behavior. I am sure she would have rather come under other circumstances but her husband and only child were not available to bring her. They had both died many, many years ago. The look on my Aunt's face made me want to cry. It was the last time any of us saw my Aunt. She died alone in a nursing home in Florida. It was the last time my Father would be together with his two siblings. My Mother was relentless in her cruel treatment of my Aunt.

"Welcome to the world of our childhood," I said to my children who were appalled at my Mother's behavior. They were looking at each other aghast. My Mother was ranting and raving about a lot more than just my Aunt's visit. Everything wasn't going her way! She was definitely in mean mode. We all tried to stay out of her way.

My Sister was the only one who was able to exercise some control over my Mother and get her to calm down a little bit. I felt a huge surge of relief. For many years I had been concerned that I had judged my Mother too harshly or imagined she engaged in the behavior I have described here. Now I was free of that concern.

I was definitely a product of my upbringing. Outwardly I appeared very confident, self assured, accomplished and in control of my world. Inwardly I was always anxious with an insatiable yearning to be loved, paralyzed by the inability to trust myself or my perceptions and feeling lost and confused most of the time. I used to fluctuate from one extreme to the other – moved from one end of the spectrum to the other. As I have aged and matured I find that those two distinct personalities have moved more toward the middle and blended. I feel integrated now rather than fragmented.

"Hello Mom," I said when she answered the phone. The next thing I heard was a dial tone. I called back. This time my Dad answered the phone. My Mother had hung up the phone when she heard my voice. You see I had committed the unimaginable sin of inviting my parents to move to the city where I live. My Mother would be leaving the city in which she had lived for the vast majority of her 83 years. Hopefully at some point in time she will stop being angry about the move.

I have made peace with my childhood. My Mother can occasionally still push my buttons but for the most part she and I exist in a strained truce. As an adult I understand that my parents are a product of their upbringing. I understand that they did the best they could based on their family history and upbringing. I don't know their family history for sure because that generation doesn't talk about those things. If only they did maybe they could have made peace with it before it was inflicted on the next generation. From my Dad I learned so many good things like honesty, integrity, love of learning, and more. From my Mother I received the discipline and structure I needed as a child. I understand that my Dad does love me as much as he can. Can the same be true for my Mother? Maybe. I don't think my Mother is capable of giving much love and what she is capable of she has spent on others rather than me. But I am OK with that. I try to treat her the way I would like to be treated by my children when I am her age. There is one difference. I hope that my children do things for me out of love not just a sense of duty or responsibility. Make no mistake I love my Dad dearly. As for my Mother that is a different matter. I do love her. I think there are as many different kinds of love a there are people. Maybe the key to a mutually satisfying relationship is to find someone that loves as much as you do or expresses love in ways you identify with or at least appreciates your love for him or her.

Maybe my Mother and I simply have totally different ideas of what it means to love someone. Perhaps she is showing me love and I just don't recognize it. How sad if that is true. How it could so easily have been avoided if we could just talk to each other about such things.

"Mom I think you should have your apartment cleaned twice a month instead of once a month. Should I contact Amanda and arrange that?" I said casually one day recently to my Mother. She simply got up and left the room. We never had that conversation.

It is only in working hard to overcome my childhood legacy that I have become the person I am. I am therefore thankful for those experiences. I must not leave this same legacy to my children. I must share myself with them and show my love for them. I must sometimes push to have those conversations about feelings that no one really likes to have. I love my children enough to want to connect with them and that has made all the difference in their lives and in mine.

As for my childhood, I strangely feel nostalgic about it especially for the city in which I grew up. Just thinking of my hometown evokes a whole host of unidentifiable emotions. For the most part I am happy my childhood is over. Oh I understand it was over chronologically many, many years ago. I am referring to the end of my emotional childhood. I finally am not doomed to repeat the entire trauma of my childhood in my relationships especially in my relationships with my children. My childhood wounds are contained but not gone. Some wounds can never completely heal. I have worked hard to become the image of myself I projected earlier - a strong, confident, loving, compassionate and secure woman. But I know if you scratch the surface too hard or too deeply you will still find a woman who feels unloved and unlovable. That is the legacy of my childhood.

CHAPTER FIVE

Step Parenting – Impossible Relationships?

It struck me that it was a very strange thing to think about at that particular moment. It was just a few moments ago that Warren and I resolved our divorce after two years of acrimony. As I was walking to my car from the courthouse I realized that I would never see or hear from them ever again. I would never know if they graduated from college, married, and had children. Why did I care? It seems to me that under certain circumstances a connection can never happen no matter how hard we try. Even in the best of times of our marriage a connection never happened between Warren's two daughters and I. Circumstances can make it impossible. That was the case here I think.

It was ten years ago – the first time I met them, Teresa and Louise. They were young girls at that time and very timid and shy. They had come to my house to spend the day. Somewhat sheepishly they examined everything in the house carefully. They tried to do it so I wouldn't notice. After checking everything out in the house they wanted to go swimming. That seemed like a good idea. Participating in an activity together usually is a good ice breaker. It is certainly beats standing around trying to make conversation with a stranger.

"Where the heck is Wentworth, Mississippi?" I asked Warren after the girls had returned home. I had never heard of it. That is where his daughters lived. It is a town of about 100,000 people. I had absolutely no point of reference to understand living in such a small town in the South. I would later discover, to my surprise, that our lack of such a common experience would be significant. In this day and age of so much national and international travel, communication and information it struck me as so odd that this difference could be so powerful.

"The girls are coming to visit for the summer," Warren told me. They would be coming to the megalopolis of Southern California. Warren and I had married and moved there a few months earlier. They had spent vacations there before so it was familiar to them. For my family it was a new full time living environment. We had visited there but never lived there. There were a lot of firsts and new beginnings that summer. It was definitely too much change all at once but I was blind to the need to introduce change carefully in those days. Maybe this was a result of my impatient nature. I wanted everything to be resolved as fast as possible or maybe "in place" would be a better phrase.

It was, to put it mildly, crazy that first summer. We had six kids living with us ranging in age from 6 to 21. We, the parents, or at least I, were walking around on egg shells. I can't speak for Warren. I so wanted all of us to somewhat gel, i.e., to at least arrive at an amiable tolerance of each other that had the potential to blossom into something more when everyone matured. I understood it was a difficult process. I had been through it before. I did not want to adopt the attitude of let's wait to enjoy ourselves until the kids no longer come to visit or no longer live with us. I am not sure what Warren thought because we really didn't talk about it. I should have pressed him to communicate about it but people's children are such a sensitive topic. We did what I imagine most second marriage couples do – we muddled through without any thoughtful plan. Maybe we were just too involved in enjoying being with each other to formulate a plan. Did we naively think that because we were happy the children would follow suit? It is hard to believe we could think that! That first summer ended up being all about damage control.

"I'm not going to do it!" I heard someone shout downstairs. I heard some more commotion downstairs. It sounded like someone was screaming or crying. When I got to the kitchen Teresa was standing by the dishwasher with her head bowed down. The phone was in her hand. Her shoulders were shaking. In between sobs she was able to blurt out, "I have to unload the dishwasher!" I hate it here. I want to go home," she continued. By that time the commotion had drawn an audience – pretty typical for those early days of the marriage "Did you call your mother because you have to unload the dishwasher?" I shrieked. "Everyone is pitching in and helping out. You need to the same," I said not very nicely I'm sure. I left before I said more I would regret. The crowd dispersed. I have no idea if Teresa ever unloaded that dishwasher. I went upstairs to finish getting ready to go to the office. I was already late.

I am sure it started earlier but this was the first time I really saw it. Of course on the drive to the office I went over everything about that scene in my mind. I remember observing that my kids, except for my youngest –the six year old, were elated. Warren and Louise were silent. I know that when I spoke to Teresa she reeled to look at me with eyes filled with hatred and loathing. I knew previously there was some animosity but this was something more. Did it start that morning? Is that when the animosity turned to loathing? No, I think it started on our wedding day. On that day Teresa looked like she was attending a funeral not a wedding. She never said she was unhappy but then she didn't need to. Her demeanor said it all.

I had intentionally asked very little of Teresa that first summer. Before this explosion Warren and I had discussed nicely with Teresa on many occasions that she had to help out at the house. Everyone had some assigned responsibilities. Her response was that she didn't have to do any chores at home and she didn't see why she should do any here. She managed to avoid doing anything for several weeks but eventually my children started getting angry. Children always feel like they are doing more than their siblings. It is much worse when the other sibling is a step-sibling. Truthfully Teresa was not doing anything. I had made a point of observing her for a few weeks because I didn't want to be favoring my children or being unduly harsh on Warren's children. I wanted to be fair. Warren acknowledged Teresa wasn't doing anything. We discussed that she needed to pitch in. Warren was going to insist that she do some chores. I guess he must have insisted that morning. Maybe I finally insisted with him. So what happened during the first overt breakdown of the summer? I got angry, lost it and I yelled at her. As I drove to the office, I remember regretting my behavior and asking myself what it would take to make things work. I wasn't asking for the moon. I just wanted everyone to tolerate each other. Even that may have been asking too much as I found out later. As soon as I got home that night I should have gone downstairs and apologized to Teresa for my outburst but I didn't.

If only we didn't have to go about the business of living, working, paying bills, housework, yard work and other relationships we might be able to handle the matter of step parenting and blending families better. I believed that all six of the offspring would eventually at least gracefully accept the situation as long as we treated them with respect and we cared about them. If we just had the right foundation it could all work. Maybe I just wanted that to be true.

When I got home that night I tried to discuss the situation with Warren and how to repair the damage and make it all work better. He had, sometimes, an authoritarian attitude toward parenting. He thought Teresa should do as she was told. I think his way of dealing with the situation was to stop asking her to do anything if in fact he ever had. I knew I couldn't ask her to do things. When I pressed the issue of Teresa's attitude and refusal to help with Warren his response was, "You are just jealous that she is much better kid than your kids, so you want to pick on her." She deserved special treatment because she was so perfect was the attitude that was never directly said – only implied. I could accept that for me but not for my children. I wasn't going to send them a message that they were not as good as Teresa.

I know that at some later time I did apologize to Teresa for my behavior. She was silent but her eyes and facial expression adequately conveyed the loathing and hatred she felt for me. Did I really think an apology would make a difference or change anything? Maybe it would plant a seed. I hoped so.

Listen, I would say to myself, your own kids hate you when they are teenagers. Take that and add to it that you are not the parent, they are away from familiar surroundings, their mom is fueling the fire of animosity or at least not helping quench the flames, they are struggling with the huge changes in their own lives brought on by adolescence and the divorce, they spend very brief periods of time with us, they are subjected to different standards and expectations from their parents. Is it possible to overcome any of that to form at least a truce with your stepdaughter? The tension that first summer was palpable.

"Everyone please come for dinner," I shouted. Slowly they all eventually trickled in. As soon as we sat down the phone rang. Warren answered it. "We just sat down for dinner. Can she call you after we finish eating?" Warren said. Then he was silent, apparently listening. "No you can't talk to her right now. She will call you later. Please stop calling here twice a day. The girls are fine. They will call you if they want to talk," he said and then he was silent again. "I asked them to call you earlier today. They didn't want to," Warren said and then there was more silence. We could all hear the shrieking from the other end of the phone. Warren hung up the phone and sat back down at the table. Teresa looked angry and embarrassed. We ate dinner although that phone call definitely created tension. I am certain that is what their mother intended to do. The girls' mother would call several times a day. After the call the attitude of the girls was dramatically worse. Later their mother got them each a cell phone so they could talk and whisper to her alone in their bedroom. I could always tell when they had talked to their mother.

Wasn't it my responsibility to make it all, the family that is, work? Didn't that include making sure his kids had a good time while visiting us? I knew, at the time, I shouldn't be taking all this on myself. After all they were his kids, not mine. Shouldn't he be primarily responsible for them? When he dropped the ball shouldn't I have just let it go? Why is it that my generation of women still feels it is solely our responsibility to make the family work? I was definitely fully indoctrinated into that way of thinking.

As I am writing this I feel overcome with such a sense of failure. I find myself going down that all too familiar path thinking what I could or should have done differently as a step parent and wife that would have changed the outcome. You know the "what ifs" of life. Is that a just a curse of my generation of women? Am I just set on self flagellation? Am I so arrogant or stupid as to think that the functioning of the family unit rests entirely with and on me? Why can't I stop doing this to myself? I don't sense that this next generation of women will have those same issues although I have no facts to base that on - just superficial observations. What a relief! The absence of such behavior in the younger generation would be a good thing!

Teresa was 14 that first summer. Louise was 7 at the time. Louise made friends and seemed to enjoy her time in California. We kept her busy with activities that she said she wanted to do. She was definitely difficult. She would challenge everything multiple times before she conceded that you meant business. But she had acted like that before the marriage. It was manageable because it could be dealt with in a direct fashion. There was unacceptable behavior and consequences for it. The simplicity after dealing with Teresa was like a breath of fresh air. Louise's behavior would unfortunately escalate and morph into something much more serious as she got older. But for now, for the most part, she enjoyed her visits with us. Still there were issues.

"Louise scratched me," he said between sobs, clutching his neck. Gary, my youngest child, was 6 at the time – a year younger than Louise. He was trying to explain more about what happened but he was crying so hard I couldn't understand him. I was able to pull his hand away from his neck. There were three huge, deep, red scratch marks on his neck –the kind made by fingernails. I drew a sharp breath. "She wanted the toy that I had," Gary explained. I am so glad none of the older kids are here I said to myself.

"Louise, come in here," Warren shouted from the other room. Gary continued to cry and hold his neck. I think he was crying more as a reaction to the overt act of hostility than the physical hurt.

"Louise you shouldn't do that," I heard Warren tell her. Now go find something constructive to do." After Warren and I were alone I demanded to know, "Is that the extent of the consequence?" Warren looked annoyed. "Oh you know Louise. She is a good kid, very bright. She is just a bit feisty. You're overreacting. Kids do these things. They fight," Warren said. I was pretty angry to say the least. As a stepparent I knew that if I disciplined Louise that would cause huge resentment. But what about the resentment Gary was feeling - I saw the incredulous look on his face – that she didn't get a punishment for behavior he knows he would have been severely disciplined for. I'll talk to Gary and Warren later I said to myself. I told Louise – I tried to be calm but I am sure I wasn't - that such behavior was unacceptable in our house. We did not resolve conflict with physical fights. Her sullen look told me that she could have cared less about what I had to say.

There was no discussing the situation with Warren later. I got the same explanation the he had previously given. In my view Warren's lack of response left me no choice. I was not going to make excuses or provide pat rationalizations to my children for the behaviors of others as I had in the past. So I gave an honest explanation to Gary – probably too honest for a six year old. He was going to have to accept something that was patently unfair. He would have to accept, for the time being, that there were two sets of rules in the house – one for Louise and one for him. I said he would, in the end, be a happier adult because he learned to behave. Louise would have problems. That did not go over well with a six year old. He was pretty angry with me. After all he didn't understand that I really could not discipline Louise even though I wanted to. If I tried I think there would have been more incidents like the one with Gary.

I know Warren was embarrassed that his daughter had acted in such a manner and did not want to admit that to me. I understood that but Warren's handling of that event severely undermined his relationship with Gary and with the other kids including his oldest daughter, Teresa.   As I look back I realize it also slightly, detrimentally affected his relationship with me although at the time I think there was too much going on to be able to see that. I say slightly because by that time in my life I was resigned to accepting that type of behavior from divorced fathers.

"Time for bed," I said to Louise as I entered her bedroom. She looked up at me and continued with something she was doing on the bed. "What are you doing?" I asked. "I am counting my pieces of candy," she said. "Why are you doing that?" I asked. I figured she wanted to make sure no one had taken any. "My Mom gave me this candy before I left. She said I could eat one piece everyday and then when the pieces were gone I wouldn't have to stay here anymore. I could go home," Louise said triumphantly. I didn't say anything.

Favoritism and unfair treatment create divisions and rifts in every family. But the detrimental effect is exacerbated in a family trying to blend. Any damage was going to be more difficult to undo. It reminded me of trying to glue something together when there was a foreign substance in the glue. The foreign substance can prevent the glue from working or it can simply create an imperfect bond. In biological families it was more likely to create an imperfect bond. In stepfamilies it can prevent bonding. Warren didn't seem interested in seeing the damage that had been created when he failed to discipline Louise for scratching Gary. Isn't it the accumulation of the "minor" incidents that eventually leads to the breakdown of relationships or prevents them from developing?

Why did Warren feel compelled to compete over who has the better child? In my experience, in a second marriage the husband's children are always prettier, smarter, and better behaved than yours. They always can find acceptable excuses for the atrocious behavior of their kids but can find no excuse for even minor infractions committed by the wife's children. The wife's children often seem to get punishments that oftentimes exceed the nature of the "crime". The husband's children rarely get any punishment even if the "crime" is severe. Do they feel guilty for the divorce? Do they feel guilty because they are only a part time dad to their own children? Are they afraid the kids won't want to visit if they discipline them? Do they really believe their kids are better than yours? The worst part is there is no way you can talk to them about the disparity in the treatment with your husband. Any attempt to discuss the issue results in accusations being hurled that you are jealous because his kids are smarter, more popular, better behaved than yours. The subliminal message is that you are simply not as good a parent as he is. Eventually you just throw up your hands in frustration. What else is there to do?

I was not going to let Warren's attitude and way of handling discipline with his daughters vis-a-vis Gary effect Gary's self esteem. It is not that I care if he thinks his kids are better than mine. I know they are not. It is that I don't want my kids to think that or think that I believe that. I knew that going along with different sets of treatment or standards would be interpreted by my children that I agreed that his kids were better than mine. I had let that happen in my previous marriage. My girls always felt inferior to Brian's daughter. I should have done something about it back then. Oh I had my reasons but none of them were really any good. I just didn't understand the extent of the damage at that time. Now I knew. There are severe consequences to remaining silent. This is why I said what I did to Gary. I had no way of knowing if what I was doing was the right thing to do or not. Step parenting was conducted on the basis of trial or error.

There were very few, if any, days without some type of incident that first summer. Louise's had her outbursts of bad behavior. Teresa somehow managed to escape doing any chores. Teresa was a princess and expected to be treated as such. I think this was a spillover from the way she was treated back in Mississippi. My older kids recognized and accepted this before I did. I ended up complying. How much was too much change to ask of Warren's children that first summer? I certainly didn't know the answer. I didn't want to set an expectation that they would be treated differently from my children but I didn't want to push too hard that first summer. It was quite a daily dilemma. Almost every day presented a new challenge.

How should I handle this with Warren? Is this disparate treatment of children just something a woman has to endure in a second marriage? After three marriages this seemed to be a pattern. Are there any men out there that recognize these issues and will discuss and work to resolve them? Do women in a second marriage do this as well? Warren's children weren't with us on a full time basis. Shouldn't I just endure it? Was it fair or right to ask my children to endure it as well? Was there any way to work this out? In exasperation, I eventually told Warren that I would concede that his children were better in every way than mine but still the competition never ended.

"Mom, I am missing some money," my teenage son, Samuel, told me. "Louise took it." I think he said "stole it". After the normal inquiry into whether the facts actually supported the accusation it appeared to be true. Louise of course denied it. That was not the first or last time that Louise would "take "something that did not belong to her. It was not the first or last time she would tell a lie. Warren repeated his mantra to me, "I was overreacting. My kids did bad things. My son just didn't like Louise and was trying to get her in trouble. There is no way she could have done that." Trying to address any of Louise' behavior became like viewing the replay of a very bad movie. I was left to deal with the anger of my children, as behavior for which they would have been severely punished, went unnoticed when committed by Louise.

Were Teresa and Louse jealous because they were not the top dogs but just one of a pack? Were they jealous that they did not have all of their dad's attention now or had to share it with someone other than their mother? Did they genuinely dislike me? Were they mad at the world because of the changes in their lives they did not want and over which they had no control? Did they just need time to adjust to the huge changes in their lives or were they simply unable to adjust? Was some of this just normal growing pains exacerbated by the fact that their lives were being witnessed and dealt with by a stranger? Were there real changes in their parent's behavior since the divorce or changes in their life in Mississippi? Were there genuine character flaws or behavioral issues that pre-existed the divorce? Was this just a symptom of a bad or weak relationship with their father that was exacerbated by the divorce and remarriage?   Was their mother creating animosity by conveying a message that visiting their dad was a punishment that they would have to just get through? I would suggest that it could be all or any of the above or any of many more possible reasons. Take your pick? Does it really matter? I used to believe that a fix was possible if we can just pinpoint the reason. I don't believe that now.   There were too many factors working against blending this family including too many factors over which Warren and I had no control.

We all struggled on for seven years. As I write this I imagine the scene from the dust bowls of the Great Depression with people struggling to move forward against the force of an overpowering wind. They are walking into the wind. They keep trying to move forward but they either get nowhere or move backward. That aptly describes the situation with Warren and I as dealing with issues regarding the children spilled over into our relationship starting that first summer and thereafter. No matter how hard I tried things got worse over the next seven years.

As Teresa grew up and matured she seemed to stop loathing me. Louise more than took her place. Teresa and I even had a few good conversations and times together – brief and rare but there nevertheless. At one point in time she had even wanted to come live with us but I think that was because she wanted to escape how bad things were back in Mississippi. It wasn't that she really wanted to live with us. That says a lot about how bad things were back in Mississippi.

"Your mother stole all my money. She cheated me. She has tried to take you kids away from me," I heard him say. I poked my head in to see that Warren was talking to Teresa. She wasn't saying a word but I could see it written all over her face. I wondered why he didn't look at her face. Didn't he see it – the hostility, rage even hatred directed at him. The ex spouse bashing was a ritual that occurred during every visit. I tried but I was powerless to stop it.

Was it any wonder that Teresa had come to intensely dislike her father?

I have seen this happen in many, if not most divorce, situations. I often wonder why parents do this. Are the divorced parents really engaged in a contest for the affection of the child? Are there any possible winners in this contest? Are the parents looking for validation of their view of the divorce and how they had been wronged? Do they want the child to pick sides like in a baseball game? Do they really think the kid will like them better than the other because of things they tell them? And if the child did what difference would it make? Fortunately this type of behavior usually stops once things settle down after the divorce and some time has passed.

Warren and his ex-wife were in a hate fest which lasted for the seven years of our marriage. I am almost certain that Teresa heard the same type of things from her mother about Warren. The saddest part is that Teresa desperately needed to share with Warren the difficulties she was actually having with her mother in Mississippi. She never could or did. As with most children of divorce she learned to keep secrets. Teresa just soldiered on with her life in Mississippi with her mother who it turned out was abusing prescription drugs and alcohol. It was no surprise when Teresa turned 18 that she simply stopped coming to visit Warren. She never answered or returned Warren's phone calls. He of course never connected her refusal to visit or even talk to him to any of his behaviors. In his view her mother had simply turned her against him. I guess that was an easy way out. Warren always liked to find the easy way out.

Gary was the only one living with Warren and I on a full time basis. My three oldest children were all living elsewhere. The three oldest children tolerated Warren. I think thcy would have spent more time at home if he weren't there but that is one of the prices a mother pays for a second marriage. I knew that going into this marriage. I thought they would do more than tolerate Warren as time when on but unfortunately the tolerance turned to loathing. Their loathing seemed to track the demise of our marriage.

Warren and I had our issues with my children as well. Gary was young enough that he was accepting and even welcoming of Warren. They were still struggling with their own adolescent issues that had been exacerbated by their father's death. My son, Samuel had no sense of direction to say the least. My youngest daughter, Ellen, had her own demons to deal with. She didn't discriminate. She was mean to everyone during those years. My eldest daughter was away at college and went out on her own after graduating.

Warren was good at helping with my children when we first got together. In fact that is one of the things I liked so about him. As I look back on it I am not sure Warren was so much helping me as he was implementing his own agenda. As soon as he came into our lives my two middle children were sent away to military school. Mind you that was a good thing for them but I wonder now if Warren pushed for that because it was a good thing for them or him. In spite of Gary's excitement over having a father Warren eventually managed to derail any relationship with him. Still I think Warren genuinely tried to have a relationship with my children in the beginning. He just wasn't very good at it.

"You want me to choose between you and my son?" I yelled at Warren. Warren looked at me angrily but he said nothing. "I choose my son," I emphatically replied as I grabbed Samuel's hand. Warren turned and walked away. "Mom, Mom stop," Samuel said. He seemed very embarrassed. Funny that I can't remember exactly what precipitated this exchange but I can still see us all so clearly standing and arguing in the hallway of the house we lived in after we were first married. Samuel had done something to make Warren angry. I think he had sided with Teresa over something Warren had said or done to her. Warren ordered Samuel to get out of the house for good.

Teresa did make friends in our neighborhood. And I think her refusal to visit initially was partly because of the huge contrast between Warrenville, Mississippi and Southern California. It was too much for Teresa. She got her driver's license in Mississippi. But she never wanted to drive when she was visiting us in California.

She never said why but I think that the traffic and freeways intimidated her. She didn't want to go to summer school in California. She never said why but I think the competition intimidated her. Kids would go to the community swimming pool wearing makeup and decked out like run way models. Teresa felt intimidated by all of that as well. California can have that effect on people.

Teresa and Louise continued to visit regularly. Warren and his ex wife always got into a huge fight before they came for a visit. The girls always arrived with a rather hostile attitude. Teresa stopped coming to visit once she turned 18. Louise continued to visit. Louise's behavior deteriorated dramatically over the seven year period. I found myself wondering at the intense transformation. I became acutely aware of changes mostly as a result of the deterioration of her relationship with my son, Gary.

In the beginning Louise and Gary seemed to enjoy each other's company. She had always fought with and been somewhat mean to him but it was manageable. Louise tried to hide her nastiness from me and his siblings but we all knew it was happening. Gary tolerated her visits well. Gary just had such a feeling of self worth and self confidence that Louise could not undermine it no matter how mean she was to him. I think that aggravated her more than anything and spurred her onto greater levels of meanness. As time went on, she no longer tried to hide her meanness toward him. She no longer made any effort to get along with him or to put up an appearance for Warren and me that she liked him. She was openly hostile to Gary and everyone else.

I don't remember how many summers it was before Louise's behavior changed. The visits blur together. Every summer I went through the same laundry list of possible causes as if this would help. Was it just that she was now a teenager? Was it that things at home in Mississippi were difficult and the anger and frustration was spilling over? Was this really her personality that she had hidden for all those years? I thought we had really made an effort to create summers for her that she would enjoy. We took her wherever she wanted to go. We enrolled her in a multitude of summer programs she wanted to attend. We arranged for her to have friends from Mississippi and California visit her. Was it wrong to have her come to visit at all? Warren was ready to give up on the visits before I was. I should have let him.

"I got an I pod," Louise exclaimed. Then she was silent. "No, I hate it here. I can't have a good time with her here." Louise was talking on the phone to a friend from Mississippi. We had just finished celebrating Christmas and she told me she wanted to tell her friend what a great Christmas she had. Warren was against buying Teresa or Louise many gifts for Christmas. He didn't believe in celebrating Christmas or so he said. His other reason was that they were too spoiled by their mother and didn't need any more gifts. I suggested that we just agree to have them spend every Christmas with their mother and have them come visit the week after. Warren wouldn't agree to that. At the last minute I would, against his wishes, buy them a few nice things believing, as Warren said, that they would have their "real" Christmas with their mother in Mississippi. Real I guess means lots of gifts? I dreaded the Christmases when they would be with us for the actual holiday. This gift issue was so stressful on top of everything else that normally went along with their visits and the holidays. This was not the first time I had heard Louise say something like this to a friend in Mississippi. It was, however, the last time I would care.

The last year of our marriage I gave up on having any relationship with Louise or even trying to make her visits enjoyable for her. Nothing seemed to work. I felt like I was trying to make this work with her all by myself. And in fact I was. It was around this point in time that I started to realize that Warren didn't really care about Louise or even Teresa. I don't think I admitted that to myself until much later. I think I had been trying, albeit very unsuccessfully, to make up for his lack of attention or interest. Of course I was doomed to fail. In retrospect I should have just let things run their course.

Warren said, before at least every summer visit, that his girls shouldn't come to visit. I should have agreed instead of insisting they come. "How can you give up on your own kids?" I would ask him. I should have let him do what he wanted. I realize now that I was wrong to insist that they continue to visit. I don't think it would have changed the outcome for Warren or his children but it would have stopped delaying the inevitable. Why did I insist on trying to create a relationship where there was none? Was it totally altruistic on my part or was I just afraid to admit that the man I was married to really didn't care about his own children? I wish I had faced that truth earlier. It would have made a significant difference in my life even if it didn't in the lives of his children.

"Did you have a good time?" I asked Gary. He was only 10 years old so you could still get him to engage in a conversation when you asked that question. He and Louse had been at a neighborhood sleepover. "Yeah, except for Louise telling everyone how mean I am to her and how she hates me," he responded. I guess she didn't just tell people that about me.

During her last summer visit I found myself withdrawing from any interaction with Louise. She and Gary rarely interacted anymore. I found it impossible to make any connection with her. I guess Gary did too. Warren had been ignoring her for years. Warren seemed to withdraw even further from her as time went on. He would drive Louise and pick her up from activities and friend's houses. At one point in time he had been more involved but slowly he had withdrawn from all responsibilities except for the custodial ones. I am ashamed to say that the summer of her last visit and the last summer of our marriage I rarely spoke to her.

As the marriage deteriorated Warren's treatment of Gary deteriorated as well. Perhaps Warren had never really bonded with Gary. I thought he had. Maybe it is just that Warren's stress spilled over into his relationship with Gary. Warren had done that with his own children as well. It struck me as odd that Warren's bond with Gary could be so easily severed. Was it because Gary was not Warren's biological child? I don't think so. I think it was just the nature of Warren's relationships. He so alienated Gary that Gary didn't want to have anything to do with him after the separation and divorce. The relationship had become destructive and so I did not force Gary to see Warren. I tried to leave the door open for Gary and Warren to have a relationship in the future but, after several years, Gary has not budged in his determination not to see Warren.

I tried so very hard to hide the stress of the divorce from Gary. I so did not want to involve him in it anymore than I had to. Warren apparently repeated what he had done with Teresa and Louise. He started bad mouthing me to Gary. I would have thought Warren would have learned his lesson from his experiences with his own daughters. Sadly that was enough, along with the history of neglectful treatment in the last years of our marriage, to break the tenuous bond between Gary and Warren. I was sadly surprised at how quickly and thoroughly the bond was severed.

I wanted so desperately for Gary to have a "Dad". I guess in my rush to give him a "Dad" I had picked the wrong one. There is such a small window of opportunity in which a child can bond with a step parent I think. Gary was still in that age range when Warren and I married. I have seen a few success stories of children bonding with a step parent. But to do that the adult has to put aside his or her own feelings and agenda in the interests of the child at least for a time. I am afraid not many adults can do that. Warren certainly couldn't.

In going into this marriage with Warren I had lowered my expectations significantly regarding a relationship with a stepchild. I thought I had learned from my previous experience and mistakes. Maybe a step parent can build a relationship under certain circumstances but I didn't have those or couldn't create those in my marriage with Warren. I think I tried. The critical missing factor in my attempt to create some type of positive relationship with Warren's children may have been the absence of a good relationship between Warren and his daughters and our inability to communicate about issues regarding all the children but especially his daughters. When I first met Warren it appeared to me that he had a good relationship with his daughters. Was that just another illusion about

Warren or did the stresses created by the divorce and remarriage undermine that relationship? The truth is that I didn't give myself time to really find out if Warren's relationship with his girls was real. I rushed headlong into this relationship and formed opinions based on just initial impressions rather than long term observation. I tend to do that. Impatience in relationships is one of my major faults.

As I look back I wonder if I am just a glutton for punishment, an eternal optimist or simply want to have a relationship in a world in which, the reality is, my potential male mates will have children. Why did I agree to become a stepparent again? Hadn't I already learned that it was an impossible situation?

It was one of those incredibly hot desert days – so hot that you feel almost as if you can't breathe. It was after all the middle of July in a city located in the heart of the desert. Brian had invited my children and I to spend the day at the local water park with his daughter and him. It was to be the first time we would meet her. She was five years old. I don't remember too many details of that day since it happened more than 20 years ago. It does strike me as odd the things I do remember from my past. I can remember clearly Brian, ever so gently, applying sun block to Bridget's little body so her delicate skin would be protected while we all enjoyed the water park. She was very quiet, shy and well behaved. We all had a great day together.

Before and after we were married, Brian faithfully stuck to his visitation schedule with his daughter, Bridget. She spent every other weekend, one night a week, certain holidays and some time in the summer with us. This was possible because we all lived in the same city. Bridget was his second child although his other daughter was grown. Bridget was born when Brian was a bit older than what used to be the national average. He was in his 40s.

Brian was so good with my children. From the very beginning he seemed to love them and treat them as if they were his own. That was not an easy thing to do as there were three of them under the age of 7 and they were very active. I was so appreciative of his love for them. It made me love him even more. Brian seemed to understand that we were a package deal. To me his love for my children was an extension of his love for me. I never felt he resented them. What a wonderful gift to have someone love you and your children.

We formed a family and by that I mean a group of people who have their differences and issues but who cared enough about each other to work them out. We had a bond, a connection that tied us all together. This may have only been possible because the father of my children had abandoned them. That bond was only disrupted by the regular visits of Bridget.

When Bridget visited Brian and I would become ensconced in separate camps. How did it become his daughter and him versus my children and me? It definitely didn't start out that way. Somewhere along the way we split apart. As time passed the camps become increasingly separate and hostile.

I can still hear Brian say, "Bridget got straight "As. Bridget got a good conduct award at school. Bridget gave up several parties with friends to come for the weekend. Bridget always does as she is told...." At the dinner table the conversation centered on Bridget, her accomplishments and how wonderful she was. Some things were directly said and some were implied. But the result was the same. Bridget was a better person, student, etc. than my daughters. They were lesser persons than Bridget. I could see it on their faces. I could see it in Brian and Bridget's faces. As I sat at the dinner table I wondered if I should say something good about my daughters. Didn't that just feed this competition? I didn't want to compete. I didn't want to start a fight. Would anything change if I did say something? The look on the face of my daughters struck like a knife in my heart, especially Ellen. Her self esteem was so fragile already. I would talk to them later – after dinner.

"We have to cancel our dinner plans for this coming Saturday with Eloise and Martin," Brian said. "We have had that planned for weeks," I replied. "Why do we have to cancel?" I asked. "Bridget is coming to visit this weekend and I don't want to go out while she is here," Brian replied. "We can go out after she is in bed," I replied. Brian refused to do that. We were always doing things together with the children during the day. But Brian and I could not go out alone at all during the weekends when Bridget visited. I understood that we did not want to go out every weekend but I resented that our schedule totally revolved around Bridget's visits. This resentment was partly fueled by the fact that when I would try to get out of going to some business event because I wanted to spend some time with my children Brian would get angry. I thought we could find a little more balance. Eventually we did.

"Can you do something special with Bridget this weekend – bake cookies, etc.?" Brian asked. I was expected to make Bridget's visits special. Some things were said directly by Brian. Most requests were unspoken. Bridget was the "princess" and we were all expected to treat her as such. She was a perfect child or so we were told. I don't think Bridget believed this. She didn't, for the most part, act that way. This was all Brian's doing.

Bridget spent every other weekend with us. Each time she visited I planned special activities to do with her and for her. We baked cookies and cakes. We sewed. We watched special movies with her. We had outings together. Through all of this I tried to establish a relationship with Bridget. But after a few years nothing happened. A feeling of love or even affection or respect never developed. A bond never developed. Sometimes I felt she was just putting in her time until she could go home. Bridget's attitude towards me was one of tolerance. I think that was mutual. She was a wonderful child but we never developed a real bond.

Was Bridget concerned that if she enjoyed her visits at our house or liked me she would be disloyal to her mother? Was it that I did not want to be disloyal to my children by loving Bridget? Did we really not like each other? Was she jealous of my relationship with her father? Was it all of the above and much more? Is it that she had the power to cause friction between her Dad and I and she liked to exercise that power? Is it just simply impossible to love someone else's child at least for me? Maybe I WAS JEALOUS. May be my kids were lesser people. For a while I entertained all possibilities trying to get a handle on the situation and what to do about it.

Finding a solution or maybe better a truce was a long, difficult process.

"Bridget told my friends they should hate me," Ellen said through her tears. "Sally wants to go home right now and doesn't want to spend the night because of what Bridget is saying about me," Ellen continued. Ellen was about 8 years old at the time. Brian insisted that Ellen and Bridget attend each other's birthday parties. They didn't have any friends in common as we lived in different parts of the city but they were about the same age. I wasn't sure I believed Ellen at the time so I talked to two of her friends. They confirmed what Ellen had said. I have to admit I was pretty angry. I also have to admit that there was an element of satisfaction in my anger. I had suspected that Bridget engaged in similar sneaky conduct before but there was never any proof. I was relieved that my suspicions were confirmed and I wasn't just being mean. I didn't say anything to Bridget about this.

"I don't believe you. Bridget would never do such a thing," Brian said to me in an angry voice. Brian called Bridget into the room. "Did you try to get Ellen's friends to stop liking her?" he said. Bridget was silent. Brian stormed out of the room. He wasn't really angry at Bridget. He was angry at me because I had refused to sweep this incident under the rug. I never said anything to Brian about this again. He would just get angrier. I checked in with Ellen later and she said things were going well.

"You are imagining it," Brian said. "You are just jealous that she is a much better kid than any of yours. I don't want to talk about it. You are so petty." All of these things were said at one time or another whenever I tried to talk to Brian about the disparity in treatment between Bridget and my kids. I knew I was not imagining it. Most often he would just storm off in anger when I brought the subject up. It almost destroyed our relationship and we loved each other very much.

It is interesting that this disparity in treatment never happened with Samuel. Maybe that is because Brian didn't have a biological son to compete with or compare to Samuel. Samuel had his struggles with Brian. He didn't like Brian to discipline him but then Samuel didn't like anyone to discipline him. I appreciated that Brian wanted to and was willing to help raise Samuel and the girls. Ellen was young enough that she loved and respected Brian as her "Dad". She was hurt when he treated Bridget with kid gloves often at Ellen's expense. That resentment may have exploded later but we never found that out.

"I want to have a pool party for a group of my eighth grade friends" Jessica said one day. It was summer. It seemed like a good idea. Brian was a little reluctant but agreed to the party. Brian liked to have everything in order and having a lot of kids over upset the order. The kids arrived and we let them have the pool and backyard to themselves. We were able to watch, hopefully unnoticed, from the house.

"The kids are standing on the tile edge and diving from the spa into the pool" Brian said rather angrily. I agreed that one of us needed to tell Jessica about this. I thought it could be accomplished simply and quickly. Brian thought otherwise. "Let's go out and talk to Jessica" Brian said. "Let's not talk to her in front of her friends" I said. I thought it would be best if only one of us went but Brian insisted on going and I was concerned as to how he would handle it. My concern was justified. "Jessica we need to talk to you" Brian said ominously. "Jessica your friends are too wild. They are destroying the pool and the backyard" Brian said angrily.

Jessica looked at me to see if I agreed. I didn't and I am sure she saw that in my face. Brian went on angrily for a few moments until I finally convinced him enough had been said. We exchanged some words when we got back to the house. Brian's sometimes had the attitude that since it was his house I wouldn't be upset if things were ruined. That wasn't true. I thought we needed to strike a balance between letting the kids have fun and maintaining the house. "Jessica please don't let your friends stand on the tile and jump from the spa into the pool" would have been enough I think. Jessica was resentful and angry at me that I "gave" into Brian. She never had another party at the house.

I felt like I was always walking a tightrope between what Brian considered egregious conduct and the expectations my children had based on my parenting style. Brian was much stricter than I. The children were used to my rules. A lot of things changed when Brian and I married and we all moved in together. This is one area in which Brian didn't want to take things slowly. Brian made me feel like I was giving in too much to my children and being manipulated by them when I didn't agree with his harsher punishments and stricter rules. The children felt like I was Brian's puppet. My children felt like I was betraying them when I "sided" with Brian. Brian felt like I was betraying him when I "sided" with my children. I was being tugged in both directions constantly. There was always someone who was mad at me or disappointed with me. Trying to make my marriage work and to blend a family was emotionally exhausting.

"You would never have done that if Brian wasn't around!" Jessica shouted. On many occasions she was right. How could I explain to her that perhaps my parenting skills needed improvement? I had not been the best disciplinarian in part due to the lack of time and energy for it. Once the children get used to the new rules and lifestyle things will get easier I would say to myself. But we needed more than just time to make it all work. I had a premonition that my children would always resent Brian no matter how much time passed. Some of that had to do with Brian and some just had to do with the nature of the stepparent relationship.

I have heard some "experts" say that only the biological parent should discipline a child. I found that to be somewhat impractical. There was so much happening all the time we just couldn't stop everything to wait for the other parent to arrive for the discipline. Things just needed to be addressed. Brian and I discussed how to handle certain matters especially the bigger child rearing issues. As with biological parents, we disagreed as to whether a situation merited some discipline and then what the discipline should be. That situation was just more complicated emotionally because Brian wasn't their biological father. Brian was a bit stricter than I as a parent but that had nothing to do with the status of my children as step children.

"We have to be able to talk about the children – all of the children," I said to Brian one day. Brian and I had split up for a while and one of the issues was the disparity in treatment among children and the tension and divisiveness it caused. We talked about this for the first time without Brian exploding. It was one of the things we would work on in counseling. In part I think I just needed to have my feelings recognized. My feelings seemed to be ignored in this marriage including my feelings about my children.

I can remember a psychologist saying that this attitude that Bridge was superior to my children and should be treated as such was an extension or reflection of Brian's view of himself in the marriage. I don't know if that is true but I do believe that Brian believed he wanted and how he felt was more important than what I wanted or how I felt. Of course I didn't realize that until much later. I see now that this attitude was a source of many of our disagreements. I was fighting for recognition for myself and my children.

Eventually we reached a truce. It was not a good solution but it worked. When Bridget would come for the weekend visit, she and Brian would do their own thing. My children and I would do our own thing. After Bridget left, we would all do things together again. I accepted it as the best we could do at least at that time.

"Everyone dinner is ready," I called from the kitchen. Everyone arrived at the dinner table and we sat down to eat. My parents were visiting from back east. I had been a nervous wreck all day waiting for this dinner. I didn't eat much as I was anxiously trying to get up my courage. Dinner was almost over. I would have to say something now. Putting it off would only make matters worse. "I'm pregnant!" I announced. All heads spun to look at me. No one said a word. There was an eerie silence. No words of congratulations or excitement were forthcoming even from my parents. Everyone got up and silently left the table. I didn't take that as a good sign.

My oldest daughter was 14 when I made that announcement. The other two were 12 and 11. It had been an agonizing decision for me. I had three healthy children that I had struggled to raise financially, emotionally and physically. I had been and still was to a certain extent exhausted by the demands of children, my husband, work and the home. I would be delaying the empty nest for 10 years. Brian never pressured me even though I knew he desperately wanted more children.

"If you want more children you need to do it now. The gynecologist had discovered a problem during a routine examination. He asked me to return to see him with my husband. "You have developed a medical condition for which the best treatment is a hysterectomy," my gynecologist said Brian and I as we were seated in his office. Brian and I looked at each other and we knew. We would have a child. I knew Brian would share the financial, emotional and physical responsibilities of raising a child. I so wanted to share all the joy as well the responsibility with someone. But there was an even greater benefit that I wasn't aware of at that time. It wouldn't become apparent until after Gary arrived.

"Did you see what he just did?' Ellen said to Bridget. "Let me feed him! Let me change him! Let me push him in the stroller!" the two youngest girls would say as they fought over who could do things for Gary. Samuel and Jessica were very involved as well. I often, later, would find one or several of the older children snuggled up on the couch with Gary watching a Disney movie. Everyone lingered at the dinner table to help feed him or to witness his latest accomplishment. Everyone wanted to go on family outings to the park to push Gary in the stroller or later on in the swing. The children all wanted to hang around the house in order to spend time with Gary. It helped that he was such a happy, fun baby. Suddenly these two separate "camps" had something in common. We all loved Gary.

After Gary arrived, most of the tension melted away between Brian and my children and Bridget and all of us. We had something that connected us – a bond. It was our love for Gary. We really were becoming a family now – a group of people that genuinely loved and cared for each other. I don't think that bond would have developed without Gary. Bridget's weekend visits were even enjoyable. It was another set of hands to help which everything and Bridget seemed to enjoy helping and spending time with Gary. Through Gary we were sharing our lives and ourselves. I am sure there are other ways to create that bond other than having a baby. Maybe his arrival just sped up the process.

We would need the love engendered by Gary's birth to get us through the trials we would be faced with shortly. Gary was the glue that held us all together. Without him I don't believe we would have survived as well as we did. I know I wouldn't have.

Is it possible to have a good relationship with a stepchild especially a woman with a stepdaughter? If not, can you at least reach an amicable truce? I realize now that all depended, to a great extent, on attitudes and circumstances over which I had no control. The biggest indicator may be the relationship between the father and child prior to the divorce. If it is a bad relationship the problem is insurmountable. If there is a good relationship then the other issues may be manageable. If the parties to the marriage can't discuss the situation you are doomed.

Warren and I were simply unable to contain the damage as time went on. In the end the focus of my tenure as stepparent was on coping with a situation in my house for long periods of time, over which I had no control. The hostility and disrespect of Warren's daughters toward me disrupted the household and set a bad example for my own children especially regarding the issue as how they could treat me, their stepfather and each other. The daily tension was palpable. I imagine that Louise would also have stopped coming to visit when she turned 18 but I didn't wait around to find out. Warren and I were divorced before then. I don't blame the issues with the stepchildren for the divorce but it definitely didn't help.

I have seen couples wait to marry until their respective children are grown and out of the house. Hopefully when your children are adults they want you to be happy and to have companionship. Of course I haven't tested that theory on my own family. Maybe the real answer is that the children are living their own lives and simply are not around enough to interfere. I hope there is more to it than that.

Can you ever really love someone else's child? Can a child of your spouse ever really love you? I have seen it happen where the stepchild and step parent have a mutual respect and even affection for each other. I think that depends more on the attitudes of the adults than the child. Maybe the child needs the permission of both of his parents to love the stepparents. Maybe both sets of parents need to accept each other before the child can accept the stepparents.

Bridget is an adult now. Oddly she lives now in the same city that I live in. We do see each other. There is a distance between us but perhaps that is the nature of Bridget's relationships in general. I don't see her interact enough with others to know if that is true. I just suspect it. I do know that when the conversation turns to her mother she withdraws even more. Perhaps it is a carryover from her childhood that she does not want to be disloyal to her mother by having a relationship with me. I sensed that was an issue when she was a child from some interactions Brian had with her mother. Perhaps I don't want to be disloyal to my daughters by having a relationship with Bridget. I think the emotional distance between us is a combination of many factors. We do share memories of and love for Brian. I am very glad she is a part of my life and Gary's life. I hope she feels the same way about us.

I so wish I could have talked about these things with others when I was going through it. It might have helped to hear what worked or didn't work for other stepparents. Is it our stoic nature that interferes with our ability to discuss these types of matters? Are we just too busy? Do we think by admitting we don't have it all under control that we are admitting we have failed?

I can offer only these few insights gained from my experience. I don't have any real answers as to how to make a stepfamily work. I was never very successful at it. I like to imagine that Brian and I would have been successful at blending our families if we had the time. We were certainly on the right track. The only thing I do know is that being a step parent requires more effort and energy than I have to give at this time in my life. I don't expect I will ever take on that role again.

CHAPTER SIX

What About God?

"I believe in God," I recently said to an acquaintance who was bashing religion. "I attend church regularly," I added. Oh I can't pat myself on the back for saying that because there were many, many times I was silent when the conversation turned to religion bashing. The current conversation abruptly and immediately stopped. It was a much more powerful response than words could ever be. The look on my acquaintance's face said it all. Intelligent people don't believe in God!

Why are intelligent people embarrassed to say they believe in God and/or attend church regularly? Why do others look askance at those who make that confession? Why do I respond by failing to or being embarrassed to admit my faith? Am I really less intelligent because I believe in God?

"Girls are you dressed yet?" my Mother shouted up the stairs. My Sister and I had already managed to put on our frilly new dresses, lace ankle socks and patent leather shoes. We had helped each other with buttons and buckles. We were squealing with delight. "We're coming," we shouted down. We were still putting trying to put on our hats with the ribbons streaming down. It was such an exciting time! We weren't going to Sunday school this day. We were too young to take communion but we were going to stay in the church with our parents for the entire service! We raced down the stairs. My Mother carefully inspected us. My Father and Brother were dressed in suits and ties. My Mother had on a new dress with a matching hat. My Mother, Sister and I wore white gloves.

When we arrived at the church, my parents greeted everyone in the narthex. As soon as we entered the sanctuary we were admonished to be very quiet. There was a beautiful stained glass window in the front of the church. In the middle of that window was a huge cross. The sun was streaming through that window filling the sanctuary with light and warmth. Beautiful hymns were being played on the organ. The choir members were dressed in their robes and waiting in the narthex for their procession into the sanctuary. The minister was dressed in his black vestments with a purple sash. As we walked closer to the front of the church I saw many of my schoolmates sitting with their parents and siblings and sometimes grandparents. We weren't allowed to talk to each other. They too were dressed in frilly, lacy dresses and bonnets. The boys were in suits and ties. The ushers were setting up extra chairs around the sanctuary. The church would be overflowing. After we sat down, the minister and choir proceeded up the aisle singing "Jesus Christ is risen today… Alleluia". As they entered the sanctuary we all rose and joined them in singing that hymn.

My Sister and I felt a bit wilted by the end of the service. After the service our parents visited with our friends, neighbors, parents of our schoolmates. We got to play with our friends. "Be careful with your new dress and shoes," my Mother scolded us. We didn't stay too long at church. We had to drive to our Grandparents' house which was about an hour away. You see my Aunt, Uncle and Cousins had come from far away to spend the holiday with my Grandparents and us. They did that almost every year. We would all sit down together to eat a wonderful Sunday dinner of roast lamb my Grandmother had prepared. Then we could change clothes and play with our cousins while our Mother, Aunt and Grandmother cleaned up the kitchen.

Religion or at least church was an integral part of my childhood. It was one of the foundations of our community. Our time at church was both religious and social. My Sunday school class was made up primarily of my classmates from school and my teacher was almost always the mother of one of my friends. It was an outing- a break from the monotony of being at home. We didn't have all the options for recreation the children do now. I have wonderful memories of the church of my childhood although that is not where my faith in God was born. But, perhaps the seeds were planted there.

"This is for you," my Father said handing a package to me. "I couldn't bear to throw it away when we sold the house." My Parents had recently moved out of the house in which I had grown up. I unwrapped the package. I recognized it right away. I couldn't believe he kept it all these years. Well maybe I can. My Father has always been very sentimental. The package contained something I had made one summer at Bible School. As I held it the memories of Bible School came flooding back. I was about 10 years old at the time. I was so proud of that glazed tile. I had drawn a picture of my dog on it.

In the summer we all went to Bible School. It is hard to imagine in these current times but we looked forward to those two weeks. Bible School was our break from the monotony of playing with the neighborhood kids. Neighborhood activities were fun but we wanted some variety. Many of my schoolmates attended Bible School along with me. My Mother and the mothers of my classmates were the teachers. We had arts and crafts. We learned stories from the Bible like we did in Sunday school. We had some recreation time together. The world felt safe and comfortable.

"Are we going to get to go the first day – Friday night?" I asked my Mother. "Can we go on Saturday as well? Can we play all the games? Can we buy something?" I continued to pester her. I was asking about the Fall Festival at the Church which was going to take place in a couple of weeks. My Sister and I were very excited. It was an annual event. My Mother was usually one of the organizers of that event. It took months to arrange and coordinate everything. Volunteers had to be procured and scheduled to man the many the booths and cook the dinner. The booths had to be set up by the fathers on the weekends or evenings. White elephant items had to be procured, tagged and displayed for sale. We played games and won prizes. My favorite game was throwing a bean bag into a backboard one of the fathers had made and painted. There was great food. We always had a dinner but there were snacks as well. I can still smell the sautéed mushrooms that were being prepared in electric skillets at one of the booths. I still love the smell and taste of sautéed mushrooms. It reminds me of the Fall Festival. As I think back to the church Festivals and other church events I am overcome with a feeling of warmth and comfort.

As I matured I remained involved in the church. I taught Sunday school. I participated in the high school youth group. I attended church summer camp for two weeks. I wasn't sure if I was going to be able to do that. It was an expensive camp and I overheard my parents discussing if they could afford it. In the end, they made some financial sacrifices because they thought it was important for me to attend. What a thrill!

The camp was located in the next state. It was a long bus ride but it was so worth it I thought. It had been a wonderful two weeks. We studied the Bible but we also did a lot of other things. We went sailing and water skiing on the lake. We had campfires, cooked smores, sang and talked.

"Camp is coming to a close. We want to encourage everyone to find a quiet spot and contemplate Jesus," Sally, our Church Youth Minister said to all of us. She had accompanied us on this trip. During those two weeks Sally kept asking me if I had "experienced God". I had no idea what that meant and I was feeling like a failure because "it" hadn't happened for me. This would be my last opportunity to do that. I distinctly remember finding a tree, leaning against it and closing my eyes. I thought hard about God and Jesus for a short while. Then I just relaxed and tried to tune everything out. A short while later, I jumped up and ran to find Sally. "Jesus appeared to me," I exclaimed to her. Sally was ecstatic. My experience and that of several others were announced to the whole group later that day.

"Jesus Christ appeared to me," I wrote to my parents on a postcard from camp. I think that the camp counselor must have encouraged me to write because my family never discussed these types of things. Emotional or spiritual experiences were never a topic of conversation in our family. Our conversations focused on the physical events of school, work and church.

I was on an emotional high that lasted for several weeks after I returned from summer camp. But as more and more time passed I started to doubt my experience. We had so much pressure put on us to "experience Jesus" that I started to doubt my experience was genuine. I felt the youth minister put too much emphasis on those types of experiences. It turned me off to religion. I started drifting away from church and the youth group after that. The youth minister lost interest in me. I guess I wasn't experiencing religion as she thought I should.

"We can't afford it. I won't fill out the financial aid application. Those colleges think parents should contribute huge amounts of money. It is ridiculous. We can't contribute anywhere near the amount they will want from us," my Father said. I had worked incredibly hard to have the credentials to be admitted to an Ivy League or similar University. Now my Father refused to allow me to apply. This was one of my first huge disappointments in life. I had the sophomoric notion that God could make this happen if He wanted to. In those days my faith in God was rather immature and I was angry at God. Other kids from my high school were accepted and attended the schools I wanted to go to. Their credentials were not as good as mine.

"Brad is attending a very expensive university away from home. Why can't I do the same? " I complained to my Father. "He will have to support a family," my Father said to explain why my Brother got to attend the university of his choice and I didn't. I never got the message, which I understand some of my peers did, that a woman could be anything she wanted to be. I felt alienated from the world in which I had grown up and by implication that included God. I was depressed. I lived at home and attended college. That is what my parents could afford. I wouldn't give God much thought again, if any, for at least 18 years.

Where have all the men gone? That is a question often asked by clergy. The men of my father's generation attended church. A much smaller percentage of the men in my generation attend and are involved with the Church. This next generation has even less. Sure attendance is down as a whole but that doesn't explain the conspicuous absence of the men. I knew Brian had attended church and several Bible studies before we met. I liked that about him. After I divorced when my children were very young, I started to have a vague sense that God was important. After Brian and I were married the vague sense became something more.

Something was pressing in on me kind of like a person in the airport security line who gets so close that they invade your personal space. I have had this feeling at various times in my life. I am usually busy and it is easy to ignore it in the beginning. I push it into the background hoping it will eventually go away. But usually it persists. It is kind of like being followed around by an omnipresent specter. It keeps its distance as long as I am moving but when I stop it gets close enough to really annoy me. It presses in on me more and more as time passes and I ignore it. It starts to engage in a "persistent nagging." The specter won't go away. It won't stop "nagging." I am in a constant state of annoyance. This feeling starts to interfere with my ability to enjoy my life. Eventually I can't enjoy anything I am doing. I feel like I am being suffocated. When that happens I am compelled to deal with it. There will be no peace in my life until I do. In my case I don't really know what I am being nagged to do. I have to conduct a sometimes exhaustive search. It is strictly a search by trial and error. I know when I have hit on the "right thing" because the discomfort stops. So it was that I was visited by my specter of discomfort when I was 37 years old.

At the time my "specter" was pressing in on me, my life was incredibly full or more appropriately incredibly busy. In fact I was so busy I wasn't enjoying my life. Back then, the innumerable daily demands prevented me from savoring any moments. Now my life is devoid of everything that made it so busy back then. Now I have time to savor the moments but not as many daily moments to savor. It seems that life is so out of balance. Is there any way to arrange it so that we aren't robbed of enjoyment by the overwhelming demands of making it all work? Is there any way to keep the memorable moments from clumping together like small metal fragments stuck to the end of a magnet? At that time in my life I couldn't imagine where I was going to find the time and energy to add anything else to my life. But something kept "nagging" me relentlessly.

"I want to tell you a story about a time I was disappointed," the young minister said. "I really, really wanted to go to this particular college. It was the only school that I wanted to attend. My parents forced me to apply to other schools but I just knew I would be accepted and go to the school of my choice. Sadly I wasn't accepted. I was very angry at God for a long time because I thought He could have made it happen for me if He wanted to," he said as he continued to tell history. As I sat in the church pew that morning and listened to this eerily familiar story, I kept wondering to myself why I had come to church that Sunday. At that time in my life everything was going smoothly at least by my standards. I was married to Brian. I was pregnant with Gary. I was employed in my field. Money was no longer a huge issue. The children were settled and doing well. The roller coaster ride of the previous years had become more of a train ride or almost. The trip still included travel over big mountains and valleys but they were smaller, fewer and farther between. Why then urgency to go back to church? I realized that my "specter" had stopped "nagging" me as I sat in church that morning. That was reason enough for me.

"Do we really want all that space?" I asked Brian He was so excited that I hadn't wanted to say anything for fear of spoiling this for him. I am not sure why I did ask. I knew it wouldn't change anything. It was too late in the process anyway. Brian looked at me quizzically and resumed giving instructions and orders to the construction crew. We would be moving to a new house on the other side of town in a few months. Everything would have to change including the church I would attend.

Eventually we settled into our new home. I found a church close by where Brian had attended services in the past. I remember our first visit was to attend a Thanksgiving service. Gary was about 5 months old at the time. He sat quietly on my lap during the service. It was, obviously, about giving thanks. I remember thinking that was a strange topic for us at the time. We had already received the preliminary diagnosis of Lou Gehrig's' disease, months earlier. I didn't feel like I had much to give thanks for at the time. Brian was going to die. In the early days of the illness, the church service offered me some peace but not because I experienced God there. I enjoyed the familiar hymns, the message, the chance to mediate, the rituals. I didn't connect these things to God.

My decision to attend church at this time had a rational component to it. I knew, even though I thankfully had no idea how difficult things would be, that I could not cope with Brian's by myself. I knew that I needed help. That was a big admission for me given my background and temperament which I won't repeat here. You see I had resolved that I would no longer just soldier on and suffer through difficult times. I wanted to arrive at the end feeling like I had "triumphed" not just survived. By triumph I don't mean patting myself on the back or blowing a horn of rejoicing like we do Easter morning. I am referring to getting to the end and saying something other than, "I made it" bitterly. I had no idea how to do that. The church seemed like a good place to look for that kind of help. I wasn't really thinking of it as a place to seek a relationship with God. I was thinking more in terms of finding people who could offer me some support in the ensuing months or years.

I saw it announced in the church bulletin one Sunday. A new group was forming. I think it was called "Living with Chronic Illness." That wasn't quite my situation but I decided to give it a try. I was totally new to this church so I did not know a soul – no pun intended.

I arrived at the appointed time or a few minutes late as is my habit. The door to the meeting room was closed. I wanted to secretly peek in to see what was happening but there were no windows. I put my hand on the door handle but I couldn't turn it. I let go of the door handle. I was afraid- no terrified. Was I afraid of facing my feelings? Was I afraid of sharing my life with strangers?

Oh there were so many fears back then it was difficult to know. If red was the color of fear my entire body would have glowed bright red. I was shaking. Something made me open the door a little bit. People were sitting in a circle wearing name tags. Ugh I hate name tags! The leader saw me before I could close the door and escape. I hope they don't expect me to say anything I thought as I entered the room.

We talked and prayed at the "Living with Chronic Illness" group meetings. After all this was church. I went through the motions of prayer. I didn't get anything out of it. Maybe that's because I didn't really believe anyone was out there listening or at least anyone who cared. Prayer to me was just empty words but the community of people, especially the leaders, did nourish me emotionally. That is what kept me coming back. I was staring into the dark, cold, black abyss of despair and anger. At times I was totally immersed in it. This group was a light in the darkness. It was the only light. I couldn't talk about my life in the "real world."

"Don't talk to your friends about what you are going through," a woman whose husband had recently died from Lou Gehrig's disease advised me. "If you do you won't have any friends," she continued. How sad that she was right! God not only afflicted us with terrible suffering but left us friendless and alone in the process. Why should I talk to Him? He obviously was not going to answer any of my prayers. There was no way Brian was going to get better no matter how much I prayed. I knew that. I didn't believe in miracles.

"If you put me here I will block the aisle," Brian said angrily. I looked around for another place but there wasn't any better place to put the wheelchair. It wasn't that people would get upset with us that we were blocking the aisle. The issue was that Brian felt totally exposed and conspicuous sitting out there alone in the aisle. People definitely stared at Brian from the moment we entered the church to the time we left. Brian and I got something out of the church service so it was worth the embarrassment.

The time church offered a respite from the demands of our daily lives. It was a quiet time to mediate and contemplate. We could forget, well almost, that Brian was dying. Brian and I never talked about God but something about the service and being in church touched us and brought us closer together. I can't explain it any better than that. That feeling would last for a few hours after we left until the demands of the terminal illness ravaged the feeling of comfort.

Time passed. The chronic illness group meetings ended. Brian's condition worsened. The memory of the nourishment of the group faded. Oh I stayed in touch with the leaders of the group but it didn't help. Nothing helped ease the suffering, pain and anger. Generally I was too tired to be angry. Every day was an incredible struggle physically and emotionally. I felt like a lone oxen pulling the wagon, loaded with Brian, the children, pain, sadness, anger up the steepest mountain known to mankind.

I was just surviving and I felt lucky to be doing that. My old unhealthy self, despite my best intentions, had taken control. With all of my resources being tapped to manage my daily life I did not have the strength to do anything but engage in survival mode. The abyss was looming darker, colder and blacker than ever.

Eventually it was too difficult to get Brian to church. We stopped attending. No one seemed to miss us.

Brian would move from his bed to his special chair in the corner of the TV room to the bathroom and back. If I had to leave the room, I would turn on the baby monitor which sat on the table next to him taking the other monitor with me. He was awake asking for things constantly during night. Occasionally I would try to take a nap during the day. Just as I dropped my head onto the pillow and started dreaming of my escape I would hear a noise over the intercom.

Anxiety, anger, hostility, fears, resentment ravaged our days and our lives. Trying to shelter the children from the anxiety, anger and hostility and take caring of Brian's physical needs was my job along with the typical daily chores. Brian's job was to get through each day. As each day passed his anger grew and my resentment grew proportionally. If only we could talk about it! But that never happened. Who knows if that would have even made any difference.

The number and frequency of visitors decreased in direct proportion to the increase in the symptoms of the disease. At the end Brian's only personal contacts were the children, me, an occasional visit from his sister and her husband and the weekly visit from the hospice nurse. Even the children started to avoid coming home although I would not realize that until much later.

I really didn't want to interact with Brian at all that day. For weeks now I so wished I could avoid him but I couldn't. As I entered the family room that morning, Brian looked at me with such hatred. I looked back at him with an equal or greater amount of hatred. I literally had to force myself to be in the same room with him that day. I wanted to scream at the top of my lungs, run away, and yell that I hated Brian, God, life and everyone else who is not going through what I am going through. "God I hate you," I remember saying to myself. I screamed inside my head, "How long is He going to torture us?" and "I can't take this anymore!" My well of coping mechanisms had run dry. Brian couldn't talk but I could read his eyes and feel the hatred that was spilling out of them. After our initial interaction, I tried to avoid meeting his eyes as I was afraid that he could read the hatred in my eyes as well. I used to cope by closing my eyes and imagining that I had ran away and was living alone in a cottage on the beach in some South Pacific island. That fantasy couldn't even give me any relief by this time.

"I can't make it through even one more day. I don't deserve this! I hate my life! I hate God!" were some of the things I screamed to myself that day and for many weeks before. Every pore of my body oozed hatred. Brian and I were trapped in a tomb out of which the air and light were being slowly drained until the time would come that we would suffocate in total darkness.

No matter how either of us felt or what we wanted to do the matters of daily living had to be taken care of and so it was with this particular day. I had just settled Brian into his lift chair in the TV room when the phone rang. I was surprised to hear it ring since no one ever called our house anymore. I answered it. "Hello" I said into the receiver. The voice on the other end was unfamiliar and cheerful. It had to be a wrong number. "This is Deborah from the church. I am new the new associate pastor and I realized that we have been remiss in visiting our sick church members. Would it be all right if I came to visit you right now?" she said. I automatically said, "OK." I regretted it as soon as I had uttered it but I had already heard the receiver on the other end click. I was definitely not up to having a visitor. I had no energy to talk to anyone especially not a complete stranger and especially not a minister. Brian couldn't speak at all.

About 30 minutes later the doorbell rang. I groaned. This woman literally burst into the room. She was vibrant, alive, upbeat, full of energy and smiling from ear to ear. I was offended. Doesn't she know Brian is dying I wondered to myself. Brian and I immediately exchanged a look but not one of anger or hatred. That was at least refreshing.

She introduced herself to Brian and tried to shake his hand. Good Lord I thought this woman is an idiot! Why would she try to shake hands with him? She obviously didn't know anything about us or our situation. Why was she here then? If she sensed my hostility she didn't show it. She seated herself on the sofa between Brian and me. I didn't listen to what she was saying. I was just waiting a polite amount of time before I could ask her to leave with the excuse that Brian was tired. I was determined to get her out of the house as soon as possible.

Was she actually doing that? I can't believe she would do that! I didn't notice she had it with her when she came into the house! She was actually reading to us from the Bible. I don't remember how long she had been doing this before it kicked in – my awareness of the words she was actually speaking. "I hate God," I blurted out. I looked at Brian and he had a look of shock on his face – to put it mildly. Brian chastised me with his eyes.

Deborah didn't skip a beat, "That's OK. Don't be afraid to tell God you are angry at Him. He can handle your anger. He won't punish you. He loves you," Deborah said. I think secretly I had been afraid to say that out loud for fear that God would punish me. But wasn't I already being punished? Could it get any worse? The obvious retorts to Deborah's statement popped into my head – He has some way of showing love and Maybe He could love me a little less. But I didn't say any of this out loud.

Deborah turned the pages of the Bible. She started reading some of the Psalms – the ones where the authors are calling out to God in anger because they are suffering or feel abandoned by God. I don't remember the exact Psalms. I have never been much of a Bible reader – then or now. The words of those Psalmists struck a chord with Brian and I. I connected with them and their anger over their suffering and at God. They knew or had known the depths of despair that Brian and I were experiencing and worse. As Deborah read, I felt a huge surge of relief and gratitude. We are not terrible people because we were filled with anger and hatred toward everyone and everything including or especially God. She read to us for a little while. Those Psalmists expressed my anger and despair better than I ever could. They survived their trials. Deborah showed us that it was OK to be angry even at God. God understood. He didn't abandon the psalmists. He was with them in their darkest hours.

Deborah left. Brian and I looked at each other in amazement and relief. Deborah reached into the depths of our despair and lifted us up. We were both so desperate – so pushed beyond our limits. I honestly don't know what would have happened if she had not come when she did. When she left she left behind some of the solace and peace she had brought with her. I felt it when I first met her at the door. Of course the anger and suffering would go on but it never again reached the depths of despair it had that morning. As write this I am acutely reminded that I have known the depths of despair. Words are truly so inadequate to describe it. The blackness surrounds you. It clings to you like saran wrap. Eventually there is no air. You slowly suffocate. On that day I think we were both close to taking our last breath. Deborah tore an opening in the wrapping. You will laugh. I want to laugh at myself. I hesitate to say this lest I be labeled a nut case. I have to say it. An angel visited us that day and rescued us from the depths of despair.

The days and months dragged on. I don't recall if Deborah ever came back to visit us. Something changed that day. We still had sleepless nights and we still experienced all the physical manifestations and emotional fallout of the illness. But I no longer felt totally alone, isolated and abandoned. Some days I didn't even feel so angry. I can't explain what happened. It is difficult to find words to explain the beginnings of an emotional transformation. How could Deborah's act of reading a few psalms and telling us it was OK to be angry with God change everything? It just did. Maybe it was because I was reminded that others had suffered and were suffering like we were. Maybe I needed someone to tell me that I was not being punished or singled out. This illness is something that happened for no particular reason. God had provided comfort to the psalmists in their darkest hours. I wondered what that would that look or feel like for me. Would He be there for me as well? Maybe God did exist and maybe he hadn't abandoned me.

I had no idea then but Deborah's visit opened the door to looking for and finding something more than misery and despair in this situation. I started to see my experience in terms of something other than my own personal suffering. It was part of something bigger. I don't mean some kind of a "plan. Many others were suffering and others, like Deborah, understood our despair. Deborah had mirrored God's love, understanding and support. I wouldn't understand that until much later. I was reminded that others had suffered greatly and triumphed over it. Maybe we could too. My suffering was not a punishment. I stopped seeing myself as being victimized.

This one dimensional, inert God of my childhood was gone. He was replaced with a, figuratively speaking, breathing, living entity. I could express my inner most feelings to Him. He could even accept my anger and yes hatred toward Him and not turn away from me. He understood my pain. He loved me unconditionally with a steadfast love. How did I know this? I saw it mirrored in Deborah. My rational armor was beginning to crack. I was starting to believe there was a spiritual world –a world that we can't measure scientifically but that exists nonetheless. My belief would grow and strengthen but for now it was minute. Her words were powerful but not as powerful as her presence. Her presence spoke much more than words ever could. I wish I could say more but words are so inadequate to explain it. It has to be experienced – felt. I can close my eyes and feel that loving presence. I would do that in my darkest hours.

There are very few people like Deborah. She just exuded spirituality. It oozed out of her pores. I was fortunate to have met her. This was brought home to me when some time after Brian died I went to lunch with Deborah. She couldn't talk of such mundane matters as jobs, children, husbands, etc. Her focus was elsewhere. At first I was sorely disappointed that I couldn't connect with her on that level. I was angry that she didn't treat me differently or special because of what I had been through. Then I realized that I connected with her on a much higher or more important level. I see that her love for everyone was the same. Isn't that how it should be? Her presence was inspiring and calming. Her main focus was beyond the mundane affairs of the day. Isn't that what a spiritual leader should be? We never went to lunch together again.

"I don't know what to do," I told the doctor's nurse over the phone. "Brian is sitting in his chair but he has no energy whatsoever. It seems like he might have the flu". "Do you want to take care of him at home?" she asked me. The prospect of that terrified me. "I would prefer he go to the hospital," I responded. Brian was transported via ambulance to a local hospice facility. To everyone's amazement he actually improved at hospice. He asked to leave the hospice facility. No one really knows what caused his demise that led to in patient hospice care and no one knows why he stabilized enough to come home. After his time in hospice he was totally bedridden. I arranged to have help with him at the house so he could come home.

Brian motioned with his eyes in the direction of his hand. I was in his room for our nightly viewing of "The Tonight Show" together.

I often laid my hand on top of his as I sat by the side his bed watching TV with him. His speech had been deteriorating for some time but I could still usually make out what he was trying to communicate. "Does it hurt for me to touch your hand?" I asked. He blinked his eyes once for "yes." Any touching caused him pain.

At the end we communicated with Brian by asking a series of questions. Brian would blink once for "Yes" and twice for "No." We would ask things like "Do you have an itch?" or "Do you need me to move your arm?" or "Do you need your pillow adjusted?" Usually by the time I asked the right question he had such a look of frustration and anger in his eyes that I was becoming distressed. He was exhausted from the daily struggle both mentally and physically. I could see that in his eyes.

Occasionally Brian would look at me with a pleading look in his eyes. It was a haunting look. The odd thing was that this pleading look was not tinged with the usual anger, hatred or frustration. That is why it haunted me so. There was no way I could go through enough questions to be able to find out what he wanted when it was something beyond meeting his basic physical needs. We weren't equipped to communicate beyond that level.

Even if he could communicate better I am not sure I would want to know what he was asking. I was afraid he was asking me to do something he had asked me when he first got ill. I had curtly dismissed the request. I simply could not discuss that or so I told him. There was just no way I could assist him in committing suicide. I often wondered if my reluctance had anything to do with my belief in God. I am not one that believes that committing suicide is a sin. But on some level I think it violates the natural order of things. Maybe even suffering has a life span and perhaps even a purpose in our lives.

Time dragged on. It was now close to three years since Brian's first symptoms had appeared. Brian was wretched. He couldn't move at all. He couldn't speak at all. He couldn't get out of the bed at all. All communication was reduced to responding to his grunts and asking the usual series of questions about his physical comfort in response to which he would blink. No one came to visit him. He continued to plead with me with his eyes. Every time I went into his room his eyes had that look.

I continued to ponder what the suffering and pleading look in his eyes meant. It kept whirring in my head until one day I finally understood. Brian was asking me to let him go- to let him die. It was only then I realized that I didn't want to let Brian go. I was astounded at myself! We were experiencing suffering and misery that overflowed the limits of what the human spirit could bear and yet I didn't want to let him go! I was holding onto him and Brian knew it. He was asking me to let him go. I realized that as tired as I was of the ordeal one part of me couldn't bear to be without him. I loved him very deeply. I closed my eyes and remembered what I learned from Deborah.

"You will be all right," I told myself. "You are not alone and you will find the strength to face this new loss," I said out loud to myself. I remember that someone had told me that the best way to handle fear was to turn and face it. I imagined myself turning around and staring straight into the fear of life without Brian, whatever that looked like. At times I visualized it like a black empty hole or a black ugly specter. I repeated to myself, "I am not alone and I will make it through this". After about a week of repeating this ritual I felt as if a huge weight had been lifted from my shoulders. I felt stronger. I was not overwhelmed by my fears. I could let Brian go.

I went to sit with Brian later that morning. I immediately noticed that the pleading look was gone from his eyes. We of course never spoke of any of this but Brian knew of my epiphany. Brian had been begging me to let him go. He was ready to die. Now I was ready to let him go. As I write this I think how ridiculous I was. We had both known for three years that he was going to die. All I can say is that the heart does not always accept what the head already knows. Brian died a few weeks later.

Brian had an uncanny ability to "read" me. Even before he was ill he understood what I was feeling and thinking without using words. This was both a wonderful gift and an annoyance. I first discovered this when we had just started dating. Brian had invited me to attend a barbecue given by his company. There were several hundred people in attendance. Brian was busy entertaining customers. I was socializing with the few people I knew. Someone called my name from behind me. As I looked over my shoulder to see who it was Brian came out of nowhere and whisked me away "to meet some people". "That was your old boyfriend wasn't it?" Brian asked but it really wasn't a question. Brian already knew.

Communication without words, voices, feelings, "knowledge" of things you can't see or touch, ministers as "angels", knowing, feeling with total assurance that you are not alone when you are not in the presence of family or friends was what I experienced. I imagined telling my experiences and beliefs to people. "Emotionalism run amuck," I could hear people say. "She has been through a terrible experience and is emotionally and physically exhausted," others would explain. "She has always been so rational," those who know me would repeat. It is only now many years later that I have the courage to talk of these things.

I have felt the presence of God in my darkest hours. I am sure He was there before that but I wasn't ready to see Him. It was only out of desperation that I opened my eyes so to speak. I let Him in or I recognized His presence. He is with me. I am not always consciously aware of it but when I close my eyes and stop all the hustle, bustle and distractions of daily life I feel His presence. It is a feeling of peace and calmness. Whatever my worries are they fade into the background. I am nourished and soothed by Him. At that time in my life I was very new to His presence but I still knew He would be with me during the terrible times that lie ahead after Brian died. I was still terrified but I was comforted because I was not alone. He would help me find the strength to face what I had to face and to go on with my life.

I was totally devastated by Brian's death. I remember thinking that I should have been prepared for it. I had known for three years he was going to die. In fact almost every day for those three years I thought about death. Almost every day I had pictured my life without Brian in it. Somehow I thought all that knowledge would prepare me for the inevitable. But it didn't. I guess there are some things for which we cannot prepare ourselves. There can be and often is a total disconnect between knowing something and feeling something. There definitely was in my case. Somehow my emotions had not gotten the message that Brian was going to die. Only my mind knew that. My mind was prepared but my emotions had not yet begun their journey. The power of grief struck me with the force and surprise of a tornado. It leveled me as the tornado levels houses. Over the next several years I would raise myself up and rebuild my life in increments until I could stand straight up again - almost. It has been a long, painful process.

For the three years of the illness and several years that followed I was overflowing with questions, anger and hatred. It was directed at everyone who was not going through what I was going through, at the world and at God. WHY, WHY, WHY – Why me? Why Brian? Why should my kids have to grow up without a father? Why should I be left alone again? Why did everyone desert us? The whys were infinite and so very painful. Bad things don't happen to good people. What had I done to deserve this? Why did God allow this to happen to me and my family? Why was I being persecuted? Wasn't I entitled to spend the rest of my life with Brian? I screamed for an answer. I wanted something that would make sense out of all this chaos, suffering and emptiness. I wanted an answer that would take away the pain.

It was cathartic to ask those questions. It was only after I screamed, yelled and railed at the injustice of it all that I found the answer. The answer is that there are no answers. I had to accept that there are questions to which I will never know the answer. I imagine you were expecting something much more profound. I was searching for something much more profound. There is so much suffering in the world but I don't believe that proves that God doesn't exist. I don't believe it is part of some great plan. It just is. The question of why there is so much suffering is one to which there is no answer. I can accept that without being angry at God.

I don't subscribe to the theory that this is all part of a big plan that we cannot see or understand. It is too easy. It does not require enough of us. I think that helps us to avoid those tough questions. It is only in asking and agonizing over those tough questions that we can find our faith.

I realize now that God didn't promise there would be no suffering. I had misunderstood. What He promised is that He would always be there but especially during the suffering. That is how I survived – my faith in God. That answered all my questions and quenched the fire for justice. It took a lot of years to find that answer but when I found it I also discovered incredible peace. I stopped being angry that I only had nine years with Brian. Of course I wish I had more years with him but I wasn't cheated. I wasn't entitled to anything. The nine years I had with Brian were a gift. Then I received another gift - the ability to truly appreciate the preciousness of life.

Faith is a concept that I never understood before Brian's illness. I knew of it. After all they always speak of it in church and elsewhere. I would get nervous when they would talk about faith at church as if it was something everyone else understood or possessed except me. I felt there was something wrong with me because I couldn't understand or didn't have faith. I came to realize that it was there all along but that I was looking in the wrong places.

Faith isn't knowledge that we acquire. It is not the result of an intellectual search or analysis. It can't be found if we hold onto our immature expectations of and notions about God. God does not promise us or reward us with an easy life or give us the life we want to lead. We cannot construct an artificial world and invite Him in. He will not show Himself. And in times of extreme crisis our anger blinds us to His presence. But, when I quieted my mind, abandoned old, youthful expectations and opened myself, without anger, to whatever he had in store for me, He appeared to me.

Faith is a born of a spiritual search and consists of spiritual "knowledge". It is a feeling but it is much more than a feeling. It is the knowledge that without a doubt God is always with me. How do

I know that? I have felt His presence. Some would scoff saying you "felt" His presence because you wanted to. I also believed that for a while. But I know now it is not true. How do I know that? Faith. Faith is the ability to believe in what we can't see or touch. I have no doubt that God is with me always especially in my darkest hours.

I was not alone through this ordeal. I am not alone now. Faith gives me peace. When I start to feel afraid, confused or anxious I close my eyes and feel His presence. He is my touchstone. I go to church because I feel His presence there. In church I can meditate, get myself centered and focused on what is important before I go out into the world again.

Oh sure terrible things have been and are done in the name of religion. The fact that people misuse, distort and abuse the message of God is not something that should cause me to turn away from religion-even organized religion. People don't turn their back on professional sports because some of the athletes abuse performance enhancing drugs.

"I hate God. I don't believe in Him. If He was good or if he existed He would never have let this happen to Brian," Samuel said to me one day recently. Ellen feels the same way. My children don't share my feelings. Samuel and Ellen are in their late 20s now but they are still young and have "young" notions about God. Talking about it won't convince them. They have to see it or experience it for themselves. I was fortunate that I was able to break free of the anger and bitterness.

I hope that someday they and you may know the peace that I have known. I wish for you an experience that leads you to a connection to and a faith in God, in whatever form he/she may take for you.

CHAPTER SEVEN

Unending Grief - How Do We Heal?

I ran into the room half expecting that it wasn't true. The room was exactly as I had left it an hour or so earlier. Brian was resting peacefully on the bed. I had known for three years this day would come. It was inevitable. I ran up to him and put my hand on his arm. I let out a low, muffled cry. His arm felt like a stone on a cold winters' night. I felt my body shudder. I remember being amazed that life could depart so quickly. I couldn't move. I stood staring at him. It felt as if the life had gone out of both of us in that room. I don't know how long I stood there motionless. I fell to my knees. I heard this horrible loud sound. It sounded like a wailing from some primitive creature in pain. I looked around the room. I was alone. It was coming from me! Life had returned to me with explosive force. I wailed rocking back and forth on my knees.

I wasn't in this room at the moment Brian died. But still I was with him at the moment of his death. I was attending the performance of Swan Lake by the Russian ballet. It was my first outing without Brian or the children in several years. I felt so guilty about going that I almost cancelled my plans. It was during the Dance of the Swans that Brian died. Strange how I knew that. As I raised myself up from the floor I felt the same peace I had experienced during that dance. I had been transfixed during that dance. I have never experienced anything like it before or since. It was as if the ballerinas were angels floating up to heaven. My thoughts now turned to the children. I must tell them.

I have no idea who made the arrangements to have Brian's body removed from the house. There was a police officer at the house when I arrived home so I guess he did. It didn't happen immediately and I was thankful for that. I never entered the room again while Brian's body was in there. But I wanted the children to have the opportunity to say goodbye to Brian if they wanted to. Kind of silly I remember thinking, because there is nothing in there but a lifeless, cold body.

"There is an emergency at home. I need Jessica to come home right away," I said to the manager of the store where my eldest daughter had a part time job. I didn't ask to speak to Jessica directly because I knew she would hear something in my voice. As I waited for Jessica to arrive home I called a few people including my friend Norma. I didn't want to be alone with my thoughts. Keeping busy has always served me well as a coping mechanism as long as I am careful not to let it take over. Norma was much older than I and she had already lost her husband. I knew she would understand.

"Brian died today," I told Norma. I heard a scream behind me. I turned around to see Jessica standing there white as a ghost. "I didn't get to say good-bye!" she shrieked. I caught her just as she started to collapse. We sat on the couch and talked. I don't remember what we said. I felt like I was outside my body watching these events. Someone else was talking to Jessica and doing these things, not me. Jessica elected to say good-bye to Brian. I walked her to the door of the room. I thought she might change her mind. After she went into the room I turned and walked away.

I then started calling the home of the friends of my other two children to locate them. They had a habit of not being where they said they were. Somehow I must have located them because I know that each of the three older children entered the room and stayed for a period of time before Brian's body was taken away. We have never discussed what transpired in the room during those visits. I only know that I heard that same shrieking sound that I had made and that each child emerged pale and exhausted. The sound of that shriek can still paralyze me. I know because I occasionally hear it during TV broadcasts regarding the war. It is the sound death makes in the living. To say that it sends shivers up my spine would be an understatement but I can't find words to describe its effect on me.

I never saw the children weep after that day. The funeral and viewing were not as difficult as I thought they would be. I think I was just numb and I was busy. There were people all around for that first week. I almost broke down when one of Brian's oldest friends came to the funeral home. He said hello to me, walked into a pew, sat down in that pew, quietly bowed his head and then sobbed uncontrollably. He seemed unaware that anyone else was present. Even now I can still "see" him crying uncontrollably.

"Should I have Gary view Brian's body? I asked my psychologist friend. "Wow I will have to think about that and get back to you," he responded. His answer was he didn't know. Gary was about two and half at the time. The family was having a private viewing just before the general viewing. When we arrived the casket was already at the front of the memorial chapel. The casket was open at Brian's request. He wore the suit that just a short time earlier he had purchased for a very special occasion. He had never spent that much money on a suit before. He looked very handsome then and now. The four older children were sitting a few rows back from where the casket was located. I picked Gary up in my arms and carried him up to the casket.

What do you say to a 2 year old in such a situation? Brian had been sick for Gary's entire life. Gary had accepted the man sitting in the corner of the room in the lifeless body as a normal part of his life. Often when he was sitting in that chair, Brian would ask for a drink of water. I would put the straw up to his mouth so he could take a drink. There was always a cup sitting on the table next to Brian. I would sometimes hear Brian making some fearful sounds and when I looked up I would see Gary putting the straw up to Brian's mouth. Brian's eyes were literally popping out of his head in terror. Gary kept trying to put the straw in Brian's mouth. I didn't want to yell at Gary so I would quickly cross the room and gently take the cup from Gary saying, "Daddy is not thirsty now but thank you."

Now, in the lobby of the funeral home, I tritely said, "Daddy has gone to heaven". Gary and I stayed only a moment at the casket. Gary looked at Brian and was silent. I didn't have Gary touch the body because the sensation of the cold flesh is so frightening. I carried Gary to the lobby in my arms. My Father was waiting in the lobby to take him home. As I was giving Gary to my Father he looked directly at my Father and said very matter of factly, as if he were describing the weather, "Papa, my Daddy died." My Father and I gasped and choked back tears. "I know," said my Father. My father took Gary in his arms, hugged him and took him home.

Gary seemed to accept death as a part of life. He never asked any questions about it. He never cried. He never seemed frightened by it. Maybe he was wise enough to realize that it was merely the lifeless body in which his Father was trapped that had finally given out. If only we adults could be as accepting of and unafraid of death as children. Throughout this ordeal Gary was my comfort and a source of my strength. His hugs, kisses and I love yous were like salve on an open wound. All of this emanated from a child that almost didn't come into this world because I was afraid. Thankfully the cancer appeared in my uterus when it did. If it had waited a few more months to manifest itself Gary would not have been conceived because by then Brian was already sick.

The next day we held a memorial service at our church. It was beautiful or so I was told. I didn't hear any of it. I remember walking in with the children and seeing the church overflowing. I don't remember anything else about the service except for the soloist singing "Amazing Grace." "Taps" was played at the graveside ceremony. I hadn't expected that. It stirred something in all of us because we gathered around and clung to each other with tears in our eyes. I still can't hear "Taps" or "Amazing Grace" without shedding tears – sometimes uncontrollably.

When the funeral was over the attendees all disappeared back into their daily lives. The older children returned to school or so I thought. Many, many days I don't think I would have even gotten out of bed if it weren't for Gary. He needed to be taken care of. He needed a mother to love him. That is not to say that the older children didn't. As I look back on it I realize in my grief I deserted my older children. I abandoned them. They had already been adrift without any parental supervision for some two years by the time Brian died. They lost both parents for a very long period of time. I made the wrong decisions where they were concerned. I know that now.

There was an indescribable emptiness in my life after Brian died. Some days it almost seemed as if I had imagined him. One day my life was all about caring for him and the next day he was gone. In spite of knowing that would happen it was a shock. The people who I did interact with right after Brian's death avoided talking to me about Brian and our life together. I guess they were afraid it would upset me. That reinforced the eerie feeling that he was never here and that none of it was real. I was reminded of how I used to feel when I watched that TV shows "The Twilight Zone". What was real? The song from that show can still make me feel disconnected from reality and fearful. I wanted to remember Brian and the life we shared – not forget it.

Ten years of my life seemed to vanish along with Brian. When I looked back I saw only a huge void. When I felt choked by loss, fear and emptiness I could run to the phone and call Nancy. Talking to Nancy took the edge off the pain. It had happened. Brian had been here. We had shared some wonderful years together. I wasn't losing my mind. Now Nancy is gone.

"Is this Samuel's mother?" the voice on the other end of the phone ominously asked. "Yes," I replied. "We need you to come down to the police station to pick up your son," the police officer said. This was not the first or last of such calls. The first one came when Brian was ill. I didn't tell him about it. Maybe I should have. The calls continued for quite some time after he died.

It was drugs. The police stopped Samuel and some friends while they were driving in Samuel's car. They found marijuana in a backpack in the car. It was a stroke of luck that the young man Samuel hardly knew told the police it was his marijuana. They were minors. Samuel was released into my custody. He would not face any charges. The officer could not have been any nicer. "He is a good kid with a future. He is not like the other kid who had the drugs. Take him home and keep him out of trouble," the officer said to me. I hoped he was right. I hoped I could do that.

I received a similar call or should I say many similar calls regarding Ellen. "Your daughter was driving around in a car with some friends. She has violated curfew," the voice on the other end of the phone said. "Can you keep her in jail for the night?" I asked. "No ma'm she is a minor. You have to come pick her up." Jessica was home so I left Gary and went to pick Ellen up at the police station. It was approximately 3 am. I don't know what Ellen's official punishment was but mine was to sit through an 8 hour class on a Saturday with other "bad" parents and discuss our kids' behavior. I guess I deserved that and maybe more.

"Please sit here," he said as he pointed to the chair at the head of the long conference table. The hostility in the room was palpable. Six pairs of eyes had been glaring at me since I entered the room. "I called this meeting to discuss Ellen's behavior," the assistant principal announced. "We are all aware that Ellen's stepfather has a terminal illness and that you are taking care of him at home," he said. Those were the only kind words spoken during this 30 minute meeting. You see my child, Ellen, was "stupid, incorrigible, and disruptive to the class and would never amount to anything". Oh the teachers who were present at that meeting didn't say that to me that day at least not in those words. They reserved those exact words for my daughter Ellen when she was in class. I didn't know that until later. You see she was just a bad kid and I was just a bad mother. The school and teachers were sending that message loud and clear. This was just the first of such meetings.

Is it any surprise that Ellen eventually simply stopped attending school? Oh I am not saying that is the only reason for her lack of attendance. There were a lot of other contributing factors but I would have to say the attitude of the teachers and administration probably topped the list. Who would want to go to a place everyday where you are told what a bad person you are? How different would Ellen's life be now and then if instead of berating her they had put their arm around her should and asked her if they could do anything for her? Such a simple gesture would surely take less energy than the berating did. They never did.

There was one bright spot for Ellen at school. From what I could piece together Ellen's English teacher approached and dealt with all children, including Ellen, with respect and compassion. It was no surprise that Ellen not only wasn't a troublemaker but actually did well in her class. That fact seemed to be lost on her other teachers.

"You have an appointment today with Dr. Travis. After we get home from that appointment we will have a homework session in the kitchen," I said to Ellen and Samuel. There were some objections and fighting but they went to the appointment. They both liked Dr. Travis.

After Brian died, I took the two middle children to Dr. Travis, the psychologist on a weekly basis. I followed his advice. I sat and tried to do their homework with them. I attended parent nights and spoke to individual teachers. I drove them to school myself every day. I ordered them to come home right after school. I kept them in after school activities they enjoyed. I tried to stay in touch with their friend's parents. In short, I tried to everything I could think of. But ultimately they needed me much earlier when Brian was sick and I wasn't there. It was too late for me to help them by this point but I wouldn't realize that until after we had all suffered so much more.

"No, I will not be attending any more parent teacher conferences," I said to the assistant principal. "I quite frankly don't understand your attitude," he responded. "I really can't handle any more kid bashing sessions at this time in my life," I said as I hung up the phone. That was the last time I ever spoke to him.

"Ellen we need to talk about what is going on with you." I said. I turned away for a moment and when I looked back Ellen had run out of the room and was headed up the stairs to her bedroom. "Stop right now" I screamed at Ellen as I chased her up the stairs. I caught her and grabbed her by the arm. Ellen whirled around to look at me. She had such a look of hatred, loathing and rage I was taken aback. "You are a stupid B.........." she screamed at me. I slapped her in the face. She went up to her bedroom and locked the door. It was hard finding the energy to battle with these teenagers. I realize now that they probably thought I didn't care. They were probably right some of the time. I so wanted a respite from problems for a while.

A few days later the doorbell rang. A man in a suit was standing at my door. "I am from child protective services. Your daughter Ellen came to school with a small bruise on her face. (She would pick that day to go to school!) She said you slapped her. I need to come in and look around," he said. Did I have a choice? He poked around the house for a while. Gary was asleep but he examined him very closely for bruises. Fortunately for me, prior to coming to the house, he has spoken to the social worker who had assisted us during Brian's illness. Thankfully, because of her intervention, the inquiry ended there but not before he went to see my eldest daughter, Jessica, at high school. She was humiliated to say the least. Only she could give Ellen a tongue lashing that Ellen would heed. Would we ever be able forgive each other for all the terrible things we had done and said to each other?

When I returned from work or some errands there were all kinds of unsavory people in the house –Ellen's "friends". Some of my jewelry went missing. After I confronted Ellen about her friends and the missing jewelry a few times, she simply stopped bringing friends home and she stopped spending any time at home. Samuel was always stoned.

"Ellen, Ellen wake up it is time for school", I said as I shook her. I tried to wake her up for 10 minutes or more. She would try to open her eyes but then she would fall back to sleep. I couldn't understand why I couldn't wake her up. I turned and left the room. I thought Ellen was sick or depressed. In reality, Ellen was out all night doing drugs and slept all day. I never even considered that as an option. I thought she hung around with a bad crowd and was not attending school regularly but I didn't see what was really going on. I had never done drugs so I didn't know the signs or symptoms. Maybe there was just too much going on for me to focus on what her behavior really meant. I am sure I wouldn't have known how to cope with her behavior even if I had known. I found out much later that she apparently drove one of the cars at night after I went to sleep. She was only 14.

"This is Sue in the attendance office," she said. "Samuel is not at school today." "OK" I said and hung up the phone. The phone rang again a few minutes later. "This is Sue in the attendance office" she said. "Ellen is not at school today." Those phone calls became part of my morning ritual along with my cup of coffee. I have no idea what Samuel and Ellen did after I dropped them off at school. I asked but they didn't answer me. I knew I wouldn't get a straight answer anyway. I'm not sure I could have handled the truth then if they told me. I berated them and told them they needed to attend school but I didn't do much more. Maybe part of my coping mechanism was to put my head in the sand when it came to my children. I didn't have the strength to really discipline them. Somehow I deluded myself into thinking that they were working through their grief. I had lost control over Samuel and Ellen when Brian was sick. I was stretched well beyond my limits in caring for Brian and Gary and I had not time or energy for anyone or anything else. But that is no excuse. After Brian died I could not get any control back over those two. They had been unsupervised for far too long.

The calls from the police and the school continued. I received several calls from the police department regarding Samuel. I picked him up several times from various police departments. His problems were drug related as well. He never acted out like Ellen. He was much more silent in his grief and anger. I expressed my anger and disappointment to him. I really didn't know what else to do. I feel fortunate that neither of them ended up in a juvenile detention facility. Maybe things weren't as bad as they could have been after all.

By day I was the mother of a charming preschooler attending coffees with other moms or I was working in a responsible position in the legal field. But I wasn't really part of that life. I couldn't connect to anything or anyone. I was on the outside looking in. I was an empty shell going through the motions of everyday living.

I would listen while people talked to me. I would wonder how they could be so angry because their husband left his clothes on the floor or be upset over something that was said or done by someone at the office. At that time in my life their concerns and even their lives seemed silly – not funny silly, stupid silly, insipid. I know they didn't want to hear about my life. That's good because I really didn't want to talk about it. I wanted to forget about it for a while if that was possible.

"Mom, Mom," the voice was a mix of fear, desperation and anger. Someone was shaking me. I awoke to a semi conscious state to see Jessica standing over my bed. "Ellen has a guy in her room," Jessica said. Through force of habit I looked at the clock. Gary was asleep next to me on the bed. It was 3 am. I got up and Jessica and I went to Ellen's room. The door was closed. I hesitated. I wanted to just turn and walk away but I forced myself to push it open not knowing what I would find. Ellen was standing alone in the middle of the room. "Ellen where is he?" I demanded. I turned and with a huge feeling of trepidation I pushed the door open to the closet. Ellen was not known for making good choices regarding "friends" these last few years. As I pushed open the door I wondered if I was going to have to call the police. Whew! He left when I told him to. "That was her drug dealer," Jessica said to me after he left. Well it could have been a lot worse I thought as I went back to my room and closed the door. I knew Ellen shouldn't be having guys in her room or doing drugs. (I thought it was just marijuana). I knew Jessica was disappointed in me. I know it was not Jessica's responsibility to police Ellen. I just couldn't seem to find the wherewithal to do anything about these things. I feel into an exhausted sleep.

After I escorted Ellen's "friend" out of the house and locked the door, I had put on the alarm. I never thought I would have to use the alarm to keep my kids in and their "friends" out. For a long time I thought I was the only one with the code but apparently I wasn't. Samuel and Ellen apparently knew it. It didn't matter. Knowing Ellen if she didn't have the code she would have just left and let the alarm screech. As I turned to go back to bed Jessica gave me a tongue lashing. I deserved it. "That was her drug dealer," she told me. My first thought was it could have been worse. I went into my bedroom and closed the door. If only it were that easy to shut the world out. But wasn't I already doing that?

This sounds rather matter of fact but in reality it was far from that. Ellen was in a rage that lasted several years. She screamed at me, used every conceivable expletive, called me every conceivable name and did whatever she pleased. I get exhausted just thinking about this. I don't have the emotional energy to relate the entire litany of behaviors, arguments or vicious scenes because to do so I would have to relive it at least in my mind. I simply can't do that again. Once was more than enough to live through that time with Ellen. I am not sure I even can remember it all as thankfully my memories of this have faded. I am unaware of much of what she did do as a lot of it took place away from the house. She was rarely home. When she was she reminded me of the Tasmanian devil – the cartoon character. He races through the desert spreading a lot of dust. Ellen whirled through the house, school and I imagine everyplace else spreading rage and fear wherever she went. I can still feel her anger and my fear as I write this.

"It is very difficult to turn a minor over to the care of the state but it can be done," the social worker said. She was the same social worker who had helped us through the final months of Brian's illness. I felt comfortable talking to her. I was absolutely desperate. I can't begin to describe my level of desperation. I had to be or I never would have considered such an option. "What happens to her if I do that?" I asked the social worker. I can't remember exactly what she said. All I remember is that it didn't sound very appealing. In addition, I didn't have the energy for another battle even if the outcome would be good and it appeared this outcome was not what I was looking for. Ellen needed to be under someone or something's control for her own good and mine but where was I to find that? I think it was just a fantasy I explored for a time. Just thinking I actually had an option gave me the illusion that I had some control and that made things more bearable on those particularly hard days dealing with Ellen.

I think I was patient and loving at least some of the time. Maybe I wasn't. I know I tried to calmly talk to Samuel and Ellen about how they felt and what they were going through. The minute I asked a question about how she was feeling Ellen's eyes would flash with anger and she would say something very cruel to me. Maybe she thought it should be obvious to me how she felt. She was so angry and I was unable to respond with love rather than anger. Usually we ended up in a heated argument. Perhaps I was the one acting like an adolescent. Her emotions were so raw, so exposed that just a simple question could ignite a fire of emotion expressed only as anger. Why was anger the only emotion we permitted ourselves to express? If only I had reached out and tried to hug her. I guess we were all torn down to our roots and maybe beyond. We wouldn't be able to connect until we had rebuilt some of our own foundations.

I tried to set up some structure for them and to discipline them after Brian died. I couldn't lock them up in the house. I couldn't be with them every minute of the day. I think I still cared about them but sometimes I wasn't sure. Most of the time I just wanted them to go away and leave me alone. I felt suffocated by their problems. I felt guilty because I believed if I had handled things better they wouldn't be having these problems. I had absolutely no idea what to do. If I sent them away I was afraid they would think I didn't love them or they would feel totally alone and rejected – more than I imagined they already did. Maybe I didn't love them anymore. Is it possible to stop loving your child? I didn't know the answer at that time. I didn't feel any love toward them.

Eventually I just ran out of energy to fight them and to fight for them. It was sadly a constant battle and a losing one at that. Samuel was not as overtly hostile and confrontational as Ellen. He simply, for the most part, ignored me. It was me against Ellen and Samuel or me against their "friends" or me against the school. And it was them against the world. It was a war. Everyone was losing. The calls continued to come.   The situation and the children's behavior continued to deteriorate.

"This is Krishna, Samuel's employer. Samuel has stolen a scale from the store." "A what!" I said. "A scale we use to measure the meats for the sandwiches," his employer said. "That sounds totally ridiculous. What would Samuel want with a scale for measuring lunch meat?" I asked. "They use it to weigh drugs," she replied. "I am going to report him to the police unless you pay for it," she said. I had pushed him into getting this job so he could spend his time constructively. I talked to Samuel. He denied it. My sense was that he was telling the truth. She really had no proof that Samuel had taken it. There were a lot of other young people working there. "I won't pay for it," I called his employer to tell her. "I will call the police," she said. "OK," I said and I hung up the phone. Within a few minutes I was hunched over the toilet vomiting. I called her back. "How much do you want? I will send you a check," I said. "When can Samuel come back to work?" she asked. I hung up the phone.

We all grieve in our own way. For adolescents not surprisingly they act out their grief or at least two of mine did.   I didn't understand that at the time. I thought if they were truly grieving we would be huddling together, talking and crying. Why do I continue to insist on imposing unrealistic expectations on situations and others? They only create havoc, pain and disappointment. When will I learn that? How or why would I expect my children's behavior to meet my idealized expectations? How much easier life would be if emotions fit into designated categories and were expressed by designated behaviors? Grief from death = crying and tears. As I write this I can't imagine how I could expect that to be so. There is a wrong and right way to grieve, isn't there? How arrogant of me to think so.

I looked at the children's behavior as a slap in the face. I acted as if it was personally directed at me. They were making my life difficult when I wanted to curl up in a cocoon and heal. I was resentful and angry at them. They forced me back into the world of problems way too soon. As one friend succinctly put it," You can't put an adult head on a child." Still I resented them for it. If I only I could have put my own feelings aside to see that, through their actions, they were really crying out in pain. I thought I had learned that lesson in my marriage counseling with Brian but I guess some lessons take a long time to learn or at least put into practice. How different would this difficult time have been for all of us if I had done that? I know my response exacerbated and even ignited the situation.

I never stopped loving Ellen. She was my daughter. But I could not imagine that I would ever like Ellen again or that I would ever want to spend time with her again. The phrase out of control does not even come close to describing Ellen's behavior. Ellen's anger consumed her and me and everything in her path. She was in a constant state of rage. Samuel was just a lost soul.

"Why don't you send them away?" he asked. "I have a client whose son became disrespectful and she immediately packed him off to military school. She said it was the best thing she had ever done," continued my friend. "We have children so they can be a part of our lives. We don't send them away the minute things get difficult. I don't want to send them a message that I am abandoning or giving up on them. I need to do everything I can before I take that drastic step", I replied.

Eventually I ran out of ideas. Everything I had tried had failed. I realized that I had absolutely no idea how to help them or what to do for them. I sent them both to those survival camps for a summer. They flourished there but when they returned home they reverted to their old behaviors and friends. I don't know why I didn't expect that would happen. I must have called a dozen boarding schools looking for one that would take my two children. Still I didn't want to send them away. I thought I should be able to help them. After all I was their mother. I hoped they would eventually work through their issues. As more time passed I realized that wasn't going to happen at least not before someone was seriously injured or serious damage was done. Maybe I didn't do it out of selfishness. I think I was afraid of being even lonelier if they went away. I think the crises with them prevented me from dealing with my own emotions. After all I was a crisis junkie. Maybe I was just afraid to admit failure. I talked about it and I thought about it but I couldn't find the wherewithal to send them away.

Eventually my relationship with Warren gave me the strength to do what was best for my children - to send them away. Warren encouraged and cajoled me into making the decision. I am grateful to Warren for that even though I later realized that he did not do that out of an altruistic desire to help the children or me. It is a paradox that some of the best things in life have their inception in bad experiences or impure acts. So it was with the decision to send Ellen and Samuel away to military school.

"We can do that. Yes. We would use off duty police officers to escort them to the school," the owner of the business told me. I was sending Ellen and Samuel away to a military boarding school. I knew I couldn't get them there by myself. They would simply refuse to go like the refused to do everything else I asked them to do. "Are they violent?" he asked me. "I don't know what they are capable of," I responded. "We would have to bring two officers", he replied.

I honestly don't know if, at that time, I cared what happened to them. I just wanted some peace. I was losing my ability to cope. I still had Gary who needed a functioning mother. So I paid the company to provide two off duty police officers to escort Ellen and later Samuel to the military boarding school. It was located many states away in the middle of a cornfield in a small town in the Midwest. I hoped they could keep them safe there. I definitely wasn't able to do it.

I often wonder what families who don't have those financial resources do. I was one of the lucky ones who did. Some of those families are imprisoned by the rage and violent behavior of their children. I know because that is what happened to one of the employees at the hair salon I used to go to. I can still see the desperation in her eyes as they peered out from her haggard face. For the most part she looked at the floor when she related her story as if she was acutely embarrassed by it all. I understood that feeling of failure and embarrassment that accompanies the knowledge that you are a terrible parent. Her husband was convicted of child abuse when he tried to physically restrain their daughter by grabbing her arm to prevent her from leaving the house. Thereafter their daughter had all the control as she indulged her craving for drugs and the unsavory lifestyle that accompanies that addiction. She victimized her parents. I don't know the outcome as my friend was so resentful that I had other options she stopped talking to me. I hope things somehow worked out for her family.

"We will be there about 6 am. We want to take advantage of the element of surprise. We will wake her up, get her dressed and in the car before she is aware of what is happening. Please have some clothes laid out for her," the off duty police officer told me. The night before they were scheduled to arrive I couldn't sleep. I really hadn't slept well since I made the decision. I kept wondering if I was doing the right thing. There was a knock at the door. I opened it and pointed to Ellen's bedroom door. I went and hid in the TV room. I was afraid if I saw them take her I would lose my courage. I was shaking and crying. I poked my head out for a moment to see Ellen, looking bewildered, in between two large men being escorted out the front door of the house. I went into the bathroom and threw up. The off duty police officer called me, later that day, to inform me that Ellen had been safely delivered to the school.

"Hi Mom, how are you?" I froze. It was Ellen's voice. She chatted on for a few minutes describing her physical surroundings. She never mentioned that she, just yesterday, was escorted to an isolated boarding school. "I'll call you in a few days," she said and hung up the phone. I don't remember saying much. Being silent was always much safer with Ellen. I didn't hear from Samuel for several weeks but I did speak, on a regular basis, to the administrators at the school. Samuel and Ellen were being looked after and they were as safe as they could be. There was an added bonus that they didn't even seem angry about being there. I think they were relieved and happy to be away. I should have done this sooner I thought. The grieving and healing process could now really begin for me.

We anchor a cold hard stone in the ground with a name, date of birth and date of death. Why do we do that? I could imagine Brian was just at work or away on a business trip until I saw that stone. I would run my fingers over the etching and say the name out loud. It was so permanent. It was so final. Somehow I was lying prone on the fresh dirt with my forehead pressed into the cold hard stone. My body was convulsing and tears were flooding my checks. I know because the stone was wet. At night the cemetery was a solitary place. I could sob, punch the dirt and scream. Why Brian? Why do I have to go through this? Why do I have to raise my children alone again? This is so unfair! Why did this happen to me? I hate God! I am so alone! I can't do this. I found myself there many nights. For a while every outing to attend anywhere ended at the cemetery. I now understood that a cemetery is a place for the living. It is a place where they can grieve.

I didn't live in the present much that first year after Brian died. My thoughts and my feelings were directed to and focused in the past. I lived, over and over in my mind, the events of my life with Brian. There was no chronology to it. It was a mass of jumbled images and events from our life together. As hard as I tried I couldn't bring myself back to the present. None of the memories were of any significant event. It was the simple mundane stuff of life. It played over and over again in my head like one of those old time reel home movies. It went in reverse. It went forward. It flickered. It fluttered. It came apart. It kept going. I had no control over it. It controlled me. I was helpless to guide it or stop it. Since that time I can't remember all the details as vividly as I did that first year. They have continued to fade. Maybe life is not so unkind.

No one called. No one came to visit. When the phone did ring I would run to answer it. I always, unconsciously, expected to hear it. "Hi honey, how are you?" Brian would always say when I answered the phone in the way only he could say it. Of course it was never him on the other end of the phone. If there is an emptier feeling that what I experienced when I answered that phone I don't know it or want to know it.

I remember taking Gary to a parade we used to go to with Brian every year. Samuel had marched in the parade years earlier. Gary and I were sitting on bleachers. There was a married couple sitting in front of us. I leaned forward. I couldn't stop myself. I tried. I embarrassed myself. I was an intruder. I leaned in so close my face almost touched the wife's hair. All I wanted was to listen to the conversation. Oh, I wasn't interested in what they were saying. That was of no interest to me. I was interested in how they were saying it. You see they were speaking that intimate talk married couples use. You know - part words, part silence, part looks and part body language or gestures spoken in a certain low, familiar tone of voice. I remember thinking how I wished I had skipped the parade that day.

The list of losses and losses went on and on and on. It seemed infinite. I was compelled by some unknown force to remember as many events of the past 10 years as possible in that one year. With Brian's death the entire last 10 years of my life was wiped out – gone or so I felt. When they buried Brian they buried our life together – my part included. We were both buried that day. At least the biggest part of me was buried that day. I was left to rebuild a life with the remnants. They seemed pretty paltry at the time. I am reminded of that line in Tristan and Iseult. I thought it was so stupid at the time – romantic nonsense. What was it? It went something like this, "They drank death together."

I felt buried just like Brian – buried or better yet maybe crushed beneath the weight of pain, loss, and suffering. The world, the people in it and their problems and concerns all seemed so trivial, and meaningless. People would talk to me and it was as if we were separated by a wall – a wall of grief and pain. I felt totally isolated from the world by my experience.

That first year it was as if I was dropped deep into a tunnel that was totally devoid of light. I would remember parts of my life with Brian. Each time I finished re-living a part of my life with Brian a small light would appear up ahead. Along with the memories I experienced the spectrum of emotions. Acceptance, anger, hatred, emptiness, love, regret, loneliness, depression were churning constantly inside me with me never knowing which would assert itself on any particular day or at any particular moment of a day. There were more memories of my life with Brian. More time passed. Over time all those feelings and memories coalesced into a solid stream of energy. The light in the tunnel was slowly increasing in size as I was propelled closer and closer to the end of the tunnel. There were days and periods of time when the light was extinguished again. Those were the days when I could hardly get out of bed and nights when I didn't sleep at all. Some days I felt like I glowed red with anger at God, the world, life and everyone who had not lost a loved one. Those were dark days. My hatred did not illuminate outward. It directed its red hot light inward. As the re-lived memories accumulated and the emotions were spent I was propelled toward the end of the tunnel. I emerged squinting into the brightness. I rejoined the world. The stream of light flows strong and steady most of the time now. Every now and then a portion gets jammed up and I am propelled back into the darkness and the past. But that is usually only for a brief period of time. I don't want to stay there.

I was driving to a friend's house. I was driving in one of those incredibly annoying developments where all the streets have these cutesy names and they all run in circles. I was totally lost. This was before GPS. This was the type of place where they think too many street lights detract from the ambience of the neighborhood. It was so dark I decided to stop the car and get out to read the street sign. Fortunately there was a lone street light at the corner ahead. I pulled the car over to the curb and parked in the opposite direction of the flow of traffic. I opened my car door. As I looked down to make sure I wasn't stepping into a drainage ditch I saw it. It was stamped into the concrete on that sidewalk. It was stamped into the concrete all over that city. It was the logo for Brian's construction company. It was a logo he had designed. I can remember when he first showed me that logo. He was so proud of it.

"Can I help you miss?" the man asked. I must have looked ridiculous dressed in a suit and heels at a construction site. Mud and dirt were everywhere. "I am supposed to meet Brian, the President of the company, here", I replied. The man looked at me like I was crazy, "He doesn't come to the job sites miss." Just then a white Lincoln Town car rounded the corner. Brian was at the wheel. The man shook his head incredulously and returned to his crew. That day I got my first lesson in building a sidewalk. You see Brian and I were on opposite sides of a lawsuit and Brian had agreed to explain one of the construction issues to me. We walked around the site together while he explained how to build a sidewalk. Brian was so proud when he showed me his company logo stamped in the concrete sidewalk. I can see him, smell him and feel his presence even as I write this. It is the small memories that ignite the flame of grief. I thought it would be the big days, the important days like Christmas that jolted me out of the present but I was ever so wrong. You can prepare yourself for the big days. The little memories just kind of sneak up on you. Seeing that logo stamped into the sidewalk propelled me back to that day. I started to cry.

That phone again! It was the headmaster at Ellen's military school, "Ellen was caught outside after curfew last night. She was drinking. This is her fourth infraction. She is incorrigible and we can't have her here anymore. Ellen is being expelled from school." Why wasn't Brian here to help me deal with this situation? I so wanted and needed him! By this time Brian had been gone for more than two years.

Boarding school was my last hope. Ellen's expulsion ignited the old feelings. What did I do wrong? How could I do this to my children? How did I fail them? What should I have done differently? After all bad children are a result of bad parents. I know at times I was not a good mother. I had my own demons that I visited on my children. I tried so hard not to do that. Is there any way to undo the damage? Ellen is so full of rage. Is it something I did? Is it something I failed to do? I know she needed more affection than I had energy to give her. Is there anything I could do to help Ellen and Samuel now? If I had been a better Mom my kids would have dealt with Brian's death much better. If they survived this could the damage ever be undone? Can they ever heal? Why, as parents, do we feel compelled to berate ourselves for our children's behavior? Would berating myself really help? But more importantly what could I do with Ellen now that she was being expelled from military school? That should be my focus. I couldn't change the past.

I had no good tools for coping with my own pain over the loss of Brian, much less the children's pain. Where would I have learned how to deal with all of this? Doctors will talk about the physical illness in great detail but they never address the emotional impact. I guess that really is not their role in our society. In my experience, most therapists are unprepared to discuss these issues. Maybe you need to have personal experience with terminal illness and death in order to be able to help someone.

I did have one connection to the world during this dark time. Back then I had Nancy, Brian's sister in my life. She understood the pain and loss in part because she also loved Brian very deeply. Nancy's compassion and understanding was akin to a climber being thrown a rope to pull them out of the dark abyss into which they have fallen. Nancy gave me a lifeline. Some days I just wanted to wallow in the dark tunnel of despair and grief while other days I was terrified I would never get out. Unfortunately Nancy was confined to home and absorbed more and more with her own serious health issues at the time of Brian's death.

I would visit Nancy at her house or talk to her on the phone after Brian died. She would talk for hours about every detail of her illnesses and I mean every detail. Talking about illness, any illness seemed to brighten her day. She got a glint in her eye the way newlyweds do when they talk about their loved one. I am sure that she knew more than many doctors. It was way more information than I wanted to hear. It was a little too descriptive for me as well. But I found myself sitting there listening and nodding my head. I wonder now how and why I could do that. But I then I remember.

There was an unspoken connection and bond between us. It was threaded through our conversations. We both were in the throes of pain, suffering and loss over Brian's death. I really couldn't tell you one word that Nancy said about illness or disease. I realized that I didn't really listen to the words. I "listened" to the love and the compassion coming from Nancy and she felt, I hope, something similar coming from me. She and her husband were the only persons who came to visit or offered any emotional support throughout Brian's illness and afterwards. Maybe she was the only person that could because she knew what I was going through.

After Brian's death I wanted to hibernate in the house. Dealing with the issues with the children, especially Gary forced me out into the world. Meeting new people was especially difficult. They didn't know my history. I was nothing without my history at that point in my life. I was defined or consumed by illness, death, problems. If you didn't know about death or illness you couldn't possibly know me. I felt like one of those props you see at tourist attractions that you insert your head in to and take a photo. I talked. I went through the physical motions of daily living. The rest of me was gone. If you touched me I might fall. It was as if my body was shorn off directly behind my face. I was a one dimensional being.

Fortunately for me there was a place for such a one dimensional being. Sarah called and invited me to the grief group meeting to be held at the church. I didn't want to go. I had tried ALS support groups. They depressed me. It was too many people discussing too many problems – a bitch session that for some reason didn't offer me any relief. There were far too many tales of the caregiver being stretched beyond their limits or even being emotionally abused by the ill person. We caregivers took it. Did we have a choice? That was partly what was so depressing. Our only choice was to abandon our sick spouse. Was that really a choice? Afterwards I left feeling more depressed than when I went. Maybe that group just needed some leadership I thought. In spite of that depressing experience, I couldn't tell Sarah "No." She had reached out to me several times already and I had rebuffed all of her attempts. She was a good leader. She could help me. I don't know that I thought this as much as I sensed it at the time.

"I don't want to go. I need to go." I said that back and forth constantly to myself since Sarah had called to ask me to come to the meeting at church. Why do I have to go through this same struggle every time?" I said to out loud to myself as the battle raged in my head. The war was a stalemate – no resolution. "Let's see. There is laundry in the washing machine. The dishwasher needs to be unloaded. The dog poop needs to be picked up," I continued to converse with myself. I went over my list of to do items in my head or maybe out loud. I started a few of the tasks, unconsciously hoping, I would be engaged in that task and miss the meeting. But after starting a few of the tasks on my list somehow I found myself in the car driving to the meeting. I had managed to delay my departure but I did make it, albeit late, to the first meeting of the grief group. That is one hurdle behind me.

As I entered the room, Sarah gestured to a chair next to her. After I took my seat Sarah stood up, "My name is Sarah. I lost my husband almost 8 years ago now. I still miss him." Her facial expression and demeanor were that of a person in the throes of recent grief. "Is that what I have to look forward to? Am I never going to get beyond this grief? " I asked myself. I looked at the door but there was no way to gracefully exit. I continued to talk to myself, "Is there a way I can pass on introducing myself? I hate talking about myself and my "experience". I was brought back from my conversation with myself by some more teary introductions. Sarah signaled to me to introduce myself and I said to myself, "Well, I have no choice but I am not going to cry in front of all these strangers. Take a deep breath. Talk slowly." I stood up. I said my name. The floodgates opened and I couldn't say a word. I fell back into my chair. "She just lost her husband," I heard Sarah compassionately explain to the group.

I felt much better after I attended a grief group meeting. There were no judgments in that group, just understanding and compassion. It was healing. It made me wonder if compassion and understanding can only arise out of similar or shared experiences, hurts, losses. Is that why the children and I didn't find it at school or out in the world? Would the absence of such shared experiences be a death knell for compassion? I looked up the definition of compassion in the dictionary, "Sympathetic consciousness of others distress together with a desire to alleviate it." But where does the sympathy come from? Can we only desire to alleviate it because we know how painful or difficult it is? Is this part of the reason why we seem to live in a compassionless world? These meetings started me on the road to healing.

After Brian died I experienced other losses – normal losses. My eldest daughter, Jessica, left to attend college in another state just a few short months after Brian died. Perhaps that was a blessing as she was able to escape so much of the trauma at home. She grieved in her own way as well – silently that is. I went into a tailspin upon returning from taking her to college. Each new loss ripped open the wound from the loss of Brian. Each event I couldn't share with him was a reminder of the loss. Why wouldn't the wound completely heal? Why was it so tender still? Would the bleeding ever stop?

It is difficult to explain what happens when the wound incurred as a result of Brian's illness and death was wrenched open. It reminded me of that experience we have when a cut or incision has long ago healed and only a scar remains. Unexpectedly someone touches that scar and sharp pains shoot out from it. Some doctors explain the feeling of pain as the triggering of the memory of pain that we have stored.

Two years had passed and the intense grieving was over but I still seemed much too mired in the past and too easily transported back into the past by all the memories that surrounded me. When the opportunity to move to California presented itself I thought it was a good idea. I would have a blank slate. It would be blank in the sense of a fresh start and as a way to escape being stuck in the past. It would also be blank meaning empty in the sense that most of the connections to Brian and our life together would be left behind. Nancy would remain. I would go.

Maybe it is good to have a poor memory as we age. We are angry we can't remember the wonderful celebrations of our life but it is such a blessing we can't remember the painful experiences. So it was that, over these many years, my memory of both the good and the bad experiences with Brian have faded and became fuzzy like an out of focus photograph. Still after 16 years some unexpected small event can trigger a flood of pain and grief. Grieving never ends.

I lost so much. I lost the biggest part of myself – the shared part. Brian and I shared so many close connections – history, children, home, future plans, and feelings. For a while I lost a sense of who I was. I was forced to forge not only a new life but a new self. I lost my rock and anchor, my best friend. I lost the only person in the world for whom I was #1. I was grieving for all I had lost – for myself. I grieved for him and all he suffered while he was alive. Now that could end. He was in a much better place than I.

"Mom I started smoking pot and doing drugs when Brian was sick. I just couldn't stand to come home and see him like that," Samuel told me just the other day. Brian has been gone for 13 years. Samuel still can't talk about Brian without getting emotional. In fact he really doesn't like to talk about him much at all. So I was surprised when he told me that. I didn't realize back then that Ellen and Samuel were acting out the pain of seeing Brian's suffering. Later they were grieving over his death. They avoided being home and with me at all costs. That started when Brian was ill. I didn't complain too much then. Maybe I was just relieved they were gone and not giving me a hard time at home. I am thankful they saved the worst for after Brian was gone. There was no way I could have coped with the fallout from Samuel and Ellen's grief while I was taking care of Brian. Maybe Ellen and Samuel sensed that.

Ultimately I had to and did find my way through the pain and grief in my own way and in my own time. My children did too. The first two years were obviously the most difficult. Everyone heals in different ways and at different times. There is no one or right way. If only I had known that then. Even though we have healed we all definitely have our scars. We each still grieve. The grief and loss never really end although they do become less intense and less frequent.

I am amazed that Samuel and Ellen have healed as well as they have. It has taken many, many years for them to get to this point. They are responsible for getting themselves through this. I can't take any credit. I loved them but they made the good choices and worked hard to get where they are. They deserve the credit for that. I can only love them as they continue on their own journeys of growing and healing.

I have forgiven myself, my children, God, western medicine, everyone who has not lost a loved one, everyone who showed no compassion and everything and everyone else I blamed during those dark years.

I have come to see Brian's illness and death as a gift that opened my eyes to how precious life is. I appreciate all that I have in ways I never did before the tragedy with Brian. I don't get angry because I don't have more or I don't have exactly what I thought I should have or what I wanted. I appreciate what is and I am thankful for it.

That is not to say that what happened to Brian wasn't abominable. I am only saying that to continue to see it only as an unimaginable tragedy limits and defines my life in a way I don't want to limit and define it. Focusing on loss and suffering leads to a life filled with bitterness and anger. Focusing on the experience as a gift leads to a life filled with gratitude and love. A life filled with gratitude and love helps create a better life for me and my family and hopefully in some small way a better world. Oh sure no one can do this all the time but we can start with moments can't we?

Through this experience I have learned not to judge others. It really is not for us, within limits, to judge if another's life or actions are right or wrong. Each of us handles things differently. Brian, the children and I each handled his illness differently. For a while I was so arrogant as to think I was handling it better than anyone else. They should be handling it better or they should be doing this or that I would say to myself. I judged them all harshly. That was so wrong of me. How self righteous of me!

We can only help each other along the way to the best of our ability. We don't do this by criticizing, judging, and blaming each other. We can do this by being understanding, loving and compassionate toward each other. (And yes by imposing limits and standards especially in the case of those closest to us.) And sure you can't help everyone but you can leave an impression on them that may help them sometime in the future.

I think that the obligation to help others may fall especially hard on those of us who have experienced more of the hardships in life than others. (I don't use the word obligation as something we are being forced to do but rather as an act of giving.) As we are able to move away from the pressing demands of our daily lives and have some time and energy for other things it is then we can see our way to seek and develop deeper connections with others and seek ways to help others. Is that not the best legacy we can leave to our children and the next generation?

CHAPTER EIGHT

Raising Children the Best We Know How

The phone rang. I instinctively looked at the clock before answering it. It was 4:30 am. Any time the phone rings before 7 am I am overcome with anxiety and a foreboding feeling that something bad has happened.

When the phone rang that morning my anxiety level was already on high alert as a result of my recent divorce. It had been at that heightened level for the past two years. This was the kind of omnipresent anxiety that overshadows every event even joyous ones. I was waiting for the proverbial other shoe to drop. In this situation that shoe was the next legal action my soon to be ex-husband was going to take against me. Being caught up in the courts is one of the worst things that can happen to a person. That is especially true for attorneys because we know that, more often than naught, the end result is not just or even fair. Those without personal experience still ascribe to the myth that courts of law are about justice. Even if you prevail, the energy, time and money expended on something so negative can tear you so far down you feel you can never get back up. Litigants have very little control. It has become difficult, if not impossible, to tell who is lying. They don't appear to be liars because they have convinced themselves that their version is the truth. The honest people are at their mercy in the courtroom.

"Some people just want to see the world burn" I think the butler played by Michael Caine said to Batman. I love that line because it describes so well a phenomena currently present in our society. Some people are so intent on destroying the person they perceived wronged them that that they don't care if they destroy themselves and everything else in the process. My ex husband is one of them. They are the most dangerous kind of opponent because there are no limits to what they will do to get what they want and what they want is usually revenge and to destroy their opponent. They are oblivious to the consequences of such a course of action, even the consequences to themselves. But I have digressed far too much.

The divorce and its fallout have been the source of my most recent anxiety. But I have always lived with a lot of anxiety. Anxiety overshadowed or maybe even defined my early years as a parent.

I didn't want to answer the telephone that morning. Calls at such hours rarely bring good news. But I was able to see the name of the caller displayed on caller ID. I still panicked. I picked up the phone. "I have to go to the hospital," her voice said over the phone. "Do you want me to come with you?" I asked. "No, not now. D is going with me," she said. "I will call when I need you". "I love you, "I said. I hung up the phone. I lay awake in bed for several hours until it was time to get up and take my youngest child to school. During that time I didn't really have any cohesive thoughts just a lot of anxiety.

"I need you to come now," she called to say sometime later that morning. I headed for the garage. Along the way, I stopped to clean the kitchen. I unloaded the dishwasher. I put a load of clothes in the washing machine. It was until about 45 minutes later that I remembered I was supposed to be somewhere else. No, I am not senile although my children often joke that I am.

"What you doing?" I asked myself in an exasperated voice. I talk to myself often, sometimes even out loud. I became aware that I was avoiding the trip. I was terrified to see my daughter suffer physically or emotionally. I am such a wimp when it comes to my children. I have had to learn, painfully, to step back so as not to rob them of their growing pains and experiences. They need to learn for themselves. This experience will mature my daughter, Jessica, greatly I say to myself somewhat convincingly. Still I wish I could endure the suffering for her. As I drove to the hospital my thoughts were mired in the past.

"Are you here all alone?" the nurse asked me. "Yes," I replied. I had been alone in that room for what seemed like an eternity. I think I was actually in there all by myself for about 12 hours before I was wheeled to the surgical room and moved onto a cold hard metal table. At least in the delivery room I had the company of the doctor and the nurse.

"Where are you taking her?" I asked the nurse as she was removing my newborn daughter from my arms. "She has to go to the nursery and get checked out," the nurse replied. "You can see her tomorrow," she said. I was wheeled into the recovery room where I again spent a long time period of time alone. I didn't see my baby, Jessica, again until sometime the next morning. My heart sank when they brought Jessica into my room. "Why is she in an incubator? What is wrong with her?" I shot off in panic. "It is just a precaution because of the condition you had while you were pregnant," the nurse replied. I emitted a huge, audible sigh of relief. I took Jessica into my arms. There really are no words to describe the rush of feelings you experience when you hold your newborn child.

The "script" set out for my generation provided that women got married and had children at a young age by today's standards. I had absolutely no idea what I was doing or what I was getting into when I became a parent. It makes sense that new parents typically look to their parents to learn how to parent. But I knew even before I had Jessica that such a plan wouldn't work for me. When Jessica arrived essentially all I knew about parenting was that I did not want to be a mother like my Mother. That was the extent of my knowledge along with a little bit of experience I gained from babysitting some of the neighborhood children when I was a teenager.

For me, becoming a parent was the most significant maturing experience of my life. I was totally responsible for another person. I would have to put her needs first and always think about what was best for her in everything I did. My primary focus was no longer and could no longer be myself. I don't know that I was afraid or overwhelmed by any of that. It all just seemed to be part of the natural progression of life.

Many women of my generation didn't follow the "script". They elected not to have children. I really didn't think of that as an option when I was young. I am thankful that I was blissfully ignorant of the other choice. While I enjoy the company of these women tremendously there is a chasm that divides us. They never learned to put another first. They never experienced the kind of love where you would sacrifice everything for another –your child. What a loss! From the moment Jessica was born my life would never be the same. Being a parent has brought me the most joy and the most pain in my life. It has enriched my life beyond measure.

Now my daughter was about to embark on this sobering and enriching experience herself. Life has come full circle as they say - whoever "they" are. My daughter, Jessica, is now giving birth to her first child. In fact as I write this I am sitting in her "birthing" room with her. Writing this would distract from my worries or so I hoped.

The nurse bustled into the room and checked some machines - those annoying things that kept beeping. She was very brusque with a no nonsense attitude. She never said much. "How is everything going?" I asked. "You'll make it. When I had my babies my husband was in the Navy. They knocked you out and you woke up with a baby. Those nurses gave you no sympathy," she said. Things haven't changed much I said to myself. She was my only human contact during many long hours of labor.

"Is that you making all of that noise?" I heard someone ask. I turned to see my doctor standing by my bedside. It was very dark outside now. When I arrived the sun was just coming up. She reached out and touched my arm. My entire body relaxed and I a feeling of warmth and comfort literally spread from where she touched my arm through my entire body. It was overwhelming. I was struck, in spite of all my desperation, by the power of the human touch. I feel it now as I recall that night. I have tried so hard to remember to touch my children. It is not something I grew up with so I have to remind myself to do it. My great grandfather expressed the importance of the human touch much better than I ever could:

The birthing process was, thankfully, so different for Jessica. I felt both envious and relieved. I am relieved that she will not suffer physically or emotionally as I did. She has her husband by her side and other family members when she wants. The nurses are so kind. She can dispense her own pain medication. They even gave her medication to speed up the process.

I wanted to forget my first birthing experience other than the moment when I first held that beautiful baby girl in my arms. The only time I wanted to remember is when we mothers were telling our "war stories". We would compete as to who had the worst and most painful childbirth experience. I have some pretty gruesome "war" experiences to relate. In true puritan WASP fashion I felt I had to forgo any comforts to give birth. If I had taken any medication or made it in any way easy on myself I would not have been blessed with my beautiful baby or so I unconsciously believed.

I unconsciously believed that everything in life was earned including good fortune and happiness. They are earned through suffering. Suffering has the added benefit of keeping anxiety at bay. Something bad is already happening so I didn't have to be anxious as to what misfortune lie ahead. Is this a vestige of the Biblical teaching of Adam and Eve that the price of sin is suffering?

I have always had a difficult time with the concept that love and good fortune are gifts to be appreciated and enjoyed. I had difficulty accepting such gifts, any gifts. I felt everything had to be earned including love. I also believed I had to go it totally alone on this journey. Isn't it a sign of weakness to need anyone or any help? I would never want to appear weak. These attitudes would leave a mark on my early years as a parent. I would make things as difficult as possible for myself to test myself, to earn love and good fortune and keep anxiety at bay. I was unconsciously seeking out difficult circumstances to see if I could survive them. It was a test I could never complete. Unfortunately my drive to make things as difficult for myself also made things incredibly difficult for my children. I think I was just unaware that I was operating under this principle at all. That is just how I functioned. So I was oblivious to the consequences to my children as well. You can see now why I assess myself as a terrible parent. There are other compelling reasons as well.

"There are no purple hearts given out for suffering and pain," the Jessica's doctor said. I could see, on Jessica's face that she was struggling with the concept that she will not suffer as much as she should. (Maybe she has heard too many war stories). Thankfully she is able to fight off that WASP urge to suffer. "You can control the medication with this pump," the nurse told her. "It will numb the pain and speed up the process." Jessica nodded that she understood. This to me was a triumph. Jessica was able to accept the help of modern science and the comfort offered by her loved ones.

I have anticipated this day with much joy and much fear and trepidation. I fear that my daughter will have to suffer too much or experience some life threatening complication. I am joyful that there will be a new person in this world to care for and to love. I fear that, even with all the tools of modern science, the baby may not be healthy.

I have fears about getting older. I am apprehensive about becoming a grandmother. After all grandmothers smell like formaldehyde and are totally out of touch with what goes on in the world. I don't want to be one of those grandmas nor do I want to be one of those modern grandmas who strive to look like the mother rather than the grandmother. With the birth of my first grandchild staring me in the face, I can no longer deny the passage of years simply by refusing to look closely at myself in the mirror.

Jessica's husband came into the waiting room. "We have a beautiful, healthy baby girl!" he said with such joy and relief. "Mom she is healthy!" Jessica said to me when I was able to enter the birthing room. We all had the same concerns I thought to myself. Why didn't we share our concerns with each other? Were we afraid to speak to each other about them for fear we would upset each other by discussing what in reality we all already knew. How silly to think that everyone would not be aware of the potential dangers. Worries and fears that are shared are so much less powerful I think. Oh the WASP ways are so ever powerful!

"Can you come to the hospital with me?" is what I should have asked him. Instead I was silent and David went to work – a business trip – from which he would have to be called back after Jessica was born. I did not want to appear like I needed any help. I would do it on my own. I don't think David really wanted to be present for the birth anyway. David arrived at the hospital after I had been moved from the recovery room to my hospital room. "You should have been here an hour or so ago. What took you so long to get here?" I asked. "Well I had to go home and shower before I came here," he replied. "The baby was born about an hour ago," I said to him. David stayed just a few minutes and then left. After all I was totally exhausted.

You are going to cry," Jessica said making fun of me. "No I am not," I replied as I looked into the face of the new baby. The resemblance to Jessica was absolutely uncanny at least in my mind. I felt a little numb. Memories flooded into the present and sometimes I couldn't distinguish between the past and the present. I kept repeating to Jessica, "She looks just like you!" until even Jessica got sick of hearing it. I felt like I was somewhere outside of my body watching this all happen. Maybe that is just my defense mechanism when my emotions overpower me and I can't control them.

"How did you know it was the right time to have a baby," a friend of mine asked a few months after Jessica was born. She was much older than I and had been married for many years. "We need to save more money and James has to get a better job so I can quit working," she said. She continued to tell me all the things that would have to change or occur before she would be ready to have a baby. I listened. "There is never a perfect time to have a baby. You just do it. If you wait for the perfect time it will never happen," I replied in all my immature wisdom. That turned out to be all too true for my friend. She never had a baby even though I know she desperately wanted one. I guess it was never the perfect time for her. Is it ever? Isn't dealing with the unpredictability of life a catalyst for personal growth? I am not advocating the absence of planning but, as with everything, shouldn't there be a balance? Doesn't too much planning make life stale?

"I'll be over to pick up the kids to take them to a movie," David said over the phone. In my naiveté I told the children that their father would be over tomorrow around 11 am to pick them up and take them to a movie. The two younger ones, Samuel and Ellen, were very excited. They were 3 1/2 and 5 years old. They got dressed early Saturday morning and waited patiently. They were talking about what they were going to do with him and what movie they wanted to see. At least as much as kids that age can discuss those matters. I knew they were excited and quite frankly I was looking forward to a little time to myself. I was going to sleep. "When will Daddy be here?" Samuel asked. "We are going to miss the movie," he later complained when the time came and went for his father's arrival. "He will be here. Something must have come up that caused a delay," I said.

After an hour passed with no phone call and no knock at the door I realized he wasn't coming. I should have said something to the children. I was a coward. Eventually Samuel just found something else to do besides wait for him. He went to his room and played with his matchbox cars. Ellen, who was three at the time, cried and carried on. I tried to get them interested in going out with me to a movie but they didn't want to. Their hurt was palpable.

"How could you just not show up," I shrieked into the phone when David finally did call. I was surprised at myself because I had given up on fighting with him over how he treated me but apparently

I still had the energy and grit to fight with him over how he treated the children. "You are crazy. I never told you that I was going to pick the kids up and take them to a movie," he responded. "Did I misunderstand him?" I asked myself.

I had just about gone crazy the last few months David and I lived together. We would talk, make plans or make a decision and then when things didn't go as planned he would tell me he never said that. Now I started to doubt myself again. It was actually stronger than that. I felt totally disoriented again – a feeling I had all the time the last months of living with David. Was I going crazy? Was the stress affecting me that much? Why did I even bother to say anything to him? I knew that nothing was ever going to change with him. He would never admit he made a mistake or did anything wrong. But what about the children I wondered.

Most of the time when David did show up he would take only one or two of them. "I simply can't handle all three of them or I simply can't afford to take all of them to the movie," he would say. One very radiant child would leave with him while the other would crumple up in a ball on the floor and cry. I was left with a shattered child whose pieces I tried to put back together. (Jessica, the oldest never really wanted to go with her father.) That is how I came to view my children. They were shattered into pieces at a very young age and the rest of their lives have been about putting those pieces back together. The pieces never fit back together perfectly but at least, now, all the pieces are back and in some kind of reasonable order.

"We don't want to take a bath. We want to go live with our Dad! We want to go live with our Dad!" Ellen and Samuel were chanting. I was somewhat accustomed to hearing this by now. It had been several months since their father, David, had moved out. This chant accompanied just about every request I made of the younger two to do something they didn't want to do. I gave them a bath silently, dried them off and got them into bed.

It wasn't hard to be a better parent than their father, David. I have often wondered if that is one of the reasons, unconsciously, that

I chose him. Eventually he just went away altogether. That is what I had hoped for but not until after he had made our life a living hell for quite a long time.

"Hello," I would shout as I came in the door. Usually the three children were at the front door to greet me and they would be jostling each other to try to get my attention. "Mom I need help with my homework," Jessica would say. "Mom Samuel hit me," Ellen would complain. "Mom the sitter was mean to me today," Samuel would say woefully. They would all end up shouting at me as each of them tried to get my attention. I would squeeze past them giving each a perfunctory hello and a hug before I rushed to the kitchen to prepare dinner. I know they each wanted some one on one time with me but it would have to wait until after dinner. They were all overwrought with hunger by the time I arrived home. All three of them would continue to talk to me at the same time as I prepared dinner. I would try to get them to take turns but it was pretty impossible.

Sometimes I could find a sitter who was affordable, reliable and cooked dinner but that was the exception. Sitters came and went on a regular basis. I couldn't afford daycare for three children. My children were not the easiest to take care of. Samuel and Ellen weren't keen on following rules.

"Mom, Ellen is crying again," Jessica told me. It wasn't like I didn't know. I had just walked in the door from the office. It was about 6:30 pm. I saw Ellen sitting in the hallway that connected the main part of the small house to the bedrooms. She was hugging her stuffed animal and sobbing. I stroked her head and said, "I love you. Everything will be OK. Come have some dinner now." Ellen continued to cry for the rest of the evening. I finally coaxed her into my bed about 8:30 p.m. She was exhausted. This same scene was replayed every night for months. As soon as I walked through the door she would start to cry. I was desperate to get her to stop. One night I sat down next to Ellen in the hallway and pretended to cry. The funny thing is that real tears came down my cheeks. We cried together for several nights. After that Ellen just stopped sitting in the hallway and crying. If only I had thought to do that sooner!

"How could you have lost your glasses?" I screamed at 5 year old Samuel. "I can't afford to buy you another pair right now!" I shrieked. I carried on like this for a while longer. I was definitely ranting and raving. Every extra expenditure was a crisis in those days. In fact everything was a crisis in those days. I was exhausted all the time. I was overwhelmed by the demands of daily living. Work was stressful. The divorce was dragging through the courts. I was receiving threats and being harassed by the children's father. The children were acting out and not doing well at school. The house was a mess all the time. The laundry was always piled high. We lived paycheck to paycheck. I would rush home from the office, cook dinner, and help a little with homework, get the younger two bathed and in bed, wash the dinner dishes and fall into bed exhausted hopefully by 9:30 pm. Then I would start everything over again the next day at 6:30 a.m. On the weekends we went to the grocery where some weeks we had only $25.00 for groceries. I was able to take the children on one fun outing each week. We usually went to a park or other free venue to try to have some fun. This is the environment in which my children spent their early, formative years.

During the demise of my first marriage, I couldn't wait to get out of the office at lunchtime so I could go for a drive. I would race to my car and drive into a quiet residential neighborhood not far from the office. I would park my car, put my head down on the steering wheel of the car and sob for my entire one hour lunch break. I would clean my face up or so I hoped and go back to the office. Thankfully the people at the office were gracious enough not to ask me what had happened. I think they instinctively knew I couldn't handle their questions.

"What do you mean you can't count money," I said to Jessica. "It is simple. Here is how you do it," I impatiently said in a raised voice. A five minute, hostile demonstration ensued after which I left to clean up the kitchen after dinner. Jessica struggled with that issue and others for quite a while. She didn't ask me again for any help with her homework. Of course my message to Jessica was that she was stupid even though I don't think I ever said that word.

"If you don't leave us alone I am going to disappear in the night and you will never ever see the children again!" I told David. I thought for sure he would have given up and gone away by now. It had been over 11 months since I filed for divorce. During those eleven months, David punched and hit me in front of the children. He called me at all hours of the day and night and threatened me with further violence. David regularly threatened to kill me in front of Jessica. I was absolutely desperate. I thought about this for months before I said it to David. I spend a good bit of time thinking about what state I would go to and how I would change my name so he couldn't find us. It had no effect on David. Maybe he didn't believe me. Maybe it was just a fantasy but I don't think so.

"Frank can you please speak to your brother and get him to leave us alone?" I said into the phone. I don't know how I had the courage to call him but I sensed that Frank would believe me when I told him what was happening. I hadn't spoken to Frank or anyone in David's family since a few months before I filed for divorce. Frank was the one and only person David looked up to. Why hadn't I asked for his help earlier? Was I was embarrassed or ashamed? I wasn't the one acting like a maniac. Frank was, as usual, gracious and kind. Shortly after that conversation David moved back to his home state.

The court eventually entered an order for child support. David simply ignored the court order. He never paid any child support. I wasn't surprised and really didn't much care. All I ever wanted from David was for him to leave us alone. I sensed that if I tried to enforce the child support order David would come back into our lives. The money was not worth it. Years later when I tried to collect some child support that is exactly what happened. I abandoned my claim forever.

"Samuel has been missing on his bike for several hours," the after school babysitter told me over the phone. He was 5 years old at the time. I left the office in a panic and drove around our neighborhood. I found Samuel riding his bike with some older boys in the desert. This wasn't the first or last time I would received that phone call

"Mrs. Smith this is Dr. Howard. I am the school psychologist at Remington Elementary School. We tested Samuel in preparation for kindergarten. He has a learning disability and we recommend he be placed in a special education class for a year before matriculating to the regular kindergarten class." I left the office in tears and drove home.

"M'am this is the police department. We have you son Samuel here at the convenience store. He and some other boys tried to steal some chewing gum." Samuel was seven years old at the time.

"I quit," the babysitter told me as soon as I walked in the door. "Samuel is impossible. He doesn't follow any rules. He is impossible to control. He does what he wants when he wants. He took off on his bike again today and was gone for 3 hours. I was afraid to call you again," she said in exasperation. I couldn't argue with her because it was all so true. This was the third sitter that had quit in about 4 months. As if finding them was not difficult enough – keeping them was even harder. I hoped she would agree to stay until I could find someone else.

"Samuel pack a suitcase and get in the car. You have to find someplace else to live," I said. "Where are you going?" Jessica asked Samuel. "Mom is giving me away," Samuel replied very matter of factly. After we got in the car I started to drive around our neighborhood. "Samuel you have to find another place to live unless you can agree to follow the rules," I said sternly. He was about seven years old. "Will you follow the rules?" I asked. Samuel was silent. I stopped the car. This kid is going to call my bluff I remember thinking to myself. He is the most stubborn kid on the planet.

"Get out and go knock on one of these doors and ask if you can live there," I said. Samuel didn't move. "Do you want to come home and follow the rules?" I asked hopefully. Again Samuel was silent. He got out of the car and stood at the corner holding his little suitcase. My heart sank. It was getting dark. "Have you changed your mind?" I asked Samuel. He was silent. "OK I am leaving now," I said. I drove away and around the block. My heart was racing. What was I going to do? I waited what seemed like an eternity and then I drove back to where I had left him. He was standing in the exact same spot on the corner still clutching his little suitcase. I opened the passenger door. "Do you want to come home and follow the rules?" I asked. Samuel nodded his head, "yes". He got into the car. Samuel's behavior improved somewhat after that. At least I was able to keep a babysitter for longer than a month or two. It was an abominable thing to do but I was desperate. I couldn't work unless I had a babysitter. I couldn't keep a babysitter unless Samuel behaved. Samuel's refusal to follow even the most basic rules could result in him getting hurt or worse.

Two science fair projects to be completed at the same time! Good heavens how could I find the time and money to do that. It seemed like a lost cause anyway. My children couldn't compete with the other children in their classes. All of those children had two parents with a lot more time and financial resources than I did.

We were broke all the time. Energy to find a better job just didn't exist. My energy was focused on keeping the one that I had. I couldn't let anyone see any of the stress or problems at the office – not if I wanted to keep my job. Sure some of it showed but I was always at the office and I had the requisite number of billable hours. Work was actually my salvation. I could forget about everything else while I was working, for the most part.

I would take vacation days to go on field trips and attend school programs during the day. In those days, my children were freaks. They were the only children with a single mom. I know they acutely felt the difference. The outward, physical differences were difficult for them to manage. Children don't like to feel "different."

Their emotional world was even more treacherous. These three, poor, young children were left in the sole care of an emotionally distraught and physically exhausted woman in her late 20s. Energy is such a limited and finite resource. I simply did not have enough energy to do everything that needed to be done in a day at least with any level of patience.

"You are stupid," I heard myself shriek at Jessica. The insults and shrieking didn't stop there. I don't want to remember what else I said. Some voice in my head was able to reach me through the rage. "You are just like your mother," I heard the voice say. I stopped in mid sentence. I can remember that moment with Jessica like it just happened yesterday. I was standing in the hallway of our little house in the desert. Oh my God how did I get here? How did I become my mother?" I so wanted to give my children something better! That realization propelled me to make an appointment with a psychologist I had met through work.

You see part of the problem was I knew what a bad parent looked like but I had no idea what a good parent looked like. I knew I was a bad parent and I wanted to stop. I couldn't change the stress I was under but I needed to cope with it better for the sake of my children. Still it was a difficult decision to go to therapy. I kept it a secret for many, many years. I didn't want to be seen as weak or having serious problems. I made the appointment with the therapist several times and cancelled it several times.

"Tell me about your background," Dr. M. said. "Do we have to discuss my parents? Just thinking about them makes me tired," I said. I put my head in my lap and cried for the whole hour. Thus began a long, painful process of trying to become a better parent and a better person. I did not have much time, energy or money to devote to this but Dr. M. was good enough to work with what I was able to do. I was terrified. I had absolutely no idea how to be a good parent. My kids were cursed with a horrible mother. I had not always been such a terrible parent. I think it started with the breakdown of my marriage to David. It seems that all the stress activated my bad parenting gene. Could I change myself? I was afraid that it would be an impossible task. That first year of therapy was awful. I would feel worse after each therapy session. I had to force myself to continue with the therapy. Eventually I turned the tide and I started to feel better.

At home I had always made it my main focus to provide physical stability for the kids like nightly family dinners, getting homework done, family outings and outings with friends. Of course that was all peppered with an occasional verbal bashing. Now I started devoting just 10 to 15 minutes every night to each of the children individually. This was a tip from a book a friend had recommended to me. We called these sessions "Our talking tos". That may have one of the best things I ever did as a parent. I wished then and now I had more energy for those "talking tos". Still in spite of my lack of time and energy and sometimes patience the children loved their one on one time with me. Some twenty years later they still talk about it reverently.

Some of the financial stress eased. The divorce and violence were put further and further behind me. David moved away and stopped inciting conflict. My emotions were not so raw. As I improved so did the children. Our life started to have some measure of peace and joy. Still there were persons that could destroy that feeling of peace and joy.

"Why have you been so upset these last few days?" my assistant, Michelle, asked me. I guess I was more nervous than usual. "My mother is coming to visit. She really stresses me out," I replied. "Just tell her not to come," Michelle replied. "You don't have to put yourself through that," she said. It sounded so simple when she said it. Could I do that I wondered. I agonized over what to do for several days. My anxiety increased dramatically as the day of my Mother's visit approached.

Finally I called my Mother. It took a week or so for me to get up my nerve. As soon as she answered the phone I said, "Don't come to visit me." I immediately hung up the phone. I didn't give her an opportunity to say anything. It was a terribly cruel thing to do. Neither she nor my Father ever called me back. Based on past experience I knew it was impossible to communicate with my parents about feelings or family issues.

My parents treated me badly when they would come for a visit. They would belittle me. Oh they would call it teasing. There is such a thing as teasing but it can so quickly and easily turn into belittlement and criticism. My parents did not know where to draw the line.

My Mother would cook dinner every night. How wonderful. But she would leave a huge mess in the kitchen. I would spend an hour or two cleaning up the kitchen every day when I arrived home from the office. Unless you have experienced it you really can't imagine the mess. She would drop sticky things on the floor and leave them there. She would allow things to splatter all over the stove and then not clean them off so that they baked on the top of the stove. It goes on and on. I tried to talk to her about it several times but she would simply get up and walk away. I feel that she was getting back at me for some wrongs she thinks I have done to her.

They would "tell" me I was a bad mother. Oh they wouldn't say that directly. I wish they had been direct but that has never been their style. When I would arrive home in the evening form the office they would say things like, "good parents understand that spending time at home with their children is more important than making money or spending a lot of time at the office." They would exchange that knowing look that my children were having difficulties because I was a bad mother. They were there to rescue my children from me. If I were able to trust my instincts I would have been able to recognize the subliminal messages my children and I were receiving from my parents. There was always a shroud of dishonesty around my parents and their interactions with me.

They would undermine my discipline with the children. When I would discipline the children my Father would simply ignore the consequence I had meted out. He wouldn't discuss the situation with me. He just did what he wanted to do with the children. They were more out of control when he was around, especially Samuel.

"What are you knitting Mom?" I asked her one Saturday morning. She had been ferociously working on this project since she arrived for her visit. "I am knitting a sweater for David," she replied. "He loves the color blue and I think it will able to use if on those cold mornings when he goes to play golf. I can't wait to give it to him for Christmas." She went on a for a few more minutes extolling the sweater and David. She knew that David and I were divorcing. I guess she gave it to him one of the times he came to pick up the children.

I realized only much later how terribly depressed I was when they visited and for quite a while after they left. I avoided my parents by staying late at the office. In the evenings I would retire early to my bedroom. On the weekends I stayed in my bedroom until late in the morning. At the time I thought I did this because I was happy to have some help with the children and needed a rest but there was more to it than that. I didn't think what effect this pattern of behavior might have on the children. They seemed to enjoy my parents' visits and I was happy for that.

My Mother treated my children much better than she ever treated me. When they were little she was very kind, patient and loving. In part I had maintained a close connection with them because I thought it was good for my children. I didn't want to deprive my children of the love of their grandparents but I felt I had no choice. Was it selfish of me to deprive my children of their grandparents? I think it was. In my defense, I really expected the respite to be very brief. I expected that at some point in time my parents would call and we would talk about why I did what I did. They never called.

This break from my parents helped me to recognize the detrimental behaviors they engaged in as parents. Once I saw that I was able to work to stop acting that same way in parenting my own children. I have worked to honor how my children feel. We communicate about how they feel and what they want. If they can't or won't communicate I sometimes press the issue by asking questions or trying to "read" them and their behavior. It is difficult to know when to press and when to back off. I think they have come to understand the importance of being honest about their feelings and so they work on that.

When it is appropriate I compromise over issues with my children. My parents were great at doing things to help me out like coming to take care of the children for a while. I continued that tradition but I try first to find out what it is my children would like me to do rather than just doing what I want to do for them or think they need me to do. Often my parents thought they were helping me out when in fact they were not. I try to avoid that mistake.

I hug my children regularly. Mostly I strive to be honest about how I feel and what I want and I strive to listen to what they tell me about how they feel and what they want. This was of course impossible at certain times in the lives of my children. But I think you earn your child's respect just by asking and trying even if they are incapable of communicating it to you. It starts to build a foundation. You can't connect or share with another if honesty is not at the foundation.

"It isn't healthy to allow your parents to treat you disrespectfully in front of your children. It eventually may result in your children feeling like it is OK to treat you that way as well," the psychologist told me. I had some support and comfort in taking a break from my relationship with my parents. My children lost their grandparents for a number of years. They were rather young and my parents lived far away so they didn't see them terribly often ever. I really don't remember them asking about my parents during this time but maybe I simply ignored their feelings in that regard.

As the years passed without any contact with my parents, I started to believe that what I wanted or how I felt was not important to my parents. As I have matured I have come to realize that perhaps they just couldn't deal with any emotional issues. We didn't speak to each other for more than two years. I finally initiated the contact. Brian urged me to do it. It was the right thing to do. My parents and I have never spoken about that time. We have never even acknowledged that we didn't speak to each other for several years. Maybe it is too painful for them. When they came back into our lives they treated me with much more respect. That is what I wanted for me and for the sake of my children. Maybe it was good for the children to see me set limits on my parents.

"Mom I don't want to go to visit Dad!" Jessica screamed. "You have to. We don't have a choice. It is court ordered visitation," I replied. As she and Ellen were walking up the ramp to board the plane Jessica threw up all over the ramp. "I don't want to go," she shrieked. She ran back down the ramp and clung to me. I watched as the flight attendant escorted my little 5 year old daughter onto the plane. Ellen was so excited. Their father rarely asked to see any of them. I knew that if I denied him the rare visits he requested he would resume where he had left off with the threats of kidnapping and violence. I let Ellen go. Jessica stayed home with me. Samuel wasn't asked to visit his father. Unfortunately their father proved me right a little later on. Ellen had a wonderful visit but then she always was her father's favorite.

"Can you and the children join my daughter and I for a day at the water park?" Brian asked. The children knew I was seeing Brian but this would be the first time they would meet Brian. He and I had been seeing each other for a few years by this time. We talked about our respective children all the time but I did not talk much to the children about Brian. I had learned to be careful about what I revealed. I knew I needed to take it slowly.

"Mom what is wrong?" Jessica asked me. I was folding laundry and I was feeling a bit blue. "I miss James," I said. Jessica turned and fled from the room. Right after my divorce from their father I had introduced James to the children. Somehow I just expected or assumed the children would like and accept him because I did. When he wasn't spending time with us I talked about him too much and too often. He was way too involved in our lives much too soon. Jessica especially felt very threatened. I chased after Jessica but of course she couldn't explain why she was so upset. I learned from that mistake.

Still it is amazing to me that Brian and I took everything so slowly. Neither of us had done that in the past. Everything just unfolded slowly. Maybe we just intuitively sensed that if we wanted this to work we would have to take our time. We both wanted it to work.

At the beginning, our relationship played out in fits and starts. Brian and I would fight, break up and then get back together. Our behavior was incredibly immature. Fortunately I was mature enough not to discuss any of this with the children. Brian would usually call me at the office or late at home in the evening after the children were in bed. We saw each other mostly at lunch time. If we went out in the evening I would meet him somewhere so he didn't have to come to the house.

Brian and I never discussed how to handle our relationship with our children. We just seem to instinctively know to keep our relationship a secret from them for a while. We had reached a place in our relationship where we thought we could meet each other's children. Thankfully we kept the children out of the drama of our relationship at least for a few years.

"We are going to go home now. Thank you for the great day" I said to Brian. It had been an easy, fun day. My children stuck close to me and avoided interacting much with Brian and his daughter. Still I thought the first meeting between Brian and my children was successful. Brian didn't try to force interaction with the children. I did the same with his daughter. We both had prior experience in relating to stepchildren and it wasn't a positive experience. We were both in unchartered territory. I remember thinking that day that maybe we were on the right track. The children and I didn't talk about Brian or his daughter on the ride home. I didn't bring it up since they didn't seem to want to discuss it. I wanted them to accept him and yes, if things worked out with Brian, I hoped one day they might even love him. I knew I could not force the acceptance and certainly not the love. It would have to develop slowly.

Brian seemed to love my children from that very first day. The reaction of the children was somewhat different especially after Brian and I were married. Samuel was elated to have a dad but not elated enough to accept discipline very well. Ellen was young enough that she was happy she had a dad. She accepted direction from Brian better than Samuel did at least for a time.

Jessica was quietly defiant and coped by having many friends that were the center of her world and with whom she spent almost all her time. Jessica had developed this coping mechanism shortly after the divorce. I fought it for a long while but then I accepted that I might never be close to Jessica again. Maybe she could never forgive me for all my mistakes or even like me again. We had been so close when she was young! Everything Jessica did seemed designed to distance herself from her siblings and me. She worked to distance herself even more after Brian and I were married. Jessica made sure she never had to be disciplined by Brian. She was amazingly successful at that. In spite of her best efforts she was forced to deal with Brian.

"Time to get up," I heard Brian say as he gently shook me. I must have slept through the alarm I thought as I opened my eyes. I went downstairs. "Jessica are you up?" I said through her closed bedroom door. She was always up but I wanted to be sure. I went across the hall. "Ellen time to get up." Then I knocked on Samuel's door, "Samuel time to get up." After I made my rounds I went back to my bedroom to get dressed for the office. I had to go back a few times to be sure Ellen and Samuel were actually up and getting ready for school. They had a tendency to fall back to sleep. This morning was no exception. "Get up, get dressed and get some breakfast now, "I said firmly. I don't want you to miss the school bus. "Good by Mom, "I heard Jessica say. "Bye, I said. "Good bye. Call me later" Brian said as he gave me a kiss good bye. I had to give some more nudging to Samuel and Ellen. I finally got them out the door to the school bus.

I went back to finish getting ready for work. I heard the door open a few minutes later. "We missed the bus, "Ellen said. Ugh that meant I would be late for work. "Get in the car and let's go," I said rather angrily. There was no time to clean up the kitchen. I dropped the kids off at school and raced down the freeway to work. Alicia greeted me at the office. "Don't forget we have to finish the Carter matter this morning and you have a meeting at 2 pm this afternoon but not at this office." I picked up my phone messages and glanced through them as I walked to my office. "Can you come in here for a minute I heard my boss say to me?

About 45 minutes later I left the senior partner's office to face the pile of files on my desk. The phone rang. It was a client. Later that morning I was able to give Brian a quick call. "Hey don't forget we have a dinner meeting tonight with the representatives of that company whose work I am trying to get." Brian reminded me. Oh Lord! I was going over in my head how I would get home, get the kids settled in to do homework, get them something to eat and be back downtown in time for dinner with Brian at 7:30 and then home in time to review homework and get them to bed on time. It was all done. I feel into bed about 11:00 pm. I forgot to say good night to Brian. As soon as my head hit the pillow I was asleep. That used to drive Brian crazy because he wanted some together with me at night. It just wasn't possible very often.

I was stretched much too thin. There was a lot of conflict between Brian and I in the beginning of our marriage. There were some legitimate issues of conflict and then some were created by our crappy relationship skills. I recognized that my children were being raised in a house with far too much conflict. If I wanted to reduce that conflict I was going to need some more time and energy for myself, my relationship with Brian and for my children.

I had definitely stopped parenting, for the most part, like my Mother. At least the verbal abuse had stopped. I could catch myself when I started berating the children or when I heard myself use a tone of voice that was telling them they were worthless or stupid. I learned to be ever vigilant to that behavior although I know I still slipped up. Counseling helped so much with reducing that behavior. Some of the change was just the fact that I had a lot less stress after Brian and I were married. That was true in spite of the stress of being in a second marriage. It seems that stress always brings out the worst parts of my personality. I was learning to manage my stress better even though there was still a lot more than I wanted. If I wanted to be a "good" parent I was going to have to reduce my stress even more. I elected to work part time or at least try to do that.

"Hey everyone dinner is being served!" I called throughout the house. Brian, my three children, my parents, who were visiting, and

I all sat down to the dinner table. After everyone had settled in Brian looked at me and nodded affirmatively. "Mom, Dad, Jessica, Samuel and Ellen." I said. Everyone stopped what they were doing and looked at me. "I am pregnant. The baby is due at the end of June". I said. There was dead silence. No one said a word. There were no words of congratulations. In fact nothing was said by anyone. "Can we be excused?" Jessica asked. "OK" I said. Brian and I sat alone with my parents for a few more minutes before they excused themselves to go to their room. After everyone left Brian and I looked at each other in disbelief. What just happened? Why was no one the least bit excited or even interested?

The children were already unhappy because we were going to be moving again. Now there would also be the addition of a new baby to cope with. We had already moved right after we were married. We were still in the same city but in a very different part of that city. I was against this latest move primarily because I didn't want to move the children again. Brian wanted it. It is one of those compromises we make when we are married I guess. That meant this would be the second time the children had to change schools in less than two years. All of this was way too much change but the move was planned before I was pregnant. The move wouldn't happen until after the baby was born because we had to wait for our house to be sold. We actually moved a week before Gary was born.

Within a period of one month we moved to a new house on the other side of the city, Gary was born and we received the news of Brian's terminal illness. The children spent the remaining two months of their summer vacation without any friends. Then it was off to a new high school for Jessica and a new elementary school for Ellen and Samuel. They would be in 5th and 6th grade.

"I need to see the principal," I told the school receptionist. I had stopped by the office after dropping Samuel and Ellen off at their new school. School had been in session a few weeks. "He is not available right now. You can come back later or call," she said. "It is urgent I told her." I called the principal later that day. "Mr. Smith", I said, "my children are being bullied and mistreated by other students at school." "Oh that stuff happens to new kids "he replied. "Once the kids get used to them it will stop." Over the next six months I made regular calls to Mr. Smith. I always got the same response. If only I hadn't been preoccupied with newborn Gary and Brian's illness I think I could have defended my children better

I answered the phone. "This is Mr. Smith. A young man at school is being suspended and will be giving you money for a new lunch box for Samuel." he said. "What happened?" I naturally asked. "Well the kids have been taking Samuel's lunch away from him every day and eating it or throwing it away. Today this boy urinated in Samuel's lunchbox and threw it on the roof of the school. His parents have been notified. He has been suspended from school for three days and he will pay you for the lunch box." Samuel had not told me about this. My poor son was not even getting to eat his lunch! I never heard from the boy or his parents. It didn't seem to me that the family took this misconduct very seriously but it seems it finally got the attention of the principal. I think this at least signaled the end of the bullying Samuel was receiving at school.

"Ellen you are not ready for school yet." I said to her as she sat on the couch. "I'm not going to school today," she said. "You have to go to school unless you are sick. You don't appear to be sick." I said. Ellen started to cry, "The girls at school are always mean to me. They even hit me the other day when I was on my way to class." "Why didn't you say something earlier?" I asked. "It would only make things worse if I told on them" she continued to cry. I drove Ellen to school that day. I bypassed the principal this time. I spoke directly to Ellen's teacher. This teacher fortunately took it very seriously. The behavior stopped. Ellen became "friends" with those girls. I often wondered if she was just friends so they wouldn't pick on her anymore.

Why is it that new kids have to be subjected to such treatment? Why do we accept that this will happen? Did my kids have a banner on their forehead that says "Pick on me?" I know the school failed them. The principal definitely refused to take this conduct seriously. Although the principal gave me lip service about doing something to stop the conduct his attitude was that it was natural or some rite of passage for new kids to be bullied. I could tell he thought I was over reacting. I wrestled with what I should do. Was there another option other than taking the kids out of this school? At that time I really didn't know what else to do or what else to demand of the school. My poor children had more than enough to deal with at home with Brian's illness and a new baby.

I feel responsible for the scars my children acquired as a result of this horrendous bullying. I let them down both in my inept demands for the school to deal with the issue and in my teachings. I failed to protect them from these bullies. Maybe my teachings had caused them to fail to protect themselves. Had my emphasis on treating others with respect and not fighting prevented my children from asserting themselves against the bullies? Was I too naïve regarding the behavior of school children? Should I have taught them to be aggressive and to fight? Was it just that they were more vulnerable because of all that was going on at home?

How can we teach our children to be respectful of others without having them feel like they can't defend themselves? That may be something they need to figure out for themselves when they are older. Elementary school is not the time to do that. They are way too young. All of the adults failed in our responsibilities toward them. This was definitely not a situation they could handle on their own. A lot of parents, to my surprise, just don't seem to care if their children are bullies. These parents were proud that their kid was "tough". I had learned a few years earlier, before Brian and I were even married that if the kids are bullies it is probably because they learned if from their parents. I guess I forgot that lesson.

I knocked on my neighbor's door. They lived directly across the street from me. Samuel was five years old and attending kindergarten. This was about the time David, their father, was to put it politely, "acting out." Samuel's Big Wheel had been broken by an older child in the neighborhood. Jessica had seen this neighbor's son, who was in fifth grade, riding the big wheel. Jessica had also told me that this boy teased and picked on Samuel at the bus stop and on the school bus. So I found myself at my neighbor's door. I figured that the father would be upset his son was engaging in this behavior. I wasn't angry when I knocked. The father answered the door.

"I would like to talk to you about some problems at the bus stop. I believe your son is teasing my son at the bus stop and on the school bus. Before I could say any more the father shouted, "You are a stupid B******** and your kid is an idiot." I jumped right into the fray. "Well your son broke my son's big wheel…" "Get the hell out of here" he said as he started to slam the door in my face. "I know now why he is the way he is. He better not touch my son again" I shouted back.

Every morning when I went to get in my car to go to work this neighbor would come out of his house and stare at me menacingly. This went on for a few weeks. Things didn't improve at the bus stop until I took direct action. "If you touch my son again I will find you and beat you up," I told the kid one day as he gave me the finger at the bus stop. I wasn't proud of myself for threatening a 5th grader but I didn't know what else to do. The bullying stopped after that. I guess the kid thought I looked angry or crazy enough to actually follow through on my threat. In those days I think he might have been right.

After Brian and I were married we had the kind of family life that I had always dreamed of. Oh that is not to say we didn't have our issues and fights. Marriage counseling was a must. We spent time together on the weekends as a family. We went bike riding, swimming, attended the children's sporting and school events, had dinner together every night, went out to dinner or lunch, watched TV together, went to movies, and did chores and projects together. Brian became involved with Samuel in the boy scouts. I had been involved with Samuel up to this time. But he was of the age now where he needed a father to participate with him. Ellen and Brian's daughter joined Brownies and I was the leader for a while. We went on trips together. Life was great!

But the birth of Gary is what brought all of us together. Everyone, including myself, had anticipated Gary's arrival with some trepidation. Jessica was 15 and was enormously embarrassed that I was pregnant. While I was pregnant she tried to keep me from having any contact with her schoolmates and friends. Everyone was wondering what changes it would bring to their life and place in the family. All of that simply washed away when Gary was brought home. Everyone wanted to hold him and help take care of him. We finally all really had something in common – a bond.

We all loved Gary unconditionally from the moment he came into this world. In expressing our love for him we seemed to be able to recognize and express our love for each other as well. Now everyone would linger around the dinner table to spend more time with Gary. We would all get so excited by the new things he was doing and we couldn't wait to share them with each other. We all took turns doing things for Gary including giving baths, changing diapers, taking him for walks and feeding him. Before Gary's arrival the children mostly tolerated Brian. At least they wouldn't admit they loved him. Brian loved the children but it was squelched by the guilt he felt to his own daughter if he showed he loved them too much. All the barriers to love between Gary, my children and his daughter seemed to just melt away with Gary's arrival.

After Gary's birth, it was pretty much life as usual except we spent the first six months in agonizing uncertainty until the original diagnosis of Lou Gehrig's disease was confirmed. I tried, perhaps wrongly, to protect the children from all of this by not discussing it with them and going along as if everything was OK. It was a blessing for all of us to have Gary to care for and to love. He was too young to know what was happening and I was determined to shield him from the stress and anger brought on by Brian's illness. If only I could have done that for the older children as well.

I called "911". I regretted it as soon as I had done it. Brian's anger over being ill had exploded and he hit me so hard he knocked me unconscious for a moment or two. It was dinner time and all the children were in the room when it happened. Brian was taken away in handcuffs in front of all of our neighbors who had congregated on their front lawns when they heard the police sirens. He spent the night in jail. I did talk to the kids about it this time to the extent they were able to listen. The looks of fear, anxiety and disbelief on their faces were shattering. We have never really talked about it since then.

We got up the next morning and everyone went to school as usual. I tried to be steady and dependable for them. Was that a mistake? Was I teaching them to repress their feelings? If Brian came home would they understand that violence against another person is unacceptable? Would they understand that sometimes we have to forgive our spouse's egregious conduct? Perhaps Brain being taken away by the police sent the right message that behavior has consequences. I knew Brian's violent act was a response to his death warrant but I thought I still need to send him a message that such conduct was not acceptable even under these dire circumstances. I see that now but at the time I spent an agonizing sleepless night wondering if I should end the marriage and wondering how angry Brian was going to be when he came home. Fortunately Brian didn't come home angry.

We all watched as Brian slowly and painfully deteriorated physically and emotionally. For months the only change was that his right arm dangled from his side like a broken limb hanging from a tree. He would pick it up with his left arm when he needed to move it or protect it. Then the disease progressed much more quickly. It ravaged his body. His gait slowed. He was in a wheelchair occasionally and then all the time. Then we purchased an electric wheelchair so he could get around on his own. Brian stopped going to work. He sat in the TV room watching TV all day. I showered him, fed him, and took him to the bathroom. Then came the time when he couldn't get out of bed.

The children and I really didn't talk about Brian's illness much after the day of the announcement. They were first hand witnesses to everything that was happening physically and emotionally to Brian and I. I would ask them periodically how they were doing or if they needed to talk. My questions were always met with a stony silence. In retrospect I don't know that it would have done any good to try to get them to talk. They could only process and acknowledge a little bit, if any, of what was happening. If I pressed the issue they simply tried to avoid me. They were all already trying to avoid being at the house as much as possible. I hoped they knew that I loved and cared about them even though all my time, attention and energy were monopolized by Brian and Gary. For the most part I just let them be. I hoped that was the right thing to do. It wasn't I later found out. That should have been obvious to me at the time. I deluded myself into thinking they were doing normal teenage things like spending time with their friends rather than at home.

"My husband was arrested for child abuse because he grabbed my daughter by the arm to prevent her from going out to meet her druggie friends."Melissa told me. "Now we have absolutely no control. We are afraid of our own daughter." I knew the feeling. I had people I could commiserate with but that didn't solve the problem. Ellen was totally out of control. She was leaving the house at night, doing drugs, hanging out with dangerous kids, bringing those kids into our home, sleeping all day and not attending school, calling me a "bitch" and generally creating an atmosphere of fear when she was around. She wouldn't go to counseling. The school offered no help. They wrote her off. I tried half heartedly to parent her.

Samuel was doing drugs as well - mostly marijuana I found out later. He never expressed his feelings as rage like Ellen. He was simply a lost soul. By the time he was in high school he had lost two fathers. Is it possible to recover from that?

Gary was my salvation through all of this. He fortunately was too young to understand what was happening and I worked very hard to protect him from what was going on around him at home. He was a toddler when all of this was happening. I think Gary was one of the reasons I didn't have as many fights as I normally would have with Ellen or Samuel. I realize now it wouldn't have done any good anyway. They were hell bent on self destruction. I hoped I could warehouse them somewhere safe until they were 18 and hopefully by then they would have overcome these issues. I simply didn't know what else to do.

"Are you upset that Gary doesn't cry when you leave him?" the preschool teacher asked me one day. "No", I replied. "I am happy that he knows I will come back for him and that he is OK when I am not around." This was my fourth child. I never could have said that when Jessica was little. Then I felt terribly guilty when I left her screaming at preschool as I went off to work. Taking Gary to preschool with all the other Moms of toddlers and the teachers was a blessing. Sure sometimes I was angry that they didn't have the problems I did. But I realized this chance to escape for even a few hours may have saved me. Life was "normal" somewhere. I could forget about my teenagers from hell. I understood they had been through too much. We all had. I understand now that they were coping the only way they knew how which was self medicating with alcohol and drugs. But, sometimes I was angry that they couldn't understand that I was hurting too. "You can't put an old head on a young body," my friend aptly said. They were after all young teenagers.

My children had lost two fathers before they were out of high school. I can't imagine the pain of that experience. I could try to empathize with their pain. But there was not much I could do. My feeling of helplessness was absolutely overwhelming. I had to watch my children act out their trauma and grief in ways that could cause injury to them and others. Even if they were spared physical injury their conduct would certainly have long term detrimental consequences for their future. They were going to have to find their way out of this on their own. I couldn't do much of anything for them. My role became limited to trying to keep them physically safe while they, hopefully, worked through all of this.

I had provided a terrible environment for them when they were young. They didn't have a solid foundation of love to sustain them through Brian's death. They had a legacy of verbal abuse and emotional neglect. If I had created such a foundation, maybe they would have weathered this all much better. It seems that Brian's death inflamed all the old wounds and hurts and created new ones. I berated myself for many years for being such a terrible mother. The guilt literally weighed me down but that wasn't helping them in any way.

"Hi Mom" the voice on the other end of the phone said. I was elated and terrified at the same time. "Ellen?" I asked. "Mom I am in a dorm room. I just had breakfast. We are going on a field trip today. We have more trips planned because you know school doesn't start for another month or so. "Talk to you soon" she said as she hung up the phone. I hadn't said anything. I was still in too much shock. I did not detect one bit of anger in her voice. Was she actually relieved that I sent her away? It seemed that way at least from that first phone call.

Samuel was hurt that I let him graduate from his survival program but he would have missed school if he did. He was hurt that I didn't see him before he went to the military school. We talked and we emailed and then he and Ellen came home from military school for Thanksgiving. It was such a thrill to see them disembark the plane in their uniforms. Everyone was staring at them. They seemed a little embarrassed but also a little proud. They both had huge smiles. They each gave me a big hug. Maybe I had made the right decision I thought to myself. We still had a long way to go but it seemed the healing had started. I was worried that they would take up with old friends and old ways while they were home. Samuel and I had one scene because I smelled marijuana on him when he came back from a visit to a friend's house. I don't think he was expecting me to be waiting up for him. I hadn't done that before he left. Otherwise we had a good visit and I was actually looking forward to having them home for Christmas.

"I'm not going to do drugs or drink when I am older. I don't want to make my mother cry." Gary said this to his preschool teacher during a parent teacher conference. I didn't say anything in response to the look of shock on the teacher's face. I just couldn't go into all of that. She didn't know about Gary's older siblings. What she must have been imagining went on at my house!

"Mom why don't you call me more" Jessica said one night when she called me from college. "I don't want to interfere with your life at school" I lamely replied. The truth was that I didn't think Jessica wanted to hear from me. She was so relieved to be able to escape the craziness of our house when she went away to college. I couldn't blame her. Her high school years were filled with moves, the birth of Gary, the death of Brian and the drug and alcohol abuse by her siblings. "Well will you call me at least once a week?" she asked. I was happy to comply with that request. In truth I was pleasantly surprised that she wanted me to call her. Jessica had coped with the illness and the emotional fallout by never being at home. I interpreted that to mean that she didn't really care. Fortunately I was wrong.

"I don't want to go back to military school," Samuel announced one day. He was 18. I knew in reality if I forced him to go he would just leave. If he didn't go back he was going to miss out on his senior year of high school. He wasn't doing drugs or alcohol that I noticed and I did check. "You can stay here on the conditions that you get your GED, work and go to community college" I replied. Unfortunately, for Samuel, this marked the beginning of many, many years of drifting aimlessly through life sometimes in the company of unsavory friends. Samuel regretted the decision not to return to military school. He told me so later. I responded that we all have our regrets.

"We are sending Ellen home immediately. Please make the travel arrangements. She continues to break and flaunt the rules and set a bad example for the other students. We can't keep her here" said the Dean of the military school. Just a few months ago she had been promoted to a leadership position and she was babysitting for one of her teachers. How could so much go so wrong so quickly I thought as I hung up the phone? Ellen had apparently snuck out of the dorm. She was caught drinking with some other students primarily with the boys. I don't know if this was the first time but it was definitely the last time.

I was in a panic. I had no idea what I would do with her. She couldn't live at home. Even though more than a year and a half had passed since she was sent away, she was still so full of anger and rage it just spilled out into everything she did and said. Before she went to military school she engaged in such incredibly destructive behavior I can't even begin to describe all of it. Ellen would do whatever she wanted. She was disrespectful and even hostile to everyone. She refused to go to school. She did drugs. She would be out all night and sleep all day. She hung around with the most unsavory people. She would scream at me and call me names. I just didn't think I could live like that again. I think she improved a little at school but coming home always seemed to bring out the worst in her. She could hold it together for a little while at home but then her behavior would deteriorate after just a few weeks of being around us or should I say me. I concluded that she just hated me or loathed me might be a better way to describe it. I tried a variety of methods but at the end of the day I had no idea how to get along with her.

I am not proud to say that I shuffled her off to another program. This program was comprised of psychological therapy and behavior modification. She could also get a high school diploma. Maybe she could exorcise her demons there I thought. I felt oftentimes that she was "possessed by demons." Ellen had been the sweetest and most loving of my children. Then she became the most vicious and evil. It was almost as if someone flipped a switch. It was as if she became a totally different person at around the age of 12. I never really knew if there was a psychiatric component to her behavior since after just a few visits she refused to return to the psychologist or psychiatrist.

"Ellen could you please unlock the bathroom door so Teresa can use the bathroom". I said as I pounded on Ellen's bedroom door. Teresa was my stepdaughter who was with us for her summer visitation. The bathroom connected to Ellen's bedroom and to the hallway. I tried to open the door to Ellen's room. It was locked. I knew she was inside. Ellen didn't respond to my pleas to unlock the bathroom door. I guess we made some progress I thought to myself. At least Ellen didn't scream or swear at me. I guess she did make some progress at the behavior modification program.

Ellen has progressed slowly since her return at 18 from her final program. She attended junior college and graduated from a four year university. Her behavior and attitude have improved tremendously over time but she is still Ellen and I still love her.

"Have you spoken to your father recently?" I asked Jessica. Jessica is now a young woman with a child of her own. "No I stopped calling him or taking his calls. Having him in my life really didn't add anything. He was always tries to blame you for the fact that he didn't have any contact with us for 10+ years. I know that isn't true. Ellen feels the same way." "I am sorry to hear that," is all I could think to say. Jessica has always been good at setting limits on people.

Is it nurture? Is it nature? If only we knew the answer it would relieve us parents of some much guilt. I have read some of the psychological writings on this subject looking perhaps to vindicate myself. My ideas have changed over the years. I have recently concluded that children come into the world with their personality already mapped out. Gary, who has grown up with little or no contact with his father definitely exhibits some of his behaviors. I think we can or events can cause a great deal of damage but we can't otherwise change their basic personalities. How they deal with those events will depend on who they are or "how they do themselves" as one psychologist used to say.

Believing this doesn't alleviate my guilt for all the wrongs I inflicted on my children as their parent. It doesn't wash way the guilt for the fact that, at critical times in their development, I had very little time or energy to devote to them or that I was a very lousy mother for many, many years. It does bring me some peace though. I am not 100% responsible for who they will or have become. It is a huge burden and maybe a bit arrogant of us to believe we have all the power regarding the formation of our children.

I find I fight with my children less because I no longer take full responsibility for what they do or who they have become. I don't have to prove to myself or anyone else that I am a "good" parent. I bowed out of the competition long ago not because I was wise or because I wanted to but because I had to. I couldn't compete with children like Ellen and Samuel. I felt alienated, isolated and a total failure because I had children with those problems.

Now I am grateful that I have had these struggles with my children. Grateful may be too strong a word but let's say I wouldn't undo it. Sure I wish I could have had a lot fewer issues with Samuel and Ellen but I am still thankful it happened. My ego got out of the way of my child rearing. I started thinking more about what was best for them and how I could help them and less about how their behavior reflected upon me or affected me.

In dealing with all of this I have become a much better parent and a much better person. I think my children have become much better people in the process and will be much better parents as well. Our connection to each other was definitely forged and strengthened by all we have been through together.

I try to guide them now. I try to help them to make good decisions and choices. But in the end, especially, as they mature, it is all up to them – who they become. What they become is not a reflection of what I did or who I am. I can't take all, or perhaps any, credit and I can't take all the blame. When we are young parents we are convinced that everything we do will have an effect on who they become as adults. It is all up to us alone. Eventually it boils down to them making choices about who they want to be. I think I fought so hard with them because I saw their choices and circumstances as a failure on my part. I thought if I had been a better parent they would not have these issues. I now realized that a lot of their issues are a result of how they respond to situations and some of that is just a function of who they are. I still bear some of the responsibility but not all of it.

"I have not been a very good parent." I confessed to Jessica. It had taken me months, years to get up the courage to say that to her.

She was a young adult at the time. I think I lacked the maturity to say it earlier but also I was afraid I would lose some of my parental authority if I did. How wrong I was to think that!

I felt like I had given them a crappy life and for a number of years I tried to make it up to them by overindulging them with material things. My generation has, I think, tried to compensate with our own children for the perceived failings of our parents. We have become slaves to our children's happiness. Everything, including our marriages, is sacrificed to see that our children are "happy." Children and their "needs" drive the household. Parents become emotionally and financially bankrupt giving their kids everything we think we didn't have. We think this makes us superior to our parents. I started doing this after Brian died. On some level I think I realized what I was doing but I couldn't stop it.

Acknowledging my failings to my children and asking for their forgiveness was one of the most liberating things I have ever done. It brought us so much closer. An unintended benefit was that they are now able to talk to me about their "failings" and mistakes rather than hiding them and making excuses. We can help each other because the walls have come down. I no longer pretend to be a "perfect" parent and the no longer pretend to be "perfect" children.

Why do we feel as parents that we have to maintain this image with our kids that we are above making a mistake – that we are perfect? I found, much too late, that admitting mistakes makes us stronger in the eyes of our children because we earn so much respect from them in doing so. As a bonus we set a great example for them on how to behave. I think it helped them become more forgiving of their own mistakes and faults as well.

"Ellen got expelled from the military school! She is hopeless. There is nothing else you can do for her." my Dad said angrily. I was shocked to hear this from my Father. He is so patient and loving. But I was thinking exactly the same thing when he said it. It is an option I said to myself. I have my Father's permission to write Ellen off – to give up and simply walk away from this problem child. But it was at that moment that I also realized I couldn't do that.

Perhaps I had done everything before this out of a sense of duty or a sense that good parents do these things. I don't think I had done anything out of love for Ellen for a very long time. It was exactly when I had "permission" or the option to give up that I realized I didn't want to. I couldn't give up on my children. As I found out later it was a turning point for both Ellen and me. She realized that I did love her because I didn't give up on her in that moment. I was finally able to give her what she needed – maybe – unconditional love. Isn't that the single most important characteristic of a good parent? That is the hard part – the unconditional part. Unconditional love is different from unconditional acceptance of behaviors. I understood that distinction as well by then.

"Mom you were never a bad parent" Jessica simply said. "Thankfully you have a poor memory" I responded. Jessica laughed and hugged me. I wasn't seeking absolution from my children. Oh they know I made huge mistakes. When they recite the stories of their childhood there are some that cause me to cringe when I hear what I did. What Jessica meant is that she knew that I always loved her. I wanted so to be different from my mother. I never felt loved by her. That is the one gift that I wanted to give them. It seems I may have accomplished that.

"Mom, Darren and I are moving out of state. We would like you to move there as well" Jessica said to me one day when she had come for a visit. I was shocked that she was moving. I was flattered that she would want me to live there as well. Since she went to college we had lived in different states or different parts of the same, large state. I have to admit I was a little apprehensive as to how it would work. I thought she asked me to go because she felt sorry for me. It turned out I was wrong.

"I'm pregnant." Jessica, my oldest daughter, told me. "This baby will be like Gary" she said. I instinctively knew what she meant. This baby will have a whole army of people who love and adore him/her not only through phone calls and infrequent visits but daily interaction. I didn't realize until then that Jessica appreciated and understood how wonderful the love of a family could be. After all there was a world of difference between her childhood and Gary's. She wasn't bitter or resentful at all when she said it. She sounded genuinely happy and satisfied that she could offer the same upbringing Gary had to her child. Now I fully understood why she invited me to live near her. Jessica "got it". She understood. There is absolutely no way to describe all I felt when she said that to me. Maybe the cycle has been broken. Maybe we have created a loving family unit. All the struggles and heartache of those difficult parenting years just melted away. I finally understood that love is a gift. I hope I gave it to my children and that they can, in turn, give it to their children.

I'm going to do a standup comedy act," Gary told me. He was about 12 at the time. "Are you sure you want to do that?" I asked. "What if the audience doesn't laugh at your jokes?" "I'll have to write new material then" he said." I was on pins and needles as he came on to the stage to perform a comedy routine that he had written. It happened! Gary told a joke. No one laughed. I looked over at the audience. I was afraid to look at Gary. I looked at Gary on the stage. He laughed. "I guess no one thought that was funny," he said to the audience. He proceeded to tell his next joke and everyone laughed this time. He knows that whatever happens he has the unconditional love and support of his family.

Gary has, for the most part, been surrounded by love. Gary is also just a good person. He seemed to come into the world that way. He is a loving, compassionate, intelligent, grounded kid who has amazing self confidence. If someone doesn't like him he just accepts it and moves on. If he is defeated in anything he resolves to do better next time and moves on. I struggle with those issues to this day. How wonderful that he does not!

It is one of the ironies of life that when we finally figure out how to be good parents we stop having children. I was lucky to have practiced and learned a lot before I had Gary. I set firm guidelines and discipline but he has made good choices for himself. It is a joint effort I think. I have had a lot of help from his siblings especially now that we live in the same neighborhood. They are a sounding board for me and for Gary. He gets lots of love and support from his family. In fact we all do.

Children need our love the most when they deserve it the least my Father always said. Maybe the same can be said of parents. This has been a long hard journey and I still have my huge struggles and failures even with all that I now know. It is difficult to find a balance between discipline and love – being tough and being loving. It is a constant struggle especially when your children are teenagers.

I don't seem to have to set rules or enforce them with Gary. He just seems to know and respect the limits. In that sense I am very fortunate. I think it is a good thing to have your children feel a little afraid of you or at least of the consequences you may impose. I am amazed how easily I move between what were the traditional roles of father and mother. It all just flows.

My current challenge is to start letting go of Gary. The separation has started. My talkative, engaging son is now a silent hulk. I catch myself getting hurt by Gary's silence and withdrawal. I lash out or try to manipulate him. I stop myself fairly quickly now. That type of behavior is so wrong and only serves to push him farther away. Can I weather this again? I think so. I know Gary has to have his independence. I also know that the love we all have for Gary will bring him back to us and he will realize that you can be both independent and part of a loving family. His older siblings have shown him how to do that.

As adults my children are each on their own journey. I tried to give them a good start. I don't think I did a very good job but I hope I get an A for effort. One thing I think I did do right is that I never gave up on them. Somehow I believed the power of my love would pull them back to the right path. Maybe it did. Maybe it didn't. Whatever forces were at work they are all on the right path now. Oh none of them are slated to make millions of dollars or win the Nobel Peace prize but to me they are all noble laureates. Could it or should it be any other way?

Having adult children is the most wonderful experience in the world because now life will mete out the consequences and teach the lessons. I don't have to. I can stand by them, love them, try to guide them and perhaps give some advice but my role is no longer one of disciplinarian. How liberating! As the parent of adults I have to be constantly vigilant that I do not overstep my boundaries - interfere, expect too much or offer too much advice. I try to be "present" for them – providing what it is they need from me at any particular time if I can.

My children and I are just ordinary people. We don't pretend to be anything else. It seems everyone these days wants to brag about themselves and their children. I often wonder if we are the only family that can't tout some amazing achievement or doesn't have any exceptional talent. I don't remember ever setting out to try to raise a "successful "child in the material sense. I understood my job to be to help each of my children to become the person they wanted to be. That of course included, as a given, a moral, compassionate, caring, loving, accepting, socially responsible, productive human being. I am proud to say I think all four of my children are those things and much more although each to a different degree. When did that stop being enough? I am disappointed in myself when I find I fell chagrined that my children don't have jobs or professions in which they make tons of money or don't have some spectacular artistic talent. Then I remember what really matters. They are all good people. I am free of the weight of the expectation of the world to produce "successful" offspring. I am no longer, thankfully, a competitor.

"You are a wonderful mother, I said to Jessica. "I had a good example –you" Jessica said to me. How fortunate that she was able to see me parent Gary. Being a parent to Gary was my chance at redemption as a parent. We can all escape the memory of me as the single, over worked, stressed out, exhausted, and sometimes verbally abusive mother of three young children. I was a terrible mother to them especially during that time –their formative years. But fortunately that has been replaced with the parent I have become. Maybe it is possible to break the cycle of abuse. I think we may have done it. I hope we can keep it that way for future generations.

We are all still who we are – the children and I. There was no miracle transformation of any of us. We still fight and disagree. I have learned that the best way to effect change in others is to change yourself. Of course I often forget that lesson in the heat of things. We have a strong bond or connection that we all know can never be severed. People marvel at how close we all are. Maybe the bond or connection is stronger in us as a family unit because it was tested so by our circumstances. We know, first hand, its resiliency and its strength. We treasure it. We rely on it. The enjoyment of the events of life is heightened because we enjoy them together. The hardships in life are easier to bear because we face them together. Maybe this is the secret of the "good" marriages – the love stories as well. I never in my wildest dreams imagined this could happen to me. I felt such an emptiness and longing my whole life. I have been lonely my whole life. Now I am part of a loving family. The longing is satisfied. The emptiness is gone. It can happen even for someone like me with all my problems and unhealthy and even destructive behaviors. We are truly a family. Life really doesn't get any better than this.

"Your son is dead" the police detective told her. They are sitting in the women's grimy apartment when she receives the news. "He has left you a lot of money. You can get out of this place and away from your abusive husband now" the detective continues. The woman is silent staring at the floor. She shows no emotion when she is told of the money. The detective continues "You can use the money to make a better life for yourself". The woman finally speaks, "It won't bring my son back. I gave up on my son. How does a mother do that – give up on her son?" she desperately asks the detective. He of course has no answer. It is clear that nothing can erase this mother's torment and pain. I feel her pain. I almost made the same mistake.

I really didn't appreciate it when Ellen said it to me. It was one of those things the significance of which is hidden because it is said on a regular day during such a regular conversation. "You never gave up on me," Ellen told me. "That is what got me through all of this – the fact that you never gave up on me or stopped loving me," she continued. I hugged her silently. Maybe I should forgive myself. Maybe I shouldn't see myself as a total failure as a parent after all. In spite of all my mistakes I have four wonderful children to whom I feel deeply connected. I have so much to celebrate and so much to be thankful for.

225

CHAPTER NINE

I Am the Breadwinner?

"Are you married? Do you have any children? How many? What are their ages? Who takes care of the children while you are at work? What do you do when your child is sick? What does your husband do for a living?" the interviewer shot the questions off in a rapid fire manner reminding me of a firing squad. I answered each one honestly and just as rapidly giving no explanation. He wasn't the first or last interviewer to ask me those questions. I remember thinking how hard I had worked to obtain all this education and how everything boiled down to whether I had children.

"You were naïve to answer those questions. It is illegal to ask them," my friend, to whom I was relating this story, said indignantly and angrily. Was I naive or was I a realist regarding the job market of those times? What could I really have done about it? I did think about lying but what good would that have done me. It is not like I could hide the fact that I had three young children for very long. What was the alternative? This was 1982 in the rust belt at the time of the first exodus of women law school graduates into the job market. I responded simply to my friend, "You haven't looked for work in really dire economic times, have you?"

You see I never really dreamed of being a lawyer. I had a few dreams of accomplishment when I was in high school but I allowed those to be smashed and never replaced them. I fell into going to law school. I saw it as a good way to make a living to help support my family. At that time I really wanted to stay home and be with my children. In many ways I am glad I didn't get what I wished for.

We were having lunch one day. The summer law clerks were getting to know each other. "What does your husband do for a living?" asked one of the other clerks. My husband did not have a glamorous or well paying job. I answered the question. "He is supporting you through law school so he can retire when you graduate," was the response from him. At the time I thought that was a pretty cynical view of marriage. Sadly it turned out that he was very intuitive.

I was always good at school. I thought those skills would really help me succeed in the legal field. Those academic skills were of a great use in the legal field when I first started out. That is not true anymore. Now I think they are more of a detriment. The legal field is considered to be a "profession". I looked up the word "profession" in a dictionary to see if perhaps I was expecting too much when I used that word. Maybe I should have looked that word up 31 years ago. The first two definitions relate to religion. The fourth definition refers to "a calling requiring specialized knowledge and training and often long and intensive academic training".

I was under the impression that the term "profession" as applied to the practice of law and other fields meant the work was about more than just making money. It included an element of service to the public. Perhaps with the use of "calling" the dictionary implies that. I really believed that I could help people, do some good and make a living all at the same time. I wanted to help people solve their legal problems and maybe along the way find some justice. After spending 27 years in this profession I can say things definitely did not work out that way for me.

"Can you type? Do you know shorthand? Do you know your alphabet well enough to be able to file documents accurately? Are you willing to take a typing and general skills test?" asked the representative at the temporary employment agency. I was about 7 months pregnant and they were the only place that wouldn't care about that. "Could you send me to a law firm if possible?" I asked. I didn't tell her why. I didn't want her to know that I had just graduated from law school and couldn't find a job.

The employment agency placed me in a job. I answered phones. I typed. I filed documents. I kept track of the attorneys' calendars. After a few months I left to have my third child. "Call me after you have the baby and we will see if we have some work for you as a lawyer," the senior partner told me. A few weeks after the baby was born I called him. He hired me. At my first job as a lawyer I was nothing more than a glorified clerk making $8.00 an hour three days a week. I was grateful. Silly because I don't think the pay even covered my child care expenses but I thought it would lead to something better. Finances were a huge issue for my husband and I but I had to start somewhere, didn't I?

"I told you she was pretty. Pregnancy makes you swell and retain water," the senior partner said to the junior partner as I sat in his office. This was my first day on the job as a "lawyer" and I was being welcomed to the law firm.

I wasn't treated with very much respect especially by the legal secretaries. Laurie, the senior secretary, refused to talk to me and refused to do any work for me. I would ask her a question and she would turn her back on me and walk out of the room. This happened several times in the presence of the senior partner. He recognized it but said I should just accept it. I never complained to him about it. It wouldn't have done any good. Anyway, I needed a job and some experience.

"I want you to represent the client in court tomorrow morning. It is a simple matter but it is a good way to get some experience," the junior partner said as he handed me the case file. I was so excited. I was going to make my first court appearance. That next morning the lawyers were waiting outside the courtroom for the bailiff to open the doors. Most of the other lawyers were staring at me. One of the other lawyers standing next to me started talking to me. "Are you new?" he asked. "Yes. This is my first court appearance," I confessed. "Welcome! It is really great to have you gals here doing family law work," he said kindly. "Thank you," I replied. Should I have told him I wasn't making a court appearance on a family law matter?

My generation was raised believing that all we needed to be successful was to work hard and do a good job. Performance and hard work would be noticed and rewarded. We would be offered jobs because of it. We would be promoted because of it. We would get raises because of it. Or so we thought. I didn't need a career plan. My hard work would bring success. That concept is so outdated that I laugh now as I write it. But in the early 80s that didn't seem so naive. Naive is a word you don't hear much these days but when you do it seems to be equated with stupidity. We operate in the "real world" now. For a long time I felt like I was the dumbest person in the world for believing in that myth. I was fortunate to find others like me – a few at least and then I didn't feel quite so stupid. They were people of similar age and background to me.

"I am leaving the firm to go out on my own," Stanley said. He is finally going to do it I thought to myself. Stanley was smart, very competent, very hard working, very knowledgeable and very humble. He was the "firm". After 19 years he finally left to go out on his own. I was surprised he had hung around so long. I guess he finally got tired of making money for the senior partner who rarely worked. Stanley was never financially rewarded for his hard work. But that is Ok isn't it? It was, after all, his own fault for not demanding more money and recognition, wasn't it? Stanley was a rarity. In my experience that is a role typically reserved for women but I guess there are exceptions to every rule.

"I have seen many attorneys spend a lot more hours at the office than you but I have never seen anyone work as hard as you when they are here," the senior partner said to me. By this time I had moved from the rust belt to a city in the southwest. I was working as an attorney in a small law firm. I worked like a maniac from the minute I got in the door until I left. I churned out the work and the billable hours. I rarely ate lunch and rarely socialized. I didn't think I had any choice. If I wanted to keep my job that is. I had to compensate somehow for the fact that I couldn't stay longer hours and I couldn't work longer hours if I wanted to spend any time with my children. I usually left the office about 6 pm. I did stay late a few times to see what I was missing out on. I wanted to be sure I was somehow compensating during the day for the extra hours I didn't put in at night. As soon as the staff left, the lawyers started to socialize. There wasn't any work really being done. Every now and then one of the lawyers would say he had to run to his office to finish something he had failed to finish earlier that day.

I was angry that pressure was put on me to stay late when I know there wasn't a lot of work being done in those extra hours. I guess by staying late a person was making a statement that the job was the most important thing in that person's life and they would sacrifice anything to please the higher ups. I never scored those points with my employers. I tried but I could never bring myself to sacrifice time with my children to shoot the shit with a bunch of guys I really didn't like. In reality I'm not sure they wanted me there but they wanted me to think they did. That way when it came time to negotiate raises they could hold that against me. They never said it but they didn't have to. I was angry because I knew my failure to stay late had nothing to do with the quantity or the quality of the work I did. Yet it was still held against me.

I resented the fact that the people who spent the most time at the office got rewarded, as a general rule, in the business world. Those persons were not necessarily more productive, knowledgeable or valuable. Shouldn't we reward loyalty, productivity, knowledge and not just long hours? I know one is much easier to measure than the others.

I often took work home in the evenings. I always met my deadlines. But I was still definitely an outsider because I didn't stay long hours into the evening at the office or come in on the weekends. I would have earned brownie points if I did that. I just couldn't do it even though I know that it cost me dearly. I did earn some brownie points by being the dumpee of all of the work the partners didn't get done on time, didn't want to do or had made mistakes on. As a woman I was expected to show an attitude of appreciation for having been given a job. I showed my appreciation by working harder than my male counterparts. I had to prove myself in more ways than males who had three children. There was an attitude of paternalism as well on the part of the two senior partners. I didn't find that offensive at first.

There were other benefits to hiring a mother with three young children. I was paid less than my male counterpart and I did more work than he did. I know the partners in the law firm in the Southwest were acutely aware of that. I think it is one reason they hired me. But I wouldn't know that until much later. I was just glad to have a job, any job. I never felt like I got less responsibility or I was viewed as less capable by the two partners in the firm. I was thankful for that. At least I was getting some good experience. And I would get annual raises after a knock down drag out fight. The two partners and I would square off in the small conference room and the "negotiation" would begin. There were never any hard feelings afterwards. That is just how they did business with everyone. Being treated equally in other areas at the firm and elsewhere was a different matter.

"I thought when you asked me all those questions about my children and my husband you weren't going to hire me," I said to one of the senior partners at the new firm in the southwest. I had been working there for 6 months by this time. He responded honestly, "It was a huge consideration in the hiring process. We were very worried but we decided with you it wouldn't make a difference. I am glad to see we were right". I remember thinking that this was an improvement of sorts from my first job searching experiences where I didn't even get a chance once they found out I had three children. At least I was being judged on my own merits instead of being written off simply as a mother with three small children. On one level I understood the reluctance of the small law firm to hire a young woman. At a small firm if one lawyer is absent there is not a team to cover for her. It means the other lawyers in the small firm have to stretch themselves to cover her work.

"Come into the judge's chambers. He will conduct the pre-trial conference in there," the bailiff informed us. Opposing counsel and I entered the judge's chambers. The judge was seated at his desk. We sat down in the chairs facing the judge. The judge was looking at what appeared to be the case file when we entered. Without looking up he said, "This is the time set for the pre-trial conference." He looked up from his desk directly at me. "Trial counsel was ordered to appear at this conference," he said rather angrily. "I am trial counsel, your honor," I replied. "You can't be," was the icy response. I sheepishly sat down. The judge was definitely not pleased. The trial was set to begin in a few weeks.

"I am in the early months of my pregnancy. I may have to ask to take breaks more often to visit the restroom," I said to another judge in chambers before the trial started. "We will take our regularly scheduled breaks and no more," he responded. This conversation took place about 8 years later. Things hadn't changed much at least in some courtrooms. I wasn't off to a good start with this trial judge. Things got worse.

"The objection is sustained," the judge said firmly. "May we approach the bench?" I asked. The judge reluctantly agreed. "Your honor we laid the proper foundation for the photographs. We can't introduce any more of a foundation than we already did. Why won't you admit them into evidence?" I asked. "Are you done?" the judge said icily. "You have sustained every one of opposing counsel's objections," I continued. Before I could say anything else the judge said, "My ruling stands. Let's resume the trial". It was just as well. I was afraid to challenge him any further. I thought I had pushed him far enough that day.

I was angry. I expected that that I would have to comply with every procedural rule and evidentiary rule perfectly but I had done that and he still wouldn't admit my evidence. Without these photographs I really didn't have much of a case. That night, after the trial ended for the day, I hired a photographer to take additional photos. I stayed up very late preparing this new exhibit to make it "pretty" for the judge. I presented the photos the next day at trial and offered them into evidence. "Admitted," was all the judge said. He had a very smug look on his face. This exhibit was no different that the first set of photos. The judge just wanted to make me jump through some hoops and see if I could handle the pressure.

"I didn't think you could do it," the judge said to me in chambers at the end of the trial. I think he meant make it through the trial. I think even defense counsel started to feel sympathetic toward me by the end of the trial. He didn't feel sympathetic enough not to take advantage of the situation. It was a long trial and I don't mean the number of days.

He was not the first or last judge who held me to impossible standards and made things more difficult for me than my male counterpart.

It took a lot of energy to navigate the competing demands of clients, bosses, judges, and opposing counsel. I learned early on that being too assertive or demanding would just make the judge or opposing counsel angry and backfire. At some level I had to engage in some socially acceptable female conduct. The expectation was different with each judge or opposing counsel. How I wished I could just show up and be a guy - an assertive advocate for my client. Oh sure they had to tailor their argument to the particular judge. But at least they didn't have to tailor their personality in order to be heard. Most judges expected some level of subservience or attitude of deference – kind of being grateful to them for allowing you – a woman – to be in his courtroom.

"I take one of the male partners with me to court whenever I am arguing an important motion," the female attorney said to me. "It greatly increases my chances of winning or at least of having a decision made based on the merits of my motion," she continued. She didn't seem bitter about that. I believed things would change with the passage of time and as the number of female lawyer and judges increased. I guess I was wrong. Apparently in some jurisdictions not much has changed in the past 27 years. I hoped this situation was limited to this particular jurisdiction. I was relieved that I had not imagined that I was being treated unfairly in many courtrooms because of my gender.

It wasn't only male judges who were prejudiced against women. A few cases I tried there were multiple defendants and therefore multiple lawyers. Several times I made objections or argued positions which she denied or rejected. Then my male co-counsel would stand up and say exactly the same thing I had said. She would sustain that objection or agree to his position. I think women believe that men simply know more or are better at what they do than we women are. Maybe we are socialized to believe that. I find myself doing the same thing to this day. I have to force myself to overcome that prejudice.

Should I say something or not? I really needed this job especially now. I could not afford to be fired. Would I be able to hide the situation from them? If I could hide it would I be better off? After weeks of agony, and I didn't need any more of that, I finally decided I needed to tell them. I was raised with "honesty is always the best policy" although I have come, at times, to doubt the wisdom of that teaching. In this situation it turned out to be a good decision because, right after I told them, the partners were served with a subpoena in the divorce action.

I didn't get the response I was expecting when I told them although I am not sure what I was expecting. "If we thought you might be getting a divorce we never would have hired you. Employees going through a divorce are always less productive and bring a lot of angst into the office," said one partner. The other partner continued, "Who is going to help with your kids now? How are you going to work here as a single mother of three children?" He was very angry.

Well at least I didn't get fired I thought. I knew there was absolutely no way I could let my personal issues or any issues with my children interfere with my work. I wouldn't be able to take any time off. I wouldn't have vacation for a while as I had to complete one year of employment before I could get one week of paid vacation. They watched me like a hawk for a while after that to make sure that my personal and child rearing issues did not interfere with my productivity. The pressure at the office was, at times, overwhelming. I was in no position to complain.

"Do you have a place I can leave Jessica next week? She has to have oral surgery to have 12 teeth removed. I can't miss any work to stay home with her", I said to the administrator at the summer day camp she was attending. "We can set up a cot for her in the room adjacent to my office," she replied. On the appointed day I dropped Jessica off at the summer camp with her mouth swollen and stuffed with gauze. I laid her on the cot. Jessica didn't complain about staying at the summer camp. She was always such a trooper. As I laid her down she was still sleepy from the medication. "Hopefully the medication they gave her and the pain medication will allow her to sleep all day until I pick her up", I said to myself. As I drove to the office I felt overwhelmed by worry about Jessica and guilt over what a terrible mother I was. I believed I was the worst mother in the world that day or should I say especially on that day. I think I always felt like that back then. It is just that some days the guilt was worse than others. This was definitely one of those days.

"Matt says he is too busy to handle these files. I would like you to handle them," one of the partners said as he laid the files on my desk. This happened regularly. Matt, the other associate, would complain that he was overworked. The partners accepted that from him with no questions asked. "I already have way too many cases to handle them effectively. I can't take on another matter and do a good job," I replied. The partner left my office without taking the files.

"I can't handle one more file! I am already handling over 150 matters," I exploded the next day. I slammed my hand down on a coffee cup breaking the cup and cutting my hand. The partner didn't leave the files in my office that day but eventually they found their way back one by one. I guess he figured my mood would pass. You see I should be grateful that I had a job - a divorcee with three young children to support. I knew they were right. I knew there were not a lot of options out there for me. They knew that too.

I know because I had been looking for another position as an associate attorney. I had been sending out resumes to inquires in our local legal paper. The recipients were not disclosed. The resumes were mailed to P.O. boxes. Sometime during this process one of the partners came into my office, closed the door and sat down. "If I find out you are looking for another job I will fire you!" he growled at me. He was angry. There was no doubt about that. I remained silent. He continued, "My friend said he received a copy of your resume in response to an ad he placed seeking a new associate attorney. "Don't ever do that again!" he shouted as he stormed out of my office. The advertisements all contained language that all inquires would be confidential. I guess that meant if you weren't a friend of the partner at the firm where the job seeker was already employed. I couldn't afford to lose my job. I stopped looking. I was really trapped now. At least I felt that way.

I was paid less than the male associate at the firm. I understand that is not unusual. Are we women partly to blame for the situation? I know I was. Do we place too low a value on ourselves and our abilities? Are we afraid if we ask for too much the client or customer will simply go elsewhere? Maybe they are only willing to do business with a woman if she is cheaper than her male counterpart? Are we afraid to find out if that is true? Does the same apply to employers? Do some people actually capitalize on that by hiring women because they know they can get the same or better work out of them at less than the cost of a male employee?

I have met a few women who had phenomenal confidence in their abilities and they achieved great things. They didn't seem to suffer from any self doubt. I wasn't one of them. I have met very few in my cadre of contemporaries. I, for one, am guilty of all of the above. I felt lucky to have a job as a single mother of three young children. I wasn't going to rock the boat or make any demands. If I was fired I knew it would be difficult, if not impossible, to find another position and if I did I doubted things would be any better there.

"I have something I would like to discuss with the two of you. Can we meet sometime this week?" I asked the two partners. The three of us sat down in the conference room a few days later. I wasn't particularly worried about what I was going to ask. I had been with the firm for five years. I had won a lot of tough cases at trial. I made the firm a lot of money. I was rarely absent. I worked like a maniac when I was at the office. I put out a respectable number of billable hours for a small firm. The clients liked me. I was starting to enjoy a good reputation in the legal community in general. I had been a lawyer for seven years by this time.

"I would like to work 20 to 30 hours per week so I can spend more time with my children and my new husband," I said. After several months I realized that my marriage was not going to make it with both of us engaged in very demanding professions. I also felt like I was losing my oldest daughter to bad influences. She had just started 7th grade. I wanted to have some time so I could enjoy my life and my family rather than just seeing everything as a burden or responsibility. Throughout my employment there the partners had expressed a personal interest in me although I thought sometimes it was a bit misplaced. They were a bit paternalistic toward me. I thought my employers would understand my request and I thought I had earned that concession. I didn't expect to be paid the same.

"We think you should stay home full time with your children," one of them said. Wouldn't you rather do that than work?" the other partner asked. I was taken aback.

I was not going to ask Brian to support my children and I had worked hard to get where I was. I didn't want to give all of that up. To my surprise and elation they agreed to the reduced work schedule. We discussed the revised expectations for me and negotiated a huge reduction in salary.

"I wish I could work only 30 hours a week," the one partner would occasionally complain to me after I was working reduced hours. Was he kidding or really resentful I remember thinking. He has to be kidding I said to myself. After all he is very well of financially and could work less whenever he wants to I remember thinking. Aside from his comments, the transition was fairly uneventful until the day, a few months later, when they called me into the conference room and fired me.

I showed up for work the next day but I really couldn't talk to either of the partners. I closed my office door and worked. Someone knocked at the door. I didn't want to open it in case it was one of the two partners. I was still too upset to talk rationally about any of this. Before I could respond to the knock, Margie, the receptionist, buzzed me on the intercom, "Kathy wants to talk to you. She is waiting at your door."

"Come in," I said to Kathy. I was rather surprised she wanted to talk to me. It wasn't that we didn't like each other. This was a small office so we all knew each other and we all got along fairly well. I liked the fact that there was an office policy of zero tolerance for gossip. Kathy worked for one of the partners. Kathy came in and sat down. "I am so angry that I had to come in and talk to you. The partners placed an ad looking for an attorney to replace you right after they "agreed" to your reduced work schedule. I have been opening resumes, fielding phone calls and setting up interviews for the last few months. They hired your replacement last week," she said.

When I calmed down a bit I was able to confront one of the partners. "What was the problem with the reduced work schedule?" I asked him He didn't respond. "Was there a problem with my billable hours? Was there any problem with the quality of my work?" I asked. He still did not respond. "We think you should stay home with your children now that you are remarried," he responded. I stayed at the office for two more weeks. I left without telling them where I was going even though they asked me repeatedly. They assumed I would be staying home with my children.

I often wondered why the two partners were so adamant that I stay home with my children. When their wives came into the office it was obvious that they didn't have much respect for them. That was a common attitude back then. Husbands and society, at that time, put a lot of pressure on women to stay home with their children. When the children were grown and they wanted to return to the work force there was no place for them. They were rejected by the business community. I observed that their husband and children often treated them like they were a source of annoyance. I often wondered if those women felt betrayed. I know I would have.

For my part I, like most working mothers at the time, resented stay at home moms. I resented them for all the things they had that I did not have – like free time and financial support. I regret that now. I think they resented us working mothers for all they perceived we had that they did not – like respect and control over our lives. It was an insurmountable barrier to friendship. It wasn't a huge issue, personally, because I had no time for friendships back then anyway.

Sadly we women had some much to offer each other but we didn't. We focused on what divided us rather than what united us. We were entrenched in our enemy camps. We were after all mortal enemies. At the heart of the battle was the conviction by stay at home moms that only full time mothers could raise successful, well adjusted children and have successful marriages. I think they feared that all they had sacrificed would be in vain if working moms could do the same. Their choices and existence were only justified if they produced better results than the working mothers. Their primary sources of respect were their children and the financial success of their husbands. Success in children was measured by academic and athletic achievement and conforming behavior. If working mothers could do it too what was left for them? How could they justify their choice?

As a working mother I felt a huge burden of guilt and hopelessness. How could I possibly compete with full time mothers? My sense of hopelessness was compounded by the fact that I was a single parent. I was angry at them because their life seemed so much easier than mine. As I have matured I realized it really wasn't but I didn't understand that back then when my children were very young. Their choices came with price tags just as mine did. How I wish I could have been aware of that back then. We might have been able to find some common ground and some connection.

I tried to cope with some of the male chauvinism, in those early days, by reminding myself that the majority of the men with whom I was interacting had stay at home wives. These men did not have an image of a woman as capable in the business world and certainly not in a demanding profession like law. They felt threatened by us on many levels. Part of their self image was based on the belief that they were superior to women at least in the business world. We couldn't possibly be as competent as a man. Some of their hostility stemmed from the same source as their wives.

After I was divorced many of the male lawyers would look at me with a look of pity or self righteousness as if to say, "I guess she couldn't get or keep a husband because she is such a bitch." Ouch!

For a number of years I certainly never wanted to be called the ultimate insult - a bitch and so I tried to please and placate my male opponents and co workers. I naively thought if I appeased them they would stop being so difficult and confrontational. I found out the exact opposite was true. It wasn't until I started to stand up to them and give back the treatment they dished out that I started to be treated with respect. That was a valuable lesson for me to learn and one that I needed to learn. But it can be difficult to turn off that confrontational attitude in other parts of your life.

As a woman you didn't want to be tough, assertive and demanding in your personal life. Those are traditionally male qualities, not female ones. In the personal arena exhibiting those qualities usually backfired. I would have to tone myself down for parent teacher conferences or even interaction with stay at home mothers. If I came off as too assertive, I was labeled as "one of them" and my requests would typically be ignored. So I had to develop two different personalities and remember to use them in the appropriate arena.

I learned to use my commuting time home from the office to change my personality. I would crank up the volume of my radio and sing at the top of my lungs. That seemed to help me decompress and change from being tough, assertive and demanding to exhibiting the more traditional qualities of a mother and wife. I thought, in those days, that was something I needed to do. Quite frankly I still have to be mindful of this issue in certain areas of my life.

"You are a bitch!" opposing counsel said to me. "Thank you," I responded with a smile. As I matured in my profession I relished being called a "bitch". It meant that I was doing my job of representing my client. It was only when I was assertive and refused to yield to the demands of the opposing counsel, that the insults would come. I considered the insults to be a badge of honor. Nothing would make opposing counsel angrier than when I flashed a big grin and thanked them for calling me a "bitch". There was some satisfaction in that.

Sometimes things would get out of hand. The abuse was so bad from some lawyers that I refused to talk to them on the phone or outside the presence of others. At that time, in the late 80s and early 90s, that was the exception rather than the rule.

"Would you please answer the question!" I demanded of the witness. This expert – a man in his 60s – was answering every question with a question accompanied by a hostile and snide look. This had been going on for about an hour. I finally couldn't take it anymore.

"If you weren't so stupid you would know how to ask a good question," he responded. His lawyer had a smirk on his face when he said that. I left the room shaking I was so angry. Bruce, my co-counsel, followed me out of the room, "He is refusing to answer your question and giving you a hard time because you are a woman." Bruce was a rare gem at that time – a lawyer who actually didn't believe women were innately inferior lawyers or maybe he just didn't feel threatened by us. I hadn't even thought of that. I did not want to go around with a chip on my shoulder blaming others perceived sexist attitudes for every difficult situation. I went back into the deposition room. Opposing counsel and I had a very heated discussion. Things got a little bit better afterwards. Opposing counsel knew he was breaking the rules and at some level knew he should stop. If only lawyers these days would do the same.

"F*** Y**" opposing counsel said to me when I challenged him on his interpretation of the law during a deposition. That wasn't the last time he would say it. He was a very big guy. Later on several times he leaned all the way across the table, put his face right in front of mine and said it. He called me stupid, incompetent and a lot of other things during that deposition. The other male attorney was silent. I continued to object to questions, instruct my client not to answer inappropriate questions and tried to remain calm. Oh I was rattled but I didn't want opposing counsel to see it. When the deposition was over I went into my office to hide the fact from the staff that I was shaking. You see this attorney had tried to be my friend in the beginning of the case. We talked about other cases and the law. He even leant me a few books to use. I didn't realize that he was expecting me to roll over on my client in return. I was naïve enough to believe opposing counsel could get along and be friendly and still represent their clients' interests. It made for a much more pleasant experience and created an atmosphere were attorneys could resolve conflicts without fighting and resorting to the courts. I had operated like that in the past. It appears things had changed dramatically in recent years. When I didn't do what this attorney wanted me to do on the case he became a vicious bully.

"I did tell her f*** y*** and I will do it again if necessary," this lawyer said to the judge during the hearing on my motion to appoint a referee to monitor this situation. "Motion denied," the judge said. I can't remember the reasons. The judge simply looked at me like there was nothing he could do. We would have no referee for the depositions. I remember wondering how this type of conduct could be tolerated and even accepted in the legal profession.

The entire legal profession has disintegrated, in my opinion. When I started in this profession women did have to work harder to prove themselves. It made us tougher and that was a good thing, I think. We needed to become tougher. Eventually we earned the respect of the male attorneys and judges by being good at what we did. I don't think that type of a community of mutual respect exists any longer. This has nothing to do with new attorney vs. old attorney or male attorney vs. female attorney. It is a profession that is now controlled and dominated by bullies, liars and cheaters.

It is too tiring and would require too much time to discuss any specifics. These attorneys lie about what information they produced. They lie about what you said to them. They lie about what you did or didn't do. They lie about what they did or didn't do. They lie about the facts and the law. I used to like to say about certain lawyers, "How do you know they are lying – their lips are moving." Now it is more than certain lawyers. Events are manipulated to make you look like the liar and the one obstructing the system. You are always on the defensive.

"I'm retiring early because I am just not good at lying," I heard more than one lawyer say. These dishonest lawyers wear you down. You get tired of fighting with them. You can't get a judge to listen to this stuff. In some sense I don't blame the judges. It must be akin to being a referee in the elementary school yard. How do you know who started it or who is telling the truth? How do you, as the attorney, defend yourself without looking like a whining elementary school kid? It would take more time than judges have to sort any of this out. They don't see lawyers often enough to get a sense of how they practice law. The bullies and liars know that. It is no longer a small community where lawyers can earn a good or bad reputation. These lawyers know there is not going to be any consequence to them or their clients. No one is enforcing the rules. Things are out of control. The winners are the cheaters, liars and bullies.

I used to love practicing law. It was all about facts and law and the skill of the practitioner in eliciting and presenting those facts and applying the applicable law to those facts. How did presentation become manipulation? How did being a good advocate become winning at any price or cost? How has serving our clients been replaced by service to our own bottom line? How can we change any of this? The better question may be do the majority of us want to change it?

I used to wonder how people who engaged in such behavior could live with themselves. Then I realized that using their measuring stick – winning, money and power – they are quite successful and well validated by our society. I remember when personal integrity – wanting to be regarded by your professional peers and colleagues as ethical, knowledgeable of the law, hardworking, representing your client's interests to the best of your ability and a good advocate, were the measuring sticks. My intent is not to glorify the past but rather to express concern for what this type of behavior means for our legal system and our future. It wasn't always like this. Oh that type of lawyers always existed but they were by far the minority. Now it seems that the minority has grown and become the majority.

"We are considering adding an associate attorney to our firm. Right now we have just the three partners. Would you be interested?" Carl asked me. I responded that I might be. His was a very high profile, successful law firm. It would be a good opportunity for me. "I am looking for a place where I can work fewer hours," I told him. "That may be doable," he said. I called him after I was fired from the firm because I wanted to work shorter hours. It was 1990. We met and I was hired. I was scheduled to work 9 to 3, which were the hours my children were in school. The arrangement included no lunch or breaks of any kind and a salary commensurate with a shorter work schedule. This was definitely a dream come true. I could have some time with my family and still work in a field I enjoyed on some challenging cases.

"We just received this letter concerning our client from the State of California. He received medical treatment from the State health care program. They have asserted a lien on the proceeds of the settlement for the cost of those services. I need you to write a letter to the State of California and tell them all the monies have already been disbursed," one of the partners at Carl's firm said. "That isn't true," I replied. "I know that but I want you to tell them that anyway," he responded. "I can't do that," I replied. I got up and left his office. Maybe it was a good thing I didn't have time to think about this before we discussed it. It wasn't the last time this partner would ask me to do something unethical. It wasn't the last time I would refuse. Eventually he just stopped speaking to me at all.

"I 'm going on vacation for three weeks. I need you to cover these court appearances for me. I need you to handle these cases while I am gone," Carl, the senior partner said. "But the client doesn't want me to handle his matter he wants you. He made that very clear last time I handled something on his case," I replied. Carl made no response. He left for his three week vacation.

"I 'm going to play golf today. I need you to cover this matter for me," Bill one Carl's partners said. "I am going to be out of the office this afternoon. I need you to handle some matters for me," the third partner said. "I already am supposed to be in two places at that same time. This would make three places at the same time. I obviously can't do that," I said. He turned to leave the office, "By the way a friend of mine is having some serious personal and professional issues and we are taking over all of his cases. I need you to handle those". "How many are there?" I asked. "I'm not sure but about 100 and they are really in a bad state. Crisis I would say," he replied. None of the files I took over while they were on vacation or out of the office ever made it back to the partners' desks.

"We need to talk," I said to Carl, the senior partner sometime after he returned from his three week vacation. I can't remember how many more times I said that to him. We never had that talk.

How does a woman get heard by her male business associates? They don't seem to respond to polite requests. You are simply ignored. When you get really angry they look at you in a condescending manner like you are suffering from PMS. You are still simply ignored only with more disdain this time.

Brian and I were having some serious marital problems. We had been married a year or so at this time. I guess we were treading water in our relationship. We couldn't seem to make the relationship work but we didn't want to get out of it either. There was a lot of conflict. We separated for a while. We finally agreed to go to counseling. After a few sessions we decided it might be good to go away together without the children. My three children were invited to visit relatives in California over Spring Break. That seemed fortuitous even though it was last minute. There was no one at the firm to discuss this with. The partners were gone on their various golf dates, vacations, etc. One of the partners would be back the week I was gone. I cleared my calendar and headed off for the week with Brian.

"Carl wants to see you right away," Alicia, the receptionist, said. It was Monday morning back at the office after a week of vacation.

The office staff was acting a bit strangely as I put my stuff in my office. I hadn't seen or talked to Carl in about a month since he had been away when I left. Even when he was in town his attendance at the office was sporadic. I went to Carl's office.

"You asked Libby to cover a meeting for you while you were gone. You told opposing counsel on a case that you agreed with him on an issue that is adverse to us," Carl fired off even before I sat down. The rapid fire listing of complaints went on for at least ten minutes. Should I interrupt him to respond to the charges individually I wondered. I was taken aback by the intensity of the attack. I eventually countered every one of the charges and Carl seemed to calm down.

Still I knew this was the beginning of the end. He had made up his mind even before I walked into the room that this was the end of our professional relationship. It hit me totally out of the blue. I was shocked. How could this happen? I was a work horse. I worked from the moment I walked in the door until I left, moving from one task to the next. I didn't socialize, talk on the phone or even go to lunch. I thought I was doing what I was supposed to do – producing work, bringing cases to resolution. I knew my resentment had been building. I couldn't handle the work of four attorneys. I was working a lot more hours than we agreed to. I couldn't get anyone to talk to me about these matters.

"Libby why would you say something like that to Carl? What things have I asked you to do that make you feel uncomfortable? Why didn't you tell me that when I asked you to do it?" I asked her shortly after leaving Carl's office. I was standing in her office. She glared at me. I continued, "Last week all I asked you to do was to cancel the meeting and if you couldn't do it over the phone to please go at the appointed time and reschedule it". Libby glowered and gloated at me. In the middle of my questions she simply walked out of the room. I never spoke to her again.

I was the office pariah after that. No one talked to me – the women didn't at least. They avoided me. Something had been boiling beneath the surface that I had missed. But then I naively avoided office politics. I would do my work and go home. Alicia and Mary Ann were still speaking to me. They told me that the women staffers were jealous of me especially Libby. Libby apparently wanted to be a lawyer but got pregnant and had to drop out of school. Legal assistants are a lawyer's best asset and I treated them accordingly. I guess it wouldn't have made any difference how I treated Libby or any of the other women in the office.

Being a women attorney was a virtual minefield. We had to deal with the issues of sexism and then the issue of competition and jealousy with women. I will never really understand why women do those things to each other? I know I am naïve. Things continued as before except only two staff members were speaking to me now.

"You need to attend this deposition tomorrow morning. I am going to be out of town," Carl, the senior partner said. "That is a really intensely litigated case that is very far along in the proceedings," I replied. "Do you think I should step in at this late date and on such short notice?" I asked Carl. I arrived at opposing counsel's office for the deposition early the next morning.

I was marshaled into the conference room by the receptionist. There were a lot of people already there. I was apparently the last one to arrive. As I entered every face turned to look at me. No one was smiling. No one said hello. No one introduced themselves to me. After a brief, curious glance they turned and continued their conversation deliberately ignoring me. As I looked around the room I was relieved to see there was one other woman in the crowd. She could help me transition into this shark pool I thought. When we took a break I started to walk toward her to introduce myself. She turned in the other direction and joined the group of male attorneys. I was left alone on the other side of the room. As I sat down I caught her glancing over at me. Her look said "I can't help you because if I do they will turn on me and make my life difficult. I am finally one of the group". As the attorneys walked out of the room talking together I sat at the table and looked over my notes. I had no idea where they were going or when they would be back. My inquiries were ignored.

"You are not dedicated enough to the firm," Carl said to me one morning after he called me into the conference room. "What do you mean?" I asked. This time I really didn't give him any time to respond, "I handle everything when you are all out of town even though I have the most inexperienced paralegal and secretary. I handle the cases assigned exclusively to me. I get everything done that needs to be done on time. I don't socialize, talk on the phone or even go to lunch. I do good work. I work at least 40 to 50 hours a week even though I am only supposed to work 30 and I only get paid to work 30. What more can I do? " "Well I am not happy any longer with arrangement we made that you would work shorter hours," Carl simply replied. "You haven't gone out of town for any trials," he said. "You never even asked me to do that. I am perfectly willing to do that," I replied. "Well I don't think your husband would like it if you went out of town for two weeks," Carl replied. "I have never implied that and it isn't true," I said angrily. "I am willing to work longer hours when necessary and I am willing to go out of town for trials. I have said this before. ," I replied. 'I simply want to have some quality time with my children and husband and working 30 hours a week makes that possible."

"All you can do is to set a good example for your children by working hard. It is the work ethic that is important. I did that for my children when they were young," Carl said. He continued, "Your children make their own choices when they become adults. For example my daughter is an alcoholic. I have washed my hands of her." I remember being struck by the matter of fact nature of that statement. There was no emotion. It was as if he were discussing the facts of a new case. I was not sure why he told me about his daughter. It seemed to negate his argument that by working more I was setting a good example for my children and thus it was good for them. Thankfully I didn't take his advice. My explanation to the senior partner at the firm that I wanted to maintain my shorter work hours – 9 to 4 or 4:30 so I could have more time to spend with my children and husband was obviously falling on deaf ears.

Unfortunately I did it. I started to cry. I know I was crying out of anger and frustration. I had done everything that was asked of me and then some. The things I couldn't do I had tried to discuss with Carl but he ignored me. "Can't we talk about this and work it out?" I asked. I knew there were no other opportunities to work shorter hours out there. I know because I had been looking.

"You have shed too many tears to continue working here," he said and got up to leave the room. I had no idea what that meant. "Oh by the way we want you to stay another four months to finish up some of the cases you are working on," he said as he left the room. I thought I was doing a bad job I said to myself as he left.

I continued working for another four months or so in a totally hostile environment. I was treated pretty badly by everyone during that time. I don't know what it is but something has always compelled me to accept lousy treatment in exchange for a paycheck. I sensed that Carl thought the fact that I was a woman contributed to the failure of our arrangement. They hired a new male associate attorney. I understand he didn't last very long either. He was followed by a number of other male associates.

"I know she does it. I have heard her on the phone and I have seen her interact with you and others, Ted said. I was so relieved. Ted did not tell me this was all a figment of my imagination. He recognized what was happening! I was elated. "Who else can I work with?" I asked. Ted paused before saying, "You know Vicki is one of those old school secretaries. She simply doesn't like working for women attorneys. You understand that, don't you? " I realized that Ted thought I should just accept this lack of respect and outright rudeness and hostility!

I did try to live with it. But it seems the more I accepted the behavior, the worse it got. Oh I tried other things as well. I talked to her nicely. I confronted her about it. But in the end it wasn't only about being treated rudely and disrespectfully. She was sabotaging the work. I felt like I was willing to and had compromised. I couldn't relinquish all of myself self respect. Is that what it would take to succeed at this firm or in this profession? How could I have a future at this firm? Ted turned a deaf ear after that initial conversation. This was the year 2000 in a totally different part of the country but I felt like I was back in the rust belt in 1982. I was getting the same treatment anyway.

Ted had just started his own practice and wanted me to join as a partner with him. I turned him down. I am not sure exactly why I did that. I have regretted that decision on many occasions. It has become my one of my quintessential profession roads not traveled. There were some concrete reasons for my refusal. My potential partner worked all the time. I didn't want to do that and if I was a partner I would feel obligated to work as hard as he did. I still had one young son at home. Ted would still be senior and I could see some real communication and management issues arising in the future with him especially after I saw his attitude regarding the principal secretary and office manager, Vicki. The practice of law itself wasn't fun anymore.

Law has become a game of win at any cost. As I said earlier, it was no longer about the facts and the law and marshalling the facts and law into the best possible argument for your client. It was about manipulating and misrepresenting the facts and law and impeding the other party's access to information. It is about manipulating the system to show the opposing party in a bad light to the court. It was about appealing to the worst aspects of a particular judge. Still I could have done it. Why didn't I? As I reflect on it I think the truth is that the desire or drive to work and succeed in law was crushed out of me many years ago.

I became so alienated by my earlier law practice experiences that I was loath to get back into that situation albeit this time with a little more control. In the early years of my career I had done everything right, I thought, and yet I still didn't reap any rewards, financial or otherwise. I do think some of it had to do with the fact that I was a woman. As a result I turned my back on my profession many years before this offer was made even though I continued to work in it. I only realized that now as I write this. Maybe my failure to make any serious money or thrive in that field was a result of many factors. All these years I thought I was just, personally, a failure.

Is it just me or do we all feel like failures unless we earn $300,000.00 a year? Is that one of the reasons why we spend so much money beyond our legitimate means? Does that sense of failure and inadequacy give rise to the attitude of superiority and entitlement which emanates from the $300,000.00+ annual wage earners? Is that, partly, what has contributed to the current attitude of "win at any cost"?

I knew one female attorney who had such self confidence I was in awe of her. She never doubted that she would be successful. She started out at a large law firm. She said she was surprised they tolerated her. They treated her like she was crazy she said. She eventually left there to start her own firm and was very successful. I never had that kind of self confidence. I tried so hard to get her to mentor me but she was, I am sure, too busy with her own concerns. Oh to be born with such innate self confidence!

"Dad I have been accepted to law school!" I said excitedly to him during our weekly phone call. "You should stay home with your children," he responded. I never got the message that I could be anything I wanted to be or do anything I wanted to do. Some women of my generation did. Men of my generation seemed to imbibe that message in their baby bottle. I received the message that "nothing was possible" outside the status quo that is I was raised believing I should get married, stay home and raise my children. I thought for a long time that is really what I wanted to do but it wasn't.

I ended up a single mom trying to make her way in the world when being a single mom was not the norm. What career goals could I have? I just wanted to make enough money to support my kids and maybe go on a vacation. It was not a very lofty goal and I often wonder if by setting my sights so low I missed out on having a career. I see women my age who have had very successful careers. I have not. I have stopped comparing myself to them. I have also stopped putting those women down in order to make me feel better about my choices. You know when you say things like, "she doesn't have children or a husband or she probably doesn't get along with her children or husband, etc."

Some women really seem to have it all – marriage, career, kids. I envy them. I couldn't do it all. As I wrote this tears welled up in my eyes. I think they are tears of disappointment in myself. It is painful to admit. I am, in many ways, a failure. If I am going to move past this failure I have to admit that to myself. I won't justify or assuage my feelings of failure by putting others down any longer.

"Well I think we are going to sell the Toyota. Your brother says it has too many miles on it and it won't make the long trip," my Father said to me during a very recent phone conversation regarding their move from my hometown to where I lived. "Dad I thought you and I already decided that you would keep that car. It will go for many more miles and you really shouldn't spend the money to get a new car right now," I replied. "I know but your brother disagrees with us. I think we will sell it," my Father replied. My sister and I refer to my brother as "the Prince."

"I went home for a visit last week. We had an 80th birthday party for my father. All of my sisters and my brother attended. It was great to be together. My brother is still drifting at age 30 but the rest of us are doing well," my friend Lisa said. "My Dad actually told me he was proud of me -well kind of – at least for him it was a huge compliment," she said looking, at least partly, pleased. "What did he say?" I asked. "My Father told me that my brother could have been President if he had my drive and energy," Lisa replied. Most of the fathers of my generation just didn't believe that we, their female offspring, could or should be successful in a realm other than the home.

For I can't remember how many years I lived with a constant sense of failure. It was more than lived with – I felt physically weighed down by it. It felt as if I was carrying a backpack full of rocks on my back. Each rock represented some defeat. I can't believe that I don't look stooped over in the photos from those years. I wasn't a good enough employee, a good enough lawyer, a good enough mother, good enough wife or good enough daughter. The idea that I should do anything just for myself or to please me never crossed my mind. We had to be super women in those days. It was expected of us. We were proving women could do and have it all.

Of course that was a total myth but we still destroyed ourselves in the process of trying to be "super woman". We may have deluded ourselves into thinking we were doing it all but if we looked beneath the surface we discovered that someone or something had been slighted or neglected. Things got worse the more you stretched yourself because eventually something snapped or broke. I was marginalized in the work place. My children had issues. I was always exhausted or beyond exhausted. I had absolutely no time for myself. I had no social life. I had no friends. I did nothing but work and take care of my children – mostly their physical needs. It wasn't even a balancing act. I was always putting out a fire because it was only when something became a crisis that I had time or energy to really devote to it. Neglecting my children would have serious and long term consequences. For me it was easiest to sacrifice my career. I thought I could take it up again later after the children were gone. I was wrong about that.

Professionally, my feeling of inadequacy and insecurity increased in direct proportion to the bragedociousness of my fellow practitioners. They were all hugely successful and earned enormous amounts of money. I was naïve enough, for a while, to believe them. I didn't really know how to brag. I couldn't bring myself to do it. Stupid I know but I can't do it. Doesn't bragging, by definition, necessarily entail some exaggeration or sometimes flat out lying? Maybe I deserved to be pushed out because I couldn't do this.

Isn't it crass to promote yourself or discuss your accomplishments and talents? That was bragging. If you were accomplished you didn't need to point it out. If you were good you would be recognized for it. Bragging was one of the ultimate sins. It was vulgar, garish and vain at least in the generation in which I grew up.

Bragging has been repackaged as self promotion and good marketing. For those of us born in the 50s there is still a stigma to bragging and it is hard to do. If you weren't raised in that era you have no idea what I am talking about and probably think "how stupid". Of course the world was smaller then. You could earn a reputation at your company or in your community. That doesn't really exist anymore and so, as much as I dislike self promotion, I have to concede it is necessary even if I can't do it. Is it any wonder we are becoming a society of narcissists?

Doesn't this conduct of touting our success easily careen out of control and impinge on other aspects of our lives as well? Doesn't it really just lead to bragging for the sake of bragging? When I was young if you were financially successful you didn't need to brag about it or flaunt it. You weren't expected to drive a VW bus but you didn't rub other people's nose in it either. The wealthy people took vacations, lived in beautiful homes, wore expensive clothes, belonged to the country club and drove expensive cars. They didn't talk about their expensive things just for the sake of talking about them. They never discussed what things cost. The fact that they had been on a wonderful vacation might come up in a conversation but it was not the focus of the conversation. But then maybe they had interests and activities other than acquiring money.

In some cases if a person doesn't brag for him or herself we do it for them. The achievement of the poor student who becomes a multi millionaire is celebrated. Certainly that is an accomplishment worth recognizing. But somehow we and maybe he or she as well, fails to recognize that he or she rose to those heights on the backs and only because of other people, including the people who work for him or her. The worker bees I call them. We never seem to celebrate them. When did we start to fail to recognize success is a team effort? Shouldn't we celebrate the contributions of all members of the team? Does this failure have unintended consequences? Do the worker bees stretch the limits of ethics and honesty in order to achieve some recognition as well? Is that partly behind this explosion of deceit, cheating and resentment?

"After working 35 years at the company all he got was a party and a crummy watch," is a statement that has been passed around in our culture. We believe that long term employees were taken advantage of by their employers. Maybe some of them were but in my Father's generation employees cared about the company and the people who worked there. The employers cared about the business and the people working in it. They were all invested in the company – personally and financially. Now we change jobs frequently but is that really an improvement?

A huge percentage of the population has the attitude that we can't be happy with our work. We are waiting until we retire or quit to really start enjoying our lives. Oh I know my Father did not love to go to work every day. But on those days he didn't want to go I think the connection and commitment he felt to the company and the other people working there outweighed any such feelings. Are things really better now? I have a feeling we will retire or "get there" and still be unhappy and dissatisfied.

Humility, loyalty, caring about the customer, being a team player are so out of fashion or style these days. We say those things in order to attract business but we don't really mean them. They are just a means to an end – getting more customers and making more money. We have to get ahead because we have to be able to drive a Mercedes, live in a huge home, go on exotic vacations, buy expensive things, retire as a multi- millionaire at the age of 55 and take personal credit for all of it. Getting ahead means stepping on or maybe better squashing the other guy. Could there be any other result once we elevated money to the level of God? Our individual need for money is number one –at the top of the pyramid. It forms the basis – it is the litmus test for all actions and decisions both business and personal.

"After 10 years I had built up a very successful employment law practice. I was invited to join a big firm. You know what that means. I would have some support. I could grow my practice even larger. I could delegate more. I could earn more. It was a great opportunity. The merger went well until about 6 months later when I was diagnosed with breast cancer. In between the rounds of chemo I would go to the office and work. My prognosis was good as we had caught it very early," Sally, my friend, was relating a story of her professional career to me at lunch one day.

She continued, "You should leave the firm. You will be punished for being sick. You have no future here. I was told this by the three female partners at the firm. I was thankful that these women came to warn me. But at the same time I couldn't help but wonder why they couldn't or wouldn't band together to stand up to the male partners. Something obviously happened in the past that caused them to reach this conclusion. They never shared with me what that was. I didn't really expect them to stand up for me but I could tell they were terrified of what might happen to them in a similar situation. I thought by standing up for me they might just change things for themselves. They felt powerless to change the attitudes and certainly the actions of the male partners. I hung in there for several months but eventually I left firm."

I recognize that what I see in my profession is going on in all professions. That makes it all the more distressful. Should I join the self promoters who care only about making money? I really can't if I want to be true to my beliefs, values and morals. Some people can divide themselves into two – the business person and the real person. But in my experience you can't leave everything at the office. These attitudes come to permeate and poison all aspects of your life. You can't just turn it off with a flip of a switch when you leave the office.

Do women really want to compete with men in a male world by becoming more like them or do we want to shape a new world that combines or maximizes the strengths of men and women similar to what a good marriage or partnership does. Is that happening anywhere? Have we given any thought to what that would look like or how to get there? Can it lead to inclusion of minority groups as well as women? Wouldn't that require we adopt an attitude which recognizes our strengths lie in our differences. Is it possible? Who wants it anyway? Have we made any progress since I started in the legal field in 1982?

I don't want to act like or be like a man in order to be successful. I don't wear pant suits in the business world. I think, in part for that reason. I feel like by doing so I am adopting the male dress code and that may lead me to act like a man in other more substantive ways. It seems to me that a lot of these recent girl power stories do just that – have the girl acting just like a man would.

"Mom can boys are lawyers too?" Samuel asked me one night at the dinner table. He was about six years old at the time. There may be some hope of effecting change. I am referring to a generation of young men raised by single, working mothers or just working mothers. Sons, perhaps much more than husbands, appreciate the challenges and sacrifices of their working mothers. These same sons eventually want to make things different and better for their wives and daughters.

"What are your career goals?" I recently asked my oldest daughter, Jessica. "I don't have a future at this company. I'm already a manager. I can't go any further unless I want to work 60 or 70 hours a week. The younger, single people are willing to do that and the ones who are willing to sacrifice their personal life in order to get ahead. I don't see the baby much during the week as it is. If I work more I will never see her," Jessica rattled off. "I don't want to be a full time mom either. I enjoy working outside the home", Jessica said.

I see my daughter is struggling with the same issues I struggled with thirty years ago. From my conversations with her and other young working mothers and women I don't see that much progress has been made in shaping a new business world. We women, who have worked in the business world for the past 30 years, seem to have had little impact on it. Oh a small number of successes have been touted. They have risen within the business structure they found themselves in. As a whole the business model is pretty much as we found it some thirty years ago. We, perhaps, fell victim to conforming to a system that was already in place and accepting things as they are in order to obtain our own personal gain. I thought we wanted to change the world.

I understand, from the media, that women have made progress in that if they work as hard as the men they can earn good money and responsible positions. Some women have proven they can not only fit in but flourish in, for lack of a better term, "a man's world." But not everyone, male or female, wants to work those hours or make the significant personal sacrifices necessary in order to "climb the corporate ladder." Have we working mothers left any mark on the business world that we entered some 30 years ago? I don't see that we have.

Where do the women like my daughter, Jessica, and her friends find opportunity or fit in? Do we care about them? Have we made any progress, in the last 30 years, in the area of balancing work and life? In order to do that don't we first need to dethrone money or the accumulation of lots of money as our principal or only goal. This value shift may be especially important in those at the top levels of the corporate or business world and may include the shareholders of a company. Perhaps the business community of my Father's generation wasn't all bad.

I hope these are challenges this younger generation will take on. Can they question and challenge the assumption that the business model of 40 hours per week for 5 days a week for everyone is the best for American businesses and employees? Perhaps they can spur the business community to change the business model to one that values things in addition to money, is concerned about the quality of life of its employees as well as its bottom line, sees inclusivity and flexibility as things to be valued, cultivates a feeling of community rather than me centeredness in the workplace and ultimately strives to find a balance between the goals of the business and the quality of life of its employees. This is just idealistic nonsense you say. Maybe but there may be a great deal of value in just discussing these issues and entertaining alternatives to the system that was created during the Industrial Revolution – about 100 years ago. Perhaps we should first ask ourselves if we want something different. I know that I do.

CHAPTER TEN

Being Squeezed – The Sandwich Generation

"Hi Mom, How are you," I said when she answered the phone. "Here's your Father," was all she said to me. Sometimes she just didn't answer me at all and handed the phone immediately to my Dad. The crime for which I am being punished is that I invited them to move to where I live. You see they are 84 years old and living in a snowy climate. My Mother is not in good health, although I wouldn't say that to her. She would be moving from the city where she has spent her entire life. They have been in the same house for 41 years. They have lived in only two houses their entire 60 years of marriage. She has always been a stay at home mother with strong ties to the church and community.

As a child I used to love to watch the movies made in the 1950s. It is amazing to me, now, that so many of them were on TV back then especially since we only had 3 channels. My favorite stars were Susan Hayward, Lana Turner and sometimes Barbara Stanwyck. I loved movies like "Stella Dallas" and "Imitation of Life". Those women sacrificed everything, including themselves, for the good of their children, husband, and family. They were so very unlike the girl power movies of today. (Although I should make a disclaimer that I haven't really watched any such movies in their entirety. I haven't even tried. I have just been told about them). Perhaps those movies did represent the attitude of the times. My Mother and her generation sacrificed themselves or things they wanted to do or have for their children and husbands. I only came to understand that recently.

"I am going to go to law school," I said to my parents during our weekly phone conversation. There was an eerie silence. "You should stay home with your children," my Father replied. My Mother said something bland and noncommittal as if we were talking about going to the shopping mall. That was pretty much the extent of our conversation about that issue – ever.

My Dad worked for 30+ years for the same company until it went out of business during the 1982 meltdown of the steel industry. He would leave for work before we left for school. When he arrived home around 6 pm he would "take a rest". My Mother prepared dinner. We all sat down and ate dinner together. Then we did homework and went to bed. My Mother would wake us each morning for school. Breakfast was on the table. We ate quickly and ran to catch the school bus. Her days were filled with volunteer and church activities while we were at school.

"Get up now right now!" I shouted as I shook him firmly. "This is the second time I have been in your room. You have to get up right now." I went back to check on Jessica and Ellen before returning to the kitchen to finish packing lunches and fixing something for them to eat for breakfast. I was back in to Samuel's room. "Samuel get up you or you are going to miss the school bus!" I shrieked. I physically removed him from the bed, got him dressed, put a piece of toast in his hand, gave him his backpack and propelled him to the front door. Jessica was already waiting at the front door to leave. I pushed Samuel out the front door behind Jessica and closed it.

Ellen was watching something on TV. I was glad she was occupied as I ran to my bedroom to hurriedly get ready for work. A few minutes later I started out the front door with Ellen in tow. I was going to drop Ellen off at the sitter before I raced to work. I opened the front door to see Samuel sitting on the front porch. "Samuel what are you doing sitting here?" I said in voice filled with panic. There was no verbal response. I grabbed him and pushed him into the car. As I drove him to school all I could think about was how I was going to be late for work. I was hoping I didn't have an early court appearance or meeting that morning.

I signed Samuel in at the school office, got back in the car, dropped Ellen off at the babysitter's house and raced to work. I was hoping no one would notice that I had arrived about 30 minutes late.

I could skip lunch to make up the time but I really couldn't stay late because I had child care available only until 6 pm.

I used to do my homework at the dining room table after my Mother had cleared away the dirty dinner dishes. My Dad was usually sitting in the living room in his favorite chair reading a book. Once my Mother cleaned up the kitchen she would join him in the living room. She loved to knit, work on crossword puzzles and play cards – solitaire primarily. My sister was often watching TV downstairs although we got so few channels I can't imagine what she could find to see. I think my brother usually did his homework in his room.

"I have a Presbytery meeting tomorrow morning. We are going to discuss World Day of Prayer. The fall festival is rapidly approaching. We have a meeting Wednesday to plan that event. Martha Harris and I are going to recruit some other women to handle individual booths. We are planning to have booths of baked goods, games, crafts and a sales booth for some white elephant items. We have been asking the congregation to drop off donations for the white elephant sales at the church," my mother rattled off. "Do people really want to buy other people's junk?" my Dad asked. My mother sighed.

"How were things at the office today?" my Mother asked. "Well the production is up at the forge. We have some new orders that have been recently placed. The union contract is up for renewal but we have a very good relationship with the members so I don't foresee any problems," my Dad replied. The sound of their voices in the background was very comforting as I turned back to my homework.

People would look at me strangely – like I was crazy. At that time of day in commuter traffic it was unusual to hear music played that loudly in a car driven by an adult. I learned to crank up my music. I would sing and dance as I sat in the bumper to bumper freeway traffic. I used my commute home as a time to unwind from the office. It took me a while to recognize how important it was to do that. The children usually heard me arrive and they would mob me at the door, all of them talking at the same time. "See you tomorrow," said the sitter as she passed me in the doorway. It was great to be missed but also a bit overwhelming.

"I'm hungry," Jessica said. "OK let me get into the kitchen and get dinner started," I replied. They would all follow me into the kitchen but invariably when I would talk to one the other two would try to talk louder or would walk away with hurt feelings. "Dinner is ready," I called. We all sat down together. That is something I insisted on. "How was school?" I asked Jessica. "You don't ask me how school was," said Ellen indignantly. "I will but I can only talk to one person at a time," I replied. "Why didn't you ask me first," Ellen whined. "Samuel why aren't you eating your dinner?" I asked. Everyone was competing for my attention and in the end they all got cheated.

"Let's go over your homework," I said as I started to clear the table. "Mom we have a project due next week and I need to buy some things at the store in the next day or two so I can get started," Jessica said. "Mom I have a play at school next week. Can you get my costume tonight?" Ellen said. "I have a note from my teacher," said Samuel as pushed a piece of crumpled paper in my hand and skulked away to his room. "Well let's talk while I clean up the kitchen and you do your homework," I replied. Of course, in reality, I was rarely that composed or even patient.

"Has everyone taken their bath?" I shouted from the kitchen. "Has everyone finished their homework?" I shouted a few minutes later. "It is bedtime," I shouted. Homework was usually done by 8 or 8:30. If I was lucky the kitchen was cleaned up by 9 or 9:30. Sometimes I had to pack lunches depending on the budget that week. I couldn't afford to pay for school lunches for two and later three children every day of the month.

I couldn't offer my children the comforts of my childhood home. I often wondered what I could or did offer them instead. Was it anything of value? Could I raise good kids when I could not provide them with what I had grown up with? How could my kids compete academically with children who had two parents one of whom was probably a stay at home mom? Jessica's project was pretty amateurish compared to the others primarily because she had done it herself without much help from me. Samuel was having behavioral problems at school. Ellen wasn't doing her homework. I was always exhausted. Did I offer anything positive? I often thought I was more of a negative influence – always tired, impatient and cranky. My life was about putting out fires at the office and at home.

"I won't be home today when you get home. I have a late meeting at the church. I should be home about 4. The Fall festival is next week and we have a lot of last minute details to take care of," she said. It was strange arriving home to an empty house that day. My Mother was always there to greet us.

"Jessica you didn't call me today when you got home from school," I said when she answered the phone. "I was really worried". "Sorry Mom I forgot," Jessica replied. "Don't do that again," I demanded. "Are you doing your homework? How much do you have?" I grilled her. "You have a call," I heard Margie say over the office intercom. "I have to go now. Please start your homework and I will call you a little later," I said to Jessica. I was too busy to call later that day. I hoped she knew she could call me if she had a problem or question.

"I am meeting with my bridge club tomorrow. I think everyone will be there," my Mother said to my Father. She then recited the names of the 12 women who had attended this same bridge group for the past 15 years. She always seemed excited to go and was so relaxed and happy after she had been with that group. How I envy her! I never developed those kinds of friendships.

"No I can't go out tonight," I said to my friend, Cindy. "I really need to get home to spend time with the kids". I never had outings with other adults. I spent all of my "free" time with the children. One day of each weekend was devoted to grocery shopping, laundry, cleaning, errands, etc. On the other weekend day we always had at least one family outing. We often went to the zoo, the park, hiking, swimming etc. We went anyplace that was free. I hoped the children enjoyed it. I am not sure I did. It was hard to enjoy my life back then. That is not to say I never enjoyed being with them. I did. Our family outings were overshadowed by the crushing weight of responsibilities and chores. My life seemed like one big "have to". I just raced from one "have to" the next. .

"Did you come to the office to get some rest," my employer said pretty much every Monday morning. In some ways the office with all its demands was a respite from the demands of raising three young children alone. Because I had "chosen" or ended up in a dead end job because I was a single mother with three young children, I could leave my work at the office for the most part. The children were 24/7. Of course I didn't realize it was a dead end job until much later.

"You and your brother got straight "As" again, "my Father said in a very pleased tone of voice. My brother and I were very well behaved children. My parents rarely had to discipline us. (Dealing with my sister was a totally different matter.) I really can't even remember ever being told what to do. We instinctively knew what was expected of us and we did it. We didn't want to disappoint or embarrass our parents or ourselves in the community. My parents or their friends were also always around to monitor our behavior and enforce the rules if necessary.

"Ellen and Spencer, I am going to give each of you a checkmark every time you don't follow the rules. I have the rules listed on this poster board. If you get ten checkmarks in two weeks there will be a huge consequence," I explained. A psychologist had recommended this system. Samuel and Ellen were difficult to discipline, to put it mildly. The babysitter seemed incapable of getting them to follow even the most basic rules. I was tired of trying to mete out some random and scattered discipline in the evenings. I hoped this could change all that and I wouldn't have to spend my evenings being angry at the children.

As I look back at my checkmark system I think I took on too much discipline all at once. I wanted the children to comply with the basic rules regarding behavior – the ones that make living together possible- like being polite, getting homework done, being kind to your siblings. I also expected them to do some minor chores and help out at the house. In retrospect I should have started with the standard behaviors and then moved to chores when those were established. My expectations were definitely too high for my children and myself in light of our circumstances. If only I had known that back then! But there were so many more deep seated issues perhaps it wouldn't have made any difference.

I couldn't be a traditional mother and father. I wasn't there after school to make sure homework was being done, limiting TV watching and monitoring the doing of minor chores. I had to deal with it all in the few hours I was home in the evenings and on the weekends. Often times I was too exhausted to try to enforce the rules. I had assumed the role of a drill sergeant always barking orders. The orders were usually ignored. But what were my choices? I so wanted to have some good, positive interactions with the children. Our weekend outings were an attempt to do just that but often those turned into military maneuvers as well. Why didn't the children, Ellen and Samuel, know and do what was expected of them like my brother and I had done? I kept hoping that would happen but it never did at least not until they were young adults. What was I doing wrong? I berated myself for many years as I searched for an answer to that question.

After all my generation was engaged in much more serious activities than our mothers, weren't we? We didn't have time for frivolous things like sewing circle meetings, bridge club or church festivals. Even if we did we would have thought there were too many other more important things to do like work and make money. We were better than our mothers because we were engaged in much more important activities, weren't we? As a young adult, I thought what my Mother did was unimportant. I also thought my Mother was "unimportant". I didn't really respect her. I didn't understand how my Mother and her peers enriched the communities and our lives. We took all of that for granted. I was blinded by my arrogance. After all I was going to do bigger and better things than she and her generation had done, wasn't I?

"Bob don't forget to take out trash tonight," my Mother said to my Father. She rarely had to remind him. Occasionally he would have his head buried in a book and forget what time or day it was. This was his only regular chore. My Father took care of the trash, household maintenance and yard work. My Mother took care of everything else.

"Hi Mom how are you?" I said recently over the phone. "Your Father has been packing boxes all week," she replied. After several months of silence she had started talking to me. What happened to cause this I wondered? I would never know. My parents' generation was never much for talking things over - important things. As a child I had to guess what was going on by studying my parents' behavior. My parents and I never overtly fought about anything. I never saw them have any disagreements in their relationship. I think they did talk things over but only when they were alone. They never actually "fought" with each other. I knew the issue was "resolved" when the unbearable tension between them would subside. Unfortunately when tension builds up over many, many years it rarely ever totally subsides. It is ever present although in varying degrees of severity. Other than the various tension levels, as a child, things just seemed to flow in my house without much discussion or dissension.

"Did you get to the grocery store today? Did you have a chance to do any laundry? The kids don't have any clean clothes for school tomorrow," I rattled off the list of things that I had asked my husband to do while he was home during the day. It had taken me a long time to ask him to do things around the house and for the children. I felt guilty every time I did ask him. He never seemed to offer or to see things that needed to be done. That would make me angry. So I would give him a list that was almost never completed. Maybe that was his way of getting back at me for asking. I would get angry when he didn't complete the list. We would argue. Usually the argument would occur in the evening when I got home from the office. Sometimes the children were awake and heard it all. Afterwards I would regret saying anything in front of the children. I knew it was wrong. Well I thought to myself I can chalk it up to another failure. I wanted to be able to come home from the office and sit down in the evening. I couldn't do that if there were chores to do. I couldn't control my irritation over my husband's failure to get anything done. I perceived it as a lack of effort or desire to do his part.

Everything with my spouse had to be negotiated. How I longed for the clearly defined roles of my parents! They never had to negotiate anything. My husband had a million excuses for why he had completed any of the tasks. He didn't understand or maybe he didn't care that certain things had to get done and if he didn't do it that meant I had to do them. For the most part, he simply ignored my requests for help. He operated from the premise that he shouldn't have to "help" me as much as I asked him to do. I did feel like I was asking for help. I hadn't developed the attitude that he wasn't helping me but he was doing his part. I still can't muster that attitude. I couldn't escape the role of the traditional wife and mother who did everything and was responsible for everything with the home and children. I validated his attitude. There was so little compromise on his part that it just didn't seem worth the effort to argue or even discuss it with him after a while. Eventually I just did everything myself. It was easier. I needed all my energy to get things done, not fight. I couldn't squander my energy or time on fighting that didn't yield any improvements or changes.

I know my spouse liked the income I brought in and we definitely needed it. But he didn't want to pay the price. The price was he would have to help with the everyday tasks. After all this was a guy whose mother ironed his underwear even in high school! What was I thinking! The problem was that I wasn't thinking. This was too much to ask of him, I think. This stuff was way beyond his abilities. I became a full time drill sergeant to my husband as well as my children. Is it any wonder I didn't like myself much in those days? Is it any wonder he didn't like me either? I didn't see I had any other choice. The physical demands of life used up all of my energy in those days.

There was no amount of negotiating that was going to change his attitude. My husband did honestly try for a while, at various times, but I think the daily responsibilities ground him down like they did me. The difference was that I felt like I had to keep going for the sake of the children. He didn't feel that way. He simply "checked out." Eventually my spouse became just one more person to do things for. He became like another child or responsibility.

I seemed to offer my children so little of what I had as a child. They never witnessed a stable marriage. I wasn't able to be home when they came home after school. I wasn't able to always help with homework and projects. I missed many of their school events and sporting events. I didn't always know their friends or parents of their friends as well as I should have. These are all things my parents did do and more. I often wondered what I did offer my children, if anything, that was comparable or as good as the stability I had as a child.

"How are you feeling?" I asked my Mother. This was before she and my Dad moved to where I live. I was calling her at the hospital. She had just had surgery to repair a broken femur. "Oh I am great. Everything is great. I don't have any pain," she replied. I knew better than to believe her. My mother is a stoic. I think that may be how her generation coped with the tragedies of their childhood and youth like the Great Depression and World War II.

I have never had an honest conversation with my Mother about anything. I think they and their generation may be totally shut off from their emotions. It is great to be stoical in the face of adversity but shouldn't it end sometime? Doesn't it interfere with our ability to understand ourselves and to connect to others? Can you connect in the absence of honesty? Did my mother's lack of honesty have anything to do with the role she played as a full time mother and wife? I often wondered if my mother, and her generation, felt they sacrificed too much or gave up too much of themselves and what they wanted in order to be a full time wife and mother. Sadly I will never have that conversation with her.

Did the role of full time wife and mother shield them and us, their children, from the harsh realities of life and allow them to create a world of their own design? Did that world enable them to be less honest with themselves and others?

I wanted to prepare my children for the "real" world. I experienced the "real" world, for the first time, as a young, working mother. I knew that everyone was not going to care about how they felt or what they wanted or help them when they needed help. That was the role of the family or at least idealistically it is. They needed to be prepared to function outside the family or so I thought.

I was waiting in line in one of those all too common doughnut shops. I was about 22 years old. There was a long line and it was not very organized. People were standing everywhere. I had been waiting a long time when I saw a gentleman who had arrived long after I did walk up to the counter and start to order his doughnuts. I was so angry but I couldn't say anything to him. I fumed in silence. As the man passed me on his way out the door I said," You know I was here long before you." He snarled at me. That was a huge step for me. I was learning to stand up for myself. In the sheltered world of my childhood we didn't have opportunities to develop those types of skills. We interacted in a very controlled environment where everyone shared our values and ideas regarding behavior and manners. We were usually in the company of one of our parents or one of our friends' parents. I couldn't be there all the time for my children.

"Hey, Stop that! You are scaring my Mother!" Jessica shouted as she banged on the window. I had just asked her if we should get out and switch cabs because this guy was driving like a maniac. I was terrified he was going to crash. That was why she banged on the window. The cab driver stopped driving like a maniac. "I am proud of you," I said to her. "Mom all my friends here in Manhattan laugh at me. They are surprised that this young woman from the southwest can handle the daily challenges of living in this city. I tell my friends that you taught me to stand up for myself from the time I was little. Sometimes I just had to because you weren't around to do it for me,"

Jessica replied. She was just 22 years old at that time. She moved to Manhattan as soon as she graduated from college. Maybe not being a stay at home mother had some benefits, I thought.

"Mommy I forgot to bring my teddy bear!" Gary said as I was driving him to daycare. He was about 3 years old at the time. "We can't go back. I have to be at work by 8:30 this morning and I cannot be late," I replied. He started to cry a little. "You will manage without the teddy bear. Life is full of challenges and disappointment. You may as well get used to it now," I harshly replied.

I wanted my children to develop the ability to be honest with themselves and others. I wanted to answer questions honestly and talk about feelings honestly at least at the level their maturity could accept and understand. I had no idea how to do that or if it would be of any benefit to my children. In doing so I know that I went way overboard for a while like what I said to Gary about the teddy bear. We didn't have the safety and security of the community like I did as a child. But that community was also rigid. The predictable flow of our daily lives rendered emotional honesty unnecessary and unattractive.

"TMI, TMI!" Jessica said laughingly in response to something Samuel had said. "What is "TMI"?" I asked. "Too Much Information," Jessica responded. I hear this expression fairly often at our family gatherings. Being honest with each other has allowed us to share our disappointments, accomplishments, our feelings and ourselves. There is a fine line between how much honesty and sharing is too much but we work on that regularly. "TMI" helps keep us in check. Perhaps this honesty was not possible in the secure and rigidly defined traditional world of my parents and my childhood. It seems the rigidity prevented communication and emotional connection. Emotions are messy, unpredictable, scary and uncomfortable. Being honest with each other has allowed me to connect with my children and vice versa. In spite of my initial mistakes I think it was a good thing to do.

In those times when I felt like I was losing it I would sustain myself with the thought that this would all be worth it if my children learned from my experiences and mistakes. They saw my generation of women try to do it all. They saw us fail. They saw us almost destroy ourselves in the process. They certainly witnessed that our marital relationships were a casualty of trying to do it all. We were caught between two worlds without any type of a road map. I hope I have provided some type of road map, however rough, to my children.

Jessica had come to visit for a weekend. "Mom I am getting married," Jessica told me. Sadly my first reaction was fear. "You haven't known him that long," I exclaimed. "Shouldn't you give it more time?" I asked. I knew that Jessica, like all of us, was going to do what she thought was best. All I could do was to express my concerns. Sadly I thought in generations past, parents used to be so excited at the prospect of their children marrying. I was terrified that she was making a mistake and would end up divorced with children. I didn't want to project the fear of my failures onto her but I couldn't escape the feeling. I know I indirectly conveyed that to Jessica.

As the band started playing we all drifted slowly into the next room. The bride and groom started dancing. Jessica and Drew were chatting and laughing as they danced. Then I saw it. A softer song started playing. Jessica ever so gently laid her head on Drew's shoulder. He tenderly enveloped her in his arms. They do love each other I said to myself as I heard the DJ asked for the parents of the bride to come to the dance floor. I guess no one told him there was only one parent of the bride present. Sadly, that was true for most of Jessica's life. That was one of those moments in life when I really missed Brian.

It is a closely guarded secret this love between Jessica and David. Or is it? I am reminded of the words of one of my former employers. "You can tell how people care about you by the way they treat you". That was a novel concept to me at the time. I was always making excuses for the lack of good treatment by my husband. He was busy, tired. It was not his nature. Everyone goes through rough times. Can you really expect someone to help all the time? Some of that was definitely just a result of who I was but wasn't some of it also a result of not knowing what to expect from a spouse in a nontraditional relationship? In a traditional relationship I was supposed to do everything for the children and to run the home. Did I really have a "right" to ask him to help? I know for a long time I felt guilty when I did. I should have been able to do it all myself. I was the wife and mother and that was my "job".

"The baby has another ear infection," Jessica said. "I am taking her to the doctor today". "You must be exhausted," I replied. "Not really. Drew and I take turns getting up with her and it was Drew's turn last night. I got a pretty good night's sleep. I was thankful for that because I have a very busy day at work today," Jessica replied. Drew doesn't feel like he is helping Jessica with her "duties". They feel jointly responsible for the child rearing and household responsibilities and they share them.

"Mom do you want to come over for dinner tonight? Drew is fixing barbecued ribs," Jessica said. "What can I do to help?" I asked as I walked in the door. "Nothing everything is under control," Jessica replied. Drew said hello as he was running some clean laundry upstairs. Jessica went out to check on the ribs. "Drew can you set the table?" I heard Jessica ask him. It just flowed like that all evening. Dinner was served. The table was cleared. The dishwasher was loaded. The pans were washed. Jessica wasn't afraid to ask Drew to do things. In fact she rarely had to ask him to do anything. She wasn't burdened with the notion that she had to do it all alone- to be super woman. I hope my experiences helped contribute to Jessica's attitude I said to myself as I drove home that night. Maybe this is a marriage that will endure and even flourish.

The burden of trying to be super women sucked all the joy out of my life. I was never a good enough mother, employee, professional, friend, sister, co worker or person. Thankfully this new generation has not fallen victim to that impossible standard. They are not afraid to ask for help. To me asking for help was akin to being a failure. I was supposed to be able to do it all and handle it all myself. I wonder if now we haven't just superimposed those expectations on the men. Do we expect them to be able to do it all – make very good money, be a supportive and loving husband, be an involved and hands on dad or be super dad? Could that be why some of them seem to be "checking out" literally and figuratively? Setting up an impossible standard can cause that to happen. I know that from personal experience.

"I wanted to marry someone as different from my Father as possible," Jessica said to me one night. I think I have done that," she declared. Oh I know there were other reasons she chose Drew but this night we happened to be talking about Jessica's Father. I think she was saying more than just that she chose someone totally different from her Father. She chose a lifestyle different from the one she grew up with.

Jessica has never really talked to me about her love for her husband. Why don't we talk about the good things about our relationships? We never seem to have trouble complaining about all the things our mate doesn't do right. Maybe love is just something that should be experienced and not talked about. I have never asked her to because I know her. Some subjects are just taboo with her. She made a pragmatic choice in a spouse I think. She wanted someone who would share the responsibilities of life. But she loves him as well. I have witnessed it.

It was a balancing act. I wanted to share enough with my children that they would not have a romanticized notion of marriage and work. I didn't want to share so much that that they never wanted to try it for themselves although I know I did do that at times. But then maybe I take too much credit. Maybe they are just much smarter than I ever was.

For many years I was mired in guilt because I couldn't offer my children the traditional upbringing I had grown up with. I was moving in the unchartered territory of a working, mostly single mother. For many years I tried to be fill the traditional female role of my youth and to be a career woman as well. It was an impossible task. I think of my generation as the "sandwich generation". The traditional female role was the bottom piece of bread. The new age career mother was and is the top piece of bread. My generation was the mayonnaise covered lunch meat between these two pieces of bread. We connected the two but we were "squeezed" in the process.

Jessica doesn't have to struggle to shed the image of the perfect mother and wife. She doesn't have to prove she can do it all by herself. She saw me race around like a crazy person trying to do it all. I was responding to outside pressure to accomplish something outside the home and the inside pressure to give my children the predictable environment I had been given. Jessica is not haunted by that same ghost. She has used the experiences of my generation to form a more realistic and fulfilling role as a wife and mother. Jessica seems to have tempered her expectations for herself and others. She also hasn't let her notion of romanticism about marriage and motherhood blind her to the realities of life and relationships. Maybe my experiences have helped her to do that. I certainly hope so.

I hear it in the media regularly. We constantly tout the business accomplishments of successful and powerful women. Let's be careful not to set that as the standard for all women like we did with "super women" for my generation. By doing that I fear we might marginalize and minimize the accomplishments of the everyday woman who does her best to balance everything. (As with all things some days she will do a better job than others.)

Shouldn't we temper our admiration of these women not because they don't deserve it but because we don't want the next generation to feel like they have failed because they can't meet that standard? If they can't meet that standard they may feel they have to choose between being a full time mother and a working woman. Haven't we fought for the ability to choose what is best for each of us and the right to be respected for our choices? Let's be careful not to trample on our advancements.

I couldn't help myself. I studied them as they interacted. Jessica invited me to a social gathering of some of her friends. The husband and wife were sitting together with their children laughing and talking. I was mesmerized. I was looking for some bit of hostility or tension in the interaction. I didn't see any. They may actually be the real deal – a genuinely loving, happy traditional family. Jessica claims they are. I am surprised at myself. I don't feel the least bit jealous of this stay at home mother. Doesn't she have what you always wanted, I ask myself. No. It is only now that I realize that I would never have been happy as a full time, traditional wife and mother like my Mother. If only I had realized that when my children were young I could have spared myself a lot of guilt and grief! Maybe it is only now I can accept it was OK to want something else.

We can each now forge our own image of motherhood and marriage. I hope my generation has formed or shaped enough of a framework of a new image that this new generation does not have to negotiate everything as we did. I hope that part of what my generation accomplished was to free our daughters of the guilt and burden of being "superwoman". I hope we have helped them to know what they want by teaching them to be honest about how they feel and what they want. I hope our example has given them permission and courage to seek out and ask for what they need and want from their spouses and children. Ultimately, I hope we have provided a rudimentary road map to start them on their journey to where they want to be.

CHAPTER ELEVEN

Have We Lost Our Way?

I hate it. Every day over and over again it invades my consciousness. I do not want to believe it. I certainly do not want to be reminded of it everyday. I can't escape it. It is in the news. It is in the newspaper. I hear it in the public conversations of everyday people. I observe it in the actions of all of us. We live in a compassionless world.

We were sitting in the lounge discussing the lesson for the day. We had been together as a group for about 3 months by then. It was a nine month course. I think there were about 16 people in the group. I really can't remember what we were discussing that precipitated the remark. Irene was always a serious person but her face hardened as she spoke. "I resent when the administration tells me to take extra time or pay special attention to a particular kindergartner because his parents are going through a divorce," she said through clenched teeth. "Why should I have to go out of my way to help people who are going through a divorce? It is their fault they are getting divorced, not mine," she spat the words out angrily. As she spoke she puffed her chest out as a sign of her moral superiority. The silence in the room was deafening. When no one murmured or made a sound, Irene looked around at the faces in the room. They were all frozen staring at her with the same incredulous expression. She was struck by the realization of what she had said. You could see it in her face. She didn't say anything else. She quietly sat down. As I looked at her face I didn't sense any regret for the feeling she expressed. I saw only embarrassment that she had made the confession here in front of all of us. After all we were in Church at a Bible study group.

Our leader at the Bible Study group was a person who exuded spirituality. It seemed to kind of seep out of her pores. She was the angel that had visited Brian and I that fateful day. After we finished staring at Irene we turned to stare at her. What could she possibly say that could reach Irene and placate the rest of us, I thought. We all waited breathlessly for some words of wisdom or for Irene, at least, to receive a tongue lashing from her. After all wasn't this a great opportunity to teach Irene a lesson? "Let's look at section two of our study guide," was all Deborah said.

I asked Deborah later about this or maybe I should say confronted her about it. Deborah explained, "I have come to know that people attend church for all sorts of reasons most of which do not include a desire to really understand and follow the teachings of Jesus. The silence of the group spoke volumes to Irene. I suspect that the school district's direct request backfired and that Irene actually treated that child worse than the other children. After today, when the administration makes that request, she will probably be more responsive."

I have to admit that, at the time, I was disappointed. Since then I think I have come to understand what Deborah already knew. If Deborah had confronted her, Irene would have been backed into a corner and would have dug her heels in more regarding her self-righteous resentment. The reaction of the group and the silence of Deborah made an impression on her. Hopefully Irene saw her lack of compassion reflected back to her through our eyes like a reflection in the mirror.

In retrospect I wish Irene's behavior had reflected back to me my own routine failure to show compassion. I was a bit too self-righteous to recognize my own failings at the time. Other people's bad behavior and "character" flaws are always so clearly visible to us. Oh if only the same were true for our own

"There but for the grace of God go I" is an expression that I used to hear a lot when I was a child. We would automatically repeat that phrase when we were confronted with or became aware of someone else's misfortune. I never hear that anymore. In fact I can't remember the last time I did hear it. Now I hear things like "They deserve it" or "I earned it and they didn't". If it isn't directly spoken, it is implied. How did an attitude of gratitude get replaced by an attitude of entitlement? Is it all a result of our cultural marketing gurus touting self indulgent and self aggrandizement quips as a way to market their clients' products? We seem to be bombarded with the slogan "You worked hard. You deserve … You earned it." Maybe after a while we started to believe that everything we have and everything we are was earned solely by our own efforts. After a while we even seem to have left out the "you worked hard" part of the equation.

I also, as a child, used to often hear, "Those to whom much is given, much is required" and "Waste not, want not". All these expressions embodied acts of selflessness – looking beyond our own individual needs and wants to something bigger – something that would benefit others and the community. Sadly those expressions and the actions generated by such sentiments seem to have disappeared from our personal and national psyche.

I promised myself I wouldn't cry. It was silly but here I was sitting in my car with tears streaming down my checks. I had just completed my route for "Meals on Wheels". It is difficult, if not impossible, to have an attitude of callousness toward the less fortunate when we volunteer to serve them and see their suffering, trials and tribulations first hand. I think our parents and grandparents understood that. Have we forgotten the simple lesson of humbly giving and serving the less fortunate? How can we want bigger cars, bigger houses and grandiose vacations when we see others who don't have the basic necessities of life satisfied? Are they really to blame and if they are does that really matter? As I cried I reminded myself to be ever grateful for what I do have and how fortunate I am. "There but for the grace of God go me" I thought as I closed the door on the last client who was mentally handicapped. How could I have forgotten to be grateful and to make service to others an integral part of my life?

Thirty years ago divorce was not what it is today. Oh I am not talking about the legal system or its ramifications. That has developed with the changing times. I am referring to the social attitudes regarding divorce. Back then, divorce was humiliating and shameful. You were a failure. It was all your fault because you didn't try hard enough to... blah, blah, blah. That "social status" of "divorce" meant the woman and her children were treated with veiled contempt. You were not required, as Hester Prynne was, to have a bright red "A" emblazoned on your chest but the treatment was somewhat similar. We were outcasts and pariahs. Irene's comment, made less than 10 years ago, is a reminder that, in some sections of our society, that attitude still exists.

"Jessica your grades have dropped. What is going on?" I asked her. She was in fourth grade at the time. She looked at me strangely and shrugged her shoulders. I could tell I wasn't going to find out what was going on from Jessica. I called her teacher and scheduled a conference. The teacher was kind enough to come to school early to meet me so that I could get to the office on time. I arrived at school around 7:45 a.m. The teacher was in the classroom. We chatted a little bit about Jessica's school work. I detected a little hostility but I was awfully tired and stressed out in those days so I thought I was imagining it. "Jessica is not doing as well as she did last year or even earlier this year and she doesn't want to come to school lately. Is there something going on with the other kids that I should know about?" I asked. "No" was the response. "Do you have any idea what may be causing this change?" I continued to probe the teacher. "No," she responded again. I asked, "Where does Jessica sit?" I have no idea why I asked that question. The teacher pointed out the location of Jessica's desk. It was located in the very last row in the far corner of the classroom. It was the desk that was furthest away from the teacher and the chalkboard. My facial expression must have reflected my surprise. Somewhat sheepishly the teacher explained, "I moved her there a few weeks ago. "Why is she sitting there if she is having problems?" I asked. "Shouldn't she be in the front of the room?" The teacher had stopped looking at me at this point in the conversation. I pressed the issue. "Why isn't Jessica sitting in the front of the classroom?" I really can't remember exactly what the teacher said. I just remember that it made no sense and seemed to be a perfectly ridiculous explanation. I trusted my instincts, for once, and said in a firm voice, "I will expect her to be moved to the front of the room right away." There was no verbal response although I did receive a brief look of contempt. "I hope I don't have to go to the principal about this," I said as I got up and left.

Jessica was moved to the front of the room. She started to enjoy going to school again and her grades improved. Was I imagining the teacher's hostility and contempt? Was I imagining that the poor treatment was a result of my status as a divorced woman? Maybe. I tended to doubt myself and my perceptions in those days. I still do. Things certainly changed for the better for Jessica after my talk with her teacher. Maybe by confronting her about her treatment of Jessica she realized what she was doing. Like Irene maybe she just wasn't aware of what she was doing. I hope that was the case.

The school Jessica attended was located in a wealthy suburban area which was primarily populated by married couples in traditional households. Fortunately for us, and unfortunately for them, it encompassed more than just those types of families. There were other similar incidents after this one. Eventually I learned to intercede before the situation got really bad or maybe I just stopped giving the teachers the benefit of the doubt. I am a slow learner. My children say I am bit naive. Maybe so. I wish I had learned that lesson sooner. My children may have been spared some pain and humiliation. Must everyone who is different pay a price? Children of divorce may not any longer be considered "different" and subjected to such treatment but others are.

I was pretty tough in those days or at least I thought I was. I certainly had to go outside the parameters of the traditional female role in order to survive and take care of my children. That required engaging in some traditional male behaviors such as direct confrontations with others. That created some anxiety for me at first but like most things in life I got used to it.

I thought I could face any situation alone. At least I had convinced myself that I could. I had to because I really had no other options. It was just the reality of my life back then. I had no safety net – no support emotionally or financially in the days when my children were very young. So I was surprised that my "invincibility" was shaken by this upcoming event. I was afraid it might turn into a confrontation. Brian was taking all of us –the children and I- to meet his family for the first time. He was very close to his family. We were going to spend Thanksgiving at his sister, Nancy's house. She had five children. Brian was bringing his daughter, Bridget and I was bringing my three.

By this time, we had met many of Brian's "friends" and taken the kids with us to business events that included family and friends. People fussed over Bridget. She was the center of attention. I remember one of my first experiences occurred when we were all invited to dinner by one of Brian's clients. We were going to this great western steakhouse. This was the kind of place I couldn't afford to take my children in those days. It was going to be a real treat for them. They were excited and so was I. Brian and Bridget came to pick us up. When we arrived at the restaurant our hosts Bob and Kim were already there. They were waiting at the entrance for us.

Kim came running over as we approached. She grabbed Bridget and hugged her. She started asking her all about school, her mom, etc. I was waiting for the greeting to finish so I could introduce myself and my children to her. The "greeting" never finished. Brian and Bob talked business at one end of the table. Bridget sat next to Kim. My children and I sat at the far end of the table. Bridget and Kim chatted and laughed together throughout the evening. Kim ordered special drinks and desserts for Bridget.

At the beginning of the evening I tried to converse with Kim but it was like penetrating a thick wall. I tried to engage my children in some conversation but they were all silent during dinner. I sat wondering if there was any way to confront Kim or anyone else about this treatment without looking petty or jealous. If there was a way I never discovered it. After all maybe I was just being petty and jealous? I know that I expect too much of people. I expected Kim to be a gracious hostess. She wasn't and I didn't know how to deal with that. As I look back I should just have asserted myself there as I had to do in the business world but I didn't know how to do that, yet, in a social situation.

So I prepared myself for a similar experience at Brian's sister's house. I knew that she was a close friend of Bridget's mother. I didn't want to get all defensive but I didn't want my children to continually receive that same message of inferiority. I spent the drive going over several scenarios in my mind as to how I would protect my children even if it meant being confrontational.

At that time I naively thought this disparity in treatment would pass as time went on. But in the years to come, Brian and I would have many a heated argument over this issue. There was definitely a subliminal message that my children were second class citizens compared to Bridget. She was prettier, smarter, better behaved than my kids or so the message went. Brian said it wasn't happening and that I was overly sensitive. I went along with that for a while in part because I doubted myself and my perceptions. Other people in our business and social world simply didn't care, were blind to it or ignored it and went along with "Brian's" program. Unfortunately my children weren't blind to it.

It really hurt to see my children treated like this especially when they would look at me with eyes that said I was supposed to protect them. It took me a while to trust myself and my perceptions. I am not exactly sure when I finally did get it. I had a huge sense of guilt for letting it go on for so long. But the critical issue for the time being was how I was going to handle this with Brian's sister? I braced myself for the worst.

Brian entered the house first. I heard someone greet him. As soon as I walked through the door I was smothered with a big hug. "Welcome, welcome. We are so glad you could be here for Thanksgiving!" I looked up to see Brian's sister, Nancy, beaming a huge smile at me. Each of my children received a similar welcome. Nancy started talking to me as if she had known me for years. She introduced my children to her brood and invited them to make themselves right at home which they did. It was a wonderful holiday. I noticed that Bridget hung back a little. I guess that she wasn't used to not being the center of attention. I felt bad for her. My children were having a great time hanging out with the "cousins".

While we were in the middle of our Thanksgiving meal there was a knock at the door. Nancy jumped up from her chair and ran over to greet a woman. The woman was dressed in tight pants and a top that didn't cover her navel. She had platinum blond hair, purple finger nail polish, bright blue eye shadow and black lipstick. She was accompanied by a small skinny toddler dressed in clothes that were a few sizes too small for him. Nancy turned and announced their arrival. "This is Kevin, my grandson and Deanna his mother. This is Eric's son." I knew something of the family history from Brian. Eric wasn't married and never had been. He had a drinking problem and couldn't hold a job or so I had been told.

"Deanna is an alcoholic and drug addict. She claims Kevin is Eric's son but I am not sure. She and Eric were together only very briefly. Deanna has trouble holding a job. She and Kevin were homeless for a while and they stayed here. She is doing better now but she hangs out with other drug addicts and I worry about Kevin," Nancy said. She spoke as if she was reciting ingredients in a recipe. I kept waiting to hear it – the judgment - the contempt for Deanna, her lifestyle and her inability to be a competent mother to Kevin. But all I detected in Nancy's demeanor and tone of voice was love and concern for Deanna and Kevin.

I was shocked that Nancy would fuss over Kevin like she did her other grandchildren! I remember thinking at the time that people like Deanna, who engage in this type of behavior, need to have some consequence so others will be deterred from such conduct. At a minimum shouldn't Deanna and, by implication Kevin, be ostracized or at least treated with a little disdain as some consequence? That is what I was brought up to believe and the attitude that would unconsciously surface. What a mean spirited hypocrite I was! Wasn't I just ecstatic that Nancy didn't treat my children any differently because I was divorced? Nancy opened her home and her heart to my children, to me and to everyone else.

"She was all about love. She didn't have a mean bone in her body," my ever sensitive eldest son, Samuel, said between sobs. It was many, many years after we first met Nancy. We were standing together at the cemetery for Nancy's funeral service. How true I thought. My eldest son was just a child when he spent a lot of time with Nancy yet her message reached him. She welcomed everyone into her home and her heart. She had health problems that were beyond horrible. She had serious issues with her own children. Yet she always smiled. She never complained. She was ever so grateful for what she did have. Most of us wrote her off as a nut case. She was out of touch with the real world we said to ourselves. I guess she was out of touch with the way the world worked. She wasn't judgmental. She didn't treat people differently based on their lifestyle, mistakes or history. Nancy lived her Christian faith. We watched as they lowered her casket into the ground. She had always been there for me. I would sorely miss her. Her love enveloped you and could take the cares of the world away.

It was another one of those (typical) days – long, lonely, painful, exhausting. No more visits from the "angel", Deborah, or anyone else for that matter, except Nancy and her husband. The phone was silent. The doorbell didn't ring. I didn't have the strength to initiate anything. And if I did what was I going to say or talk about. "Hey good morning." This morning I took Brian to the bathroom. I wiped his butt. I showered him. I fed him. I put him in his chair to watch TV. I am tired because I was up all night turning Brian in bed, taking him to the bathroom or rearranging his limbs for him. So what have you been doing today?" I said to myself. I guess I could have faked something but I didn't have the energy for that. My salvation was my time away with Gary at his activities and my visits with Nancy. That was if I could leave Brian with someone for a little while.

Before he was sick Brian was always busy with social and business functions and sporting events. He had two or three such events every week. We went to dinner. We attended weddings. We attended anniversary parties. We went on trips together. We visited people in their homes and they came to our home. Brian counted himself rich in friends. I never knew so many people before I married Brian. Brian thrived on this type of life. I would have preferred to have a little less social life.

After Brian was diagnosed with Lou Gehrig's disease, he continued to go to the office everyday and our social life continued as before. There was an outpouring of sympathy and support that was unimaginable. I was touched and a little overwhelmed by it. As the disease progressed and Brian wasn't able to get to the office or leave the house, his friends would call and come by. Brian's condition worsened. His body further deteriorated.

"Hey how is he? I'm going to come over and visit tomorrow around 10. Is that OK?" one of Brian's friends called to say. "Great. Brian will be very happy to see you and have some company," I responded. Brian was waiting anxiously the next day for his visit. It was 11 and the friend had not arrived yet. I tried to call him but I couldn't reach him. This friend didn't come the following day either. He didn't call to cancel or explain why he didn't come. "Hey Brian he probably got busy and forgot," I said. "Do you want me to call him again?" I asked. Brian was silent. I think he already knew.

I did call Brian's friend a few days later. We chatted about his life and then I asked, "Did you forget about your visit to the house the other day?" There were some excuses and evasions. "What is really going on?" I asked. I didn't want to promise Brian a visit on another day only to have him be disappointed again. I pressed the issue. The friend finally confessed, "I can't handle seeing Brian like that. It depresses me. I can't understand him when he talks. I don't know what to say to him." Other people said the same thing to me during the last part of the illness. I wanted to tell all of them, "This is not about you or how you feel. This is about Brian. He is sick, dying, scared and he needs some support and company." But I was silent.

I judged and chastised these "friends" even if only in my mind. Maybe I should have said those things. Maybe if I had they would have come to visit Brian. Maybe they just sensed my hostility and that kept them away. I so wanted Brian to have visitors! Oh later I understood that seeing Brian reminded them of their own mortality and they did not want to be reminded of that. Still somehow I wished they could have put their own feelings aside for Brian's sake. I didn't say anything to Brian about my conversation with his friend.

In those days I would still call "friends" to ask them to visit. They said, each in their own way, that same thing. I stopped calling. Brian knew that his was not a pretty disease and that his emaciated and distorted body was not a welcome sight. He was confronted with his own mortality each and every day. The lack of visitors only drove that point home. Brian stopped asking me to call "friends." He accepted they were not going to visit him anymore. It took me a little longer to accept. Maybe I never did. There was little or no relief from the drudgery and monotony of each day. Nancy, the "kook" and her husband were the only visitors. And once a week the hospice nurse came. The doorbell was silent. The phone didn't ring.

"I don't talk about my husband's illness or that part of my life with my friends because if I did I wouldn't have any friends," she said matter of factly. I had gone to her house to deliver our handicap van that Brian was now no longer able to use. She was caring for her husband who had ALS and she had two young daughters. I was shocked when she said that. I wanted to scream how can you call them friends but I was silent. As sad as I felt when she said that I thought maybe she was right – maybe she had the better attitude. I also knew that I couldn't do that. I wish I could. Maybe I would still have had friends to talk to and visit me if I could have adopted her attitude. I couldn't do that. I couldn't separate out parts of my life. Brian dying and taking care of him was my life. I didn't know how to talk about anything else.

Brian died one beautiful sunny Sunday afternoon. There was a huge turnout at his funeral. I was told that it was one of the largest, attendance wise, ever at the Church. It was standing room only and it was a huge sanctuary. I hadn't noticed. After the funeral, the doorbell was silent and the phone didn't ring. The living were forgotten along with the dead. It is as if we all had died together. Maybe we had.

"Ellen is a problem at school. We need you to come to the school for a parent teacher conference", the principal said over the phone. I arrived at the school at the duly appointed time. I entered the conference room and stared into the faces of what I assumed were Ellen's teachers. The principal conducted the meeting. "We understand that your husband is dying and you are caring for him at home," he said without emotion. We then went around the table and each teacher, with an unimaginable look of hostility, discussed Ellen using very uncomplimentary adjectives, to put it mildly.

I confronted Ellen when she came home from school. "Mom the teachers tell me I am stupid, that I don't belong in school, that I will never amount to anything and stuff like that. I can't sit there and listen to it," she should have said. "Has anyone talked to you about what is going on at home?" I should have asked. Instead our "conversation" really went something like this, "I hate you!" she screamed. I shrieked, "You stop talking to me like that I am your Mother."

If only Ellen could have expressed what was going on with her to the teachers or administration. If only I were capable of "hearing" what was going on with Ellen. We all turned a blind eye to her suffering. Somehow Ellen made it through that school year. I am sure they passed her so they wouldn't have to put up with her again the next year. Her behavior and the school's response to it got worse over the next few years. Sadly I think the messages Ellen received from the teachers and administration had as much to do with the fact that Ellen looks very Hispanic as the fact that she was acting out over Brian's illness and death. I only came to that realization many years later.

"When I was 9 years old my mother died. My father had to work very long hours to pay for the medical bills. I would not have made it through those years without the kindness of my teachers," related a man in his 60s. The local newspaper had solicited stories from people who had grown up in our city asking them to relate what it was like to live here when they were young. I calculated that the man who was relating his story would have been a boy in the 1940s. Until I read this article I thought I was just expecting too much from the teachers. Maybe I had not imagined things were different years ago. I could not help wondering, "Where have the kindness and compassion gone? Can we regain it? Have we lost our way?"

"We are sorry to hear about your loss. The teachers all signed a card for you and your family," she said looking very satisfied with herself. Brian died before the school year was over. I had bumped into one of Ellen's teachers when I was at school shortly after he died. Surprisingly she recognized me. I didn't know what to say. I was speechless. Hallmark does a good job but did this teacher really think a sympathy card could erase an entire year of cruelty and indifference? Ellen still bears the scars from that year.

Ellen never thought she could graduate from high school much less go to college. She did graduate from college. She thinks she is stupid and that somehow she got lucky. Almost 16 years later I see her self confidence and self esteem finally growing. I hope she can rise above the cruelty of the teachers and life as she continues to mature. Perhaps cruelty is too strong a word but indifference in the face of incredible hardship, vulnerability and pain may amount to cruelty. The wounds of our youth are so much deeper than those received in later years. They do leave permanent scars. It wasn't just the teachers. I failed her as well.

We moved to another state after Brian died, in part, to escape the painful memories. We moved to what, I think, is one of the most beautiful places in the world. Every day is sunny and balmy. The coastline is breathtaking. The sound of the waves is soothing. The trees and grass are green year round. The flowers bloom all year long. Everywhere you look there are beautiful and vibrant colors. If this place were a painting it would be one of Monet's landscapes. There is always a fresh clean smell as if it had just rained. The people are beautiful as well. They are successful and exude the confidence of those who have made it to the top. You are naturally seduced into wanting to belong to and be a part of that group and that place. This place is a "paradise."

But something else was present along with the incredible physical beauty. It was, for a time, hidden by the physical beauty. It was a stealthy, insidious and persistent invader. I succumbed to it without being aware of it. The part of the country we moved to is touted as being a trendsetter for the rest of the country. I hope that isn't true regarding this unfortunate "trend".

"This is our new neighbor who lives in the house previously owned by the Martins," the hostess introduced me. I was attending a neighborhood get together to meet my new neighbors. I shook a few hands. I reached out to shake the hand of one of my neighbors but hers was not extended, "Oh you are the lady who brought all the comps down in the neighborhood. You got your house really cheap," she said as she turned away from me. Welcome to paradise I thought. I didn't realize it at that time but my first introduction to the neighborhood set the tone for the years that I lived there. I thought it was just an isolated incident.

Bruce, one of my new neighbors and I enjoyed a cup of coffee together that day. Well I think the word "enjoy" fits. Bruce was, understandably starved for company and conversation. He was the full time caregiver for his wife after a stroke robbed her of her faculties. Bruce talked. I listened. "They come here and take our jobs. They get free health care and free education for their kids that I pay for it with my tax dollars. We should put them all in a bus and send them back across the border. Oh I have heard they don't have jobs and can't feed their families in their country but that is not my problem. Their country needs to fix its own problems. We shouldn't have to pay the price because their economy and government are screwed up. ..."

Bruce had a tone of rancor and hatred that was, quite frankly, a little scary. I was silent. Bruce continued on for a while in that tone until I said I had things to do. I had a feeling of despondency for a while after he left. I often wondered how someone who took such loving care of his wife could have those attitudes towards others who were also suffering or in difficult circumstances. As much as I admired Bruce for this dedication to his wife I found I avoided spending time with him.

Bruce spewed a good bit of venom but it wasn't right to avoid him. He needed companionship. The first tendrils of the vine I named "Inhumanity" had already grabbed a hold of me. It was a plant that flourished in "paradise." I chose that word after looking it up. Inhumanity means "lack of compassion or pity or an inhuman or cruel act."

"They shouldn't have kids if they can't take care of them. Why should the taxes I pay have to go to support them and their kids! (It wasn't a question). It is not my problem. It is their own fault they are where they are. I worked hard to get where I am. I didn't have an education either. They are lazy and don't want to work hard. If they worked hard they wouldn't have these problems," Ken said. It was a vitriolic spew of venom and I felt stunned like the victim of a poisonous snake bite. I was still new to "paradise." "I have some work to do now," was all I said.

In "paradise" I heard similar attitudes repeated regularly. Different people same sentiment. It reminded me a little bit of the movie "Groundhog Day."

In "paradise "we didn't see those people. You know the people who show visible signs of poverty, physical illness or disability. We read about them in the newspapers or saw them on television. Occasionally there would be a request at church to help them. "Out of sight out of mind," was the unspoken motto. They were physically and economically excluded from our world and our realm of personal experience. This was no accident. After all we intended to create a beautiful environment unmarred by any unpleasantness. I often wondered if the creators of Disneyland played a part in the creation of "paradise". The place was artificially created to look beautiful all the time. The inhabitants themselves presented beautiful physical images.

The oceans, the weather, the coastline are breathtakingly beautiful. It is paradise! As I was sitting looking out over the ocean listening to another Ken I was struck by the immense contrast. I was in the most beautiful places talking to one of its very handsome, successful inhabitants who had the soul of a troll. It seemed the more beautiful the physical surroundings the uglier were the souls of the inhabitants. It reminded me of a see saw.

I should have told them I disagreed with them and that we should care about and help others who did not have what we had. But I didn't. In part I lacked the moral courage to speak up. I was a coward. I knew I would be ostracized – quietly so but ostracized all the same. I would ask myself if it mattered that I would be ostracized. Did I really want to socialize with people who cared only about themselves and cared nothing about the less fortunate? On some level I wanted to fit in with these successful, beautiful people. Some part of me is still the girl in high school from the wrong part of town who wants to be part of the "in or wealthy" crowd.

The repercussions of speaking out could result in more concrete "punishment". I witnessed the esteemed governing body of the Homeowners' Association persecute those they didn't like or who didn't agree with them.

Wasn't I crazy to let these attitudes mar my contentedness with the physical beauty? Everyone wanted to live there. There must be something wrong with me if I didn't like it there. I was told as much by the inhabitants if I ever expressed any reservation about living in "paradise.

I had reasons, albeit lousy ones, for my lack of moral courage." I often wondered if there was something about the breathtaking beauty of the physical surroundings that seduced me into silence. That beauty can lull you into a feeling of complacency about social issues. Why think about that stuff when there is so much physical beauty to enjoy?

I knew I was betraying myself and the lessons I had learned from my experiences with Brian by remaining silent. I wouldn't have changed their attitudes if I had spoken up but I might have been able to stop what was happening to me. The small tendrils of the "inhumanity" vine were grabbing a hold of me in the smallest of ways.

I felt myself panic. This woman had dropped it right in front of me. She was about my age, maybe a little bit younger. It was there – lying just a few feet in front of me. I could have easily reached down and picked it up for her. Many years ago I would have automatically done that, without thinking. But now a battle raged in my head as to whether I should or should not do it. What reason could I possibly have for not doing something kind for another person? After a moment or two she picked up her book herself. I was angry at myself. As I walked away I thought that I would not have been afraid to yell at her for dropping the book right in front of me but I was afraid to do something kind. Telling her off would have earned me respect. Being kind would have earned me disdain. How did kindness become so passé? Aren't manners just a way of recognizing and respecting that others have needs as well as us? Is the absence of small kindnesses and manners the precursor to worse behaviors like loss of compassion?

"It is not my fault they are losing their homes. They borrowed money they could not afford to repay. They got in over their heads. No one has ever bailed me out. How could they have ever been so stupid to believe the mortgage broker? It is their own fault, no one else's," a business acquaintance said angrily to me during a discussion of the current financial situation.

"I should get a break on my $800,000.00 mortgage if they do!" one of the anchors on the national news said. Others expressed those same sentiments. Why are we so resentful if someone gets a break or benefit that we really don't need? I thought we were supposed to outgrown those adolescent attitudes as we matured into adulthood.

We, as a society, love to and are obsessed with assessing blame. It has almost become a national pastime like baseball used to be. Just watch the presentation of stories on the national news shows. We typically rush to help when a natural disaster strikes as there is no blame to assess. It is quite the opposite in other situations where we determine there was a man made causation factor. Immediately after such a tragic event the focus shifts from helping the victims to seeking the persons or organization responsible for the tragedy. What do we accomplish by assessing blame? In some limited situations some change in procedures can be effected by inquiring into an assessing "blame". But don't we take the inquiry or should I say "inquisition" well beyond the scope required to assess the need for change? Is it any wonder that any individual involved in a tragedy refuses to tell the truth regarding what happened. Honesty could help us correct the situation in the future. But correcting the situation is always secondary to publicly flogging the perceived perpetrators. What is achieved by looking for, blaming and punishing someone for every unfortunate event that happens? This obsession serves to divide us rather than unite us and I think uses up precious resources that could or should be dedicated to improving the situation. Does this preoccupation with assessing blame another by-product of our lack of compassion?

Once we assess blame the next step is to mete out some punishment. We see the relatives of victims of violent crimes seeking, in the criminal courts, the greatest punishment possible for the perpetrator. Such behavior isn't limited to the criminal courts. It happens often in family and civil courts. Punishment is a critical element of human relations. But there is a difference between punishment and revenge. The courts are used all too often as a venue to seek revenge. In those cases, the punishment is rarely severe enough to satisfy the "victim". The damage can never be undone. There is no magic pill that will "heal" or make things right again. Sometimes obtaining revenge leaves an even greater emptiness because it did not yield the anticipated result. In my experience, revenge does not bring any genuine healing or peace.

Perhaps genuine healing can only occur in the presence of forgiveness and compassion. This may be as true for nations as for individuals. Those qualities do not grow rapidly. If we are willing to spend time and resources finding someone to blame and seeking punishment or revenge why are we not willing to spend time cultivating compassion and forgiveness? Revenge and blame can be easy "fixes". They don't require any deep soul searching or effort on our part but they don't yield much relief either. The act of cultivating an attitude of forgiveness and compassion does require a great deal of effort but it will enrich our lives for years to come.

"Mom it is going to take me three more years to get my degree. How could I have been so stupid! Why did I party so much? Why didn't I study more?" Samuel berated himself. I realized as he spoke that I too had, unconsciously, been berating and blaming him. Samuel made mistakes. Samuel has suffered the consequences of his mistakes and learned from them. I share a huge part of the "blame" for his situation. I need to stop, unconsciously, berating and blaming him and myself for his failures and mistakes. "You are where you are. That is all behind us now. Let's not look back unless it helps you to move forward," I replied to Samuel. I finally meant what I said.

It is so liberating to stop blaming myself and others ad nauseum for mistakes and misjudgments. It is a lesson I have to continually relearn but it is becoming easier to live that way on a daily basis. I have developed a different attitude. I am, by nature or maybe upbringing, self righteous. Now I can usually stop myself when I start down that path. I don't feel driven to judge or "punish" the Deannas and Kens of the world or even myself or my family as much.

I am finally able to recognize my own failings, shortcomings and mistakes. Maybe that recognition has helped met to develop an attitude of compassion for myself and others. I strive to accept people for who they are or where they are in their life's maturation process or learning process. Maybe in the greater scheme of things they have suffered consequences and will grow and learn as they are capable. It is not for me to say or know. All I can do is to be true to myself and my values when I am with them. I can refuse to judge them and try to show compassion or understanding for what their situation is. Maybe that alone can effect great change.

Do we, as a society, care if we are losing our compassion? What are our core values? Are we a country that believes we should help the less fortunate or help all citizens achieve a certain standard of living or is it everyone for him or herself? If we choose to be guided only by our own self interest or everyman for himself aren't we giving up our humanity? Do you only get to enjoy only what you have earned yourself or should you be able to share, to some extent, in the collective good fortune? Should we set aside some of our own self interest for the common good? The Founding Fathers advocated the practice of "enlightened self interest." I think somewhere in the last 200 years we lost the "enlightened" part. With only self interest as our guide have we lost our way?

"The Sheriff posted a foreclosure notice on our front door of our house. It was there when I came home from school one day. You see my father lost his business. We had already sold our only car and everything else we could sell. We didn't get much because no one had any money to buy anything back then. My mother found a job as a secretary in the next town. She would leave the house at 5 am and return about 7:30 pm every day. It was an hour and a half train ride from our town to where she worked. In the dark, rain, sleet and snow she would walk to the train station from our house. Our two ill grandparents moved into our house. We took care of them. My brother and I slept in the attic because they occupied our bedrooms. I never heard my mother complain. She knew we were one of the lucky families. We were rescued from homelessness by a wealthy friend of my father's who paid off the bank and the back taxes."

I like to think my Mother told me this story but she didn't. It is a story that I pieced together over many years. Snippets of the events were related by many people except for my Mother. She never told me anything about it. I think it was much too painful for her. No one who lived through it wants to talk about or remember the Great Depression. My Mother was a young girl at the time. The events and the fear it generated have shaped her life and, for a time, the national psyche.

The generations who lived through the Great Depression don't seem to have the attitude that everything we have or don't have is entirely a result of our own efforts or lack thereof. They don't make a distinction between the victims of the Great Depression, the 9/11 tragedy and the downtrodden in our society. To them they are simply people in need. All of my relatives who experienced the Great Depression, i.e., my Grandmothers, my Grandfathers, my Aunts and Uncles, my Mother and my Father have all made community service an integral part of their lives. Their need to help didn't stop with the end of that terrible era. They give out of a sense of gratitude for all that they do have. Rarely are any of their good deeds tainted with an attitude of blame or recrimination. They give back to those who have less regardless of the reason why they have less. Perhaps they don't see all that they have as being "earned" or deserved by them. They see it as luck, fate or as a gift from God. That may be the critical lesson learned from the Great Depression.

Those expressions that I never hear any more like "There but for the grace of God go I," or "To those to whom much is given much is required," have been replaced with phrases like, "You deserve this. You are entitled to __________. After all you work hard. You earned it. " I started to pay attention to the number of advertisements that tout that enticement. It seems to have become the marketing mantra of our time. But are we, unconsciously, allowing marketers and advertisers to shape and define our culture and values? Are these mantras a reflection of the shift in our values? Are we allowing business or the making of money for ourselves to be our primary focus to the exclusion of service to our community and even family?

Families and communities are splintered geographically and philosophically in contrast to what was in place in the 50s and 60s when I was a child. A lot of physical separation is the result of relocating to find a better job. In the absence of family and community connections we become susceptible to the marketers and other pop culture forces. We lack the family and community connections and role models that show us how to live our lives in a meaningful way. Those connections keep us grounded. Those connections serve as a filter for the pop cultural messages. In its absence everything rushes at us and we become easily confused and misled. Why can't we, in these current times, seem to form communities of any sort?

"Let's set one day a month aside to volunteer together at the local food bank," I proposed to my group of friends who meet regularly for lunch. My request was met with dead silence. Why is it so difficult to get my generation to come together as a group for any purpose? We are not joiners. We don't join churches, community service organizations, bridge clubs or much of anything else. We get together for drinks and dinner with our friends. Is this another symptom of individualism run amuck? Are we afraid we will lose our individual identity by becoming associated with a group? Are we just too selfish and unyielding to make any compromise that a group may require of us? I think I am guilty of all of the above. Groups are the building block of relationships and communities. Isn't that worth any individual sacrifice?

"I want to discuss marketing the business with all of you this morning. The most important thing I have to say is that you have to tell everyone, everywhere you go what you do for a living. You never know where a business opportunity may arise. You always want to tout your accomplishments and why you are different from the other lawyers. Look at every situation as a business opportunity," the senior partner at the firm lectured us. This was his mantra. I just couldn't bring myself to do what he wanted.

In the competitive business world we strive to separate ourselves out from others. We are constantly bombarded with the message that we have to distinguish ourselves from our "competition" or our co-workers in order to get ahead. That business model has been foisted onto our social interactions. Everyone becomes competition because we are never out of work mode. We are what we do for a living. When we see others as competition we don't want to help them in the business or social environment. Every relationship becomes utilitarian. What can I get out of this relationship or how it is good for me and my business is a question we silently ask ourselves. We no longer have a sense of connection to our neighbor, our community, even our family. It can happen in spite of our best intentions. We absorb the attitudes of our culture similar to the ways single cell organisms absorb things by osmosis. It just happens without an act of volition. The callousness seems to enter your soul without your consent or knowledge. I know it happened to me.

"Do you have time for a quick cup of coffee?" I asked my friend Lucy. "Oh I have to go to a meeting that will take a few hours. Kyle has a water polo match all day. Helen has a birthday party at 1 pm and then dance lessons at 4:00 pm. In between I have a bunch of errands to run. Oh yeah. Kyle has a tutoring session after water polo. I don't think I can make it but I will call you later." Lucy replied. I had seen her, looking distressed, earlier that week at some school event. Things were not good in her life or so she said when I asked her what was wrong. I called to invite her for coffee because I thought she might want to talk about a few of those things. We never got together. When I saw her at a swim event a week later I asked, "How are things going?" "I have been too busy to think about anything," she said.

I remember thinking that Lucy had imbibed the drug of choice for the 21st century – incessant activity – "busyness". Or should I say buzziness as it reminds me of bees swarming around a hive – the constant activity and noise. After all we have to get everything checked off of our "to do list" don't we? Our "to do list" typically does not include thinking about our life, volunteering in the community outside of our children's school or doing something kind for a stranger or even a friend, at least not a kindness beyond the perfunctory..

"We are sitting in this row," the middle aged lady standing behind me barked at me. I was standing in the aisle trying to squeeze my oversized carry on in the overhead compartment. I shouldn't have been doing it and she was right to be unhappy with me. I was too cheap to pay the $25.00 to check it. I turned to look at a scowling, angry face. My immediate reaction was to tell her to "buzz off" I was trying as hard as I could to get my luggage situated. Instead, who knows why, I said, "sorry" and moved aside so she and her husband huffily could take their seats next to mine. She was still scowling. I sat down. Again for some unknown reason I asked her, "Are you going home or is this the beginning of a trip?" "Oh we are returning from a wonderful vacation to New England," she replied. We talked for the entire plane trip. I can't remember when I enjoyed a plane trip so much. We exchanged phone numbers and when I am in her area I will call her. If I hadn't taken the chance and spoken kindly to her I would have spent an hour or two in silent, probably mutual hostility. That hostility would have shaped the remainder of my day.

It seems trivial but maybe it is not. You see I am guilty of the same thing as my friend on the airplane. I carry around an attitude of hostility or abrasiveness. I can remember when I first became aware of it. I was looking in the mirror as I combed my hair. "Oh my God?" I said out loud. It can't be. I looked again. How could that have happened? I tried for several days to consciously change it but the minute I stopped thinking about it went back to the way it was. The expression on my face was set to a permanent scowl! Now I understood why I got the reactions I did when I was out in public. I observed that same scowl on the face of my Mother and Sister. Was it genetic? Was it a consequence of middle age where everything sags including, apparently, the smile muscles? Whatever it was I needed to change it. In this age of anonymity I want to present a welcoming, kind first impression.

"Where we expend our effort and time our riches will also lie," is an expression I have often heard. How trite but true! I say this to myself periodically as a wake up call. We own a lot of stuff – expensive stuff in some cases. But we are a very poor country. As I listen to the news or read the newspaper I think sometimes we might be on the verge of spiritual bankruptcy. Is our goal in life to acquire as much stuff as possible? Do we realize we are making that the primary focus of our lives? We may not admit it but we don't expend our best efforts and our time in our relationships and our communities. We delude ourselves. We reserve our best efforts for the business world and impressing people who really don't care about us. I saw this with Brian. All of his so called friends disappeared once he could no longer bestow benefits such as contracts, favors or business on them. Sadly both Brian and I thought at least some of these people were our friends. They weren't. I became very bitter after that experience. It was a long time before I would make any effort for anyone other than my family.

We stay busy so as to avoid any emotional unpleasantness in our lives. We adopt the world view that if you aren't successful it is only because of your own failings so we can avoid caring about others – strangers, family and neighbors. We are obsessed with assessing blame and with recrimination again so we can avoid doing for others. If it is their fault so we don't need to help them. We refuse to sacrifice any of our "individualism" or to compromise to be part of a group. We define ourselves more by our differences than our connections. We spend our principal energies – the best of ourselves - in acquiring material stuff and racking up business credentials. After all that is a lot easier than working at personal connections and relationships and our success is easier to measure and control.

"How does it feel to lose your entire home and all your possessions?" the news person asked this person. In the midst of this flood in North Dakota the news person was going up randomly to people and asking those stupid questions news people like to ask. This nameless man didn't give the usual and obvious reply. "I am happy to sacrifice my home to the flood for the good of the community in order to prevent other homes from flooding. I do not want others to experience the loss and pain I have experienced," he calmly said. I replayed it on my DVR to be sure I had heard what he said. I followed that story for several days but I did not see or hear anything else about the nameless man after he made that statement. Perhaps it was his choice to remain silent. That alone is very refreshing. Clearly the news covers a story until you hate hearing about it – at least initially after it happens. So in a way I am glad they did not retell of this incredible act of selflessness. We become impervious to information that is constantly repeated. This man is after all a hero in the truest sense of the word. I hope I am not the only one who thinks so. If only we could find a way to recognize and build on that as a community and a nation.

"Mom the swim team is collecting certain items to send to the service men and women serving in Iraq and Afghanistan. I want to make up a flyer to give to our neighbors asking for contributions," Gary said. He was about 12 years old at the time. He was so excited about this project. He carefully prepared a flyer and distributed it our neighbors by placing it in their mailbox of each house. He received one bag of donations that was left on our front porch before the deadline. "Gary you received a letter today," I said when he arrived home from school. Gary excitedly opened the letter. He read it and then with a look of total dejection he handed the letter to me. It read something like this, "It has come to our attention that you have placed items in certain mailboxes. That is a violation of federal law. You will be prosecuted if you engage in this conduct again." It was signed by the postmaster. I found it hard to imagine that one of our neighbors had complained to the post office concerning Gary's request for donations for the military troops but apparently someone did.

I had to leave "paradise". Eventually all I could see was the ugliness. The vine called "inhumanity" was growing in me and choking me. I was losing my core values and my guide through this life. I was lost.

The wonderful thing about our society is that we have the freedom to become who we want to be on many levels. There are few constraints anymore. However that also makes it difficult to find common ground with others in this day of overwrought individualism and self interest. If we don't think about these things, i.e., how we want to define ourselves and our society we become the puppets of the mass marketers and pop culture and at the mercy of unscrupulous individuals.

I submit our individual and collective lives would be richer if we based our actions and make our decisions from a place of compassion and humanity. If we do so the end result may be the same but the process will not be. It will not take a toll on our souls. It will not undermine or destroy our humanity. As a parent we make decisions regarding our children out of love, compassion and concern for them. As a community and society shouldn't we do the same?

We feel entitled rather than grateful. We feel we deserve our good fortune. We believe we have earned it by our own efforts. We are concerned only about ourselves. That belief system creates an attitude of callousness towards those who haven't had such good fortune. We blame them for their situation which absolves us of any responsibility to help them. Where will such attitudes take us? Is it someplace we want to go? Have we misplaced the core values that ground us and guide us through life? Have we lost our humanity? As a consequence are we lost? If so, do we want to do something to reclaim it? I know that I have a lot of work to do on myself. What about you?

CHAPTER TWELVE

The Lost Generation of Sons?

They are lost. At least it appears that way to me. They seem to wander aimlessly through life for any number of years. Often they drift from one dead end job to another with no sense of direction. Sometimes they even engage in dangerous and self destructive activities. They appear to have no sense of self - who they are. I call them the "lost generation".

"Samuel are you all right?" I asked as I bent down to pick him up off the floor. He was just five years old. My marriage to his father was breaking up or should I say it was already over – finished. It had morphed into fits and starts of fighting, name calling, withdrawal. It reminded me of an old car sputtering to turn on or come alive. It sparks, sputters and then dies. This happens over and over until finally it can't even turn over. There is just the empty whir whir of the engine as you turn the key in the ignition. That was the state of our marriage at this time. The situation escalated to violence before it finally ended. I used to wonder what David thought he was accomplishing by becoming violent. He claimed he wanted the relationship to continue. If he wanted the relationship to continue violence certainly would create the exact opposite effect. I was looking for some rational explanation for his behavior. Only later I came to understand that the violence was an expression of his rage that the relationship was ending.

Men in our culture are permitted, or at least my generation is permitted, only one emotion – anger. Every emotion they experience is expressed as or channeled into anger. A small amount of anger can sometimes slowly ooze out of his pores. More often there is so much pent up emotion that it explodes. My withdrawal from David and our relationship was definitely the catalyst for the eruption that was already boiling beneath the surface.

I was sitting on the couch. The three children were playing somewhere in the house or yard. David put his contorted face right in front of mine - only about an inch away. Instinctively I knew that it didn't matter what I said he was going to rant and rave. I listened or pretended to listen for a few minutes and then I got up and walked away. He followed me or should I say he stalked me into the hallway. Of course all the children came running when they heard the shouting. David knocked me down. Samuel was standing right next to me when I was knocked down. He went down with me and I landed on top of him. That is the event that precipitated my assisting Samuel up off the floor that particular day.

"What can I do to protect my children?" I desperately asked the therapist. "Will I be able to undo any of the damage when this is over?" I asked her. "Samuel will probably always remember the physical altercation as being directed at him," she replied. I remember feeling distraught that my children were going through all of this. I couldn't undo what had already happened. Quite honestly I was too overwhelmed at the time to really think about fixing anything in the past. I was just trying to get through the days.

"Do you remember when your father pushed me down and I fell on top of you?" I asked Samuel. He was about 26 years old at the time. "No," he replied. "Do you remember any of the violence that occurred during that time?" I asked. "No," Samuel again replied.

"Dad is sending me a birthday present," Samuel excitedly told me as soon as I arrived home from the office. "What do you think he will get me?" he asked me. Samuel went on excitedly speculating on what wonderful gift his father would send him. I remained silent. He was about six years old at the time. His father had just moved back to his home state.

"Samuel goes to the mailbox several times a day to see if his birthday gift from his father has arrived," the babysitter said. "I have tried to stop him but he insists," she continued. I didn't know what to say to Samuel. I didn't want to make excuses for his father. At that time I had not learned how to be honest with my children so I said nothing. After about two weeks Samuel just stopped going to the mailbox to look for the gift. He never mentioned the gift again and never really mentioned his father much again. That seems to be the incident that caused Samuel to sever any ties, if in fact they ever existed, he had to his father.

Even before he moved away, Samuel's father's phone calls were sporadic. He would promise to take the children somewhere. Occasionally he showed up around the time he promised. I would answer the door. Samuel and Ellen were standing a short distance behind me. They were dressed and waiting to go. I had learned not to let them answer the door. Typically the conversation went something like this. "I can't take all of them today because ....." fill in the blank. I would be standing directly in front of Samuel and Ellen as if my body created a sound barrier. "Come on Ellen. Samuel I'll take you next time." their father typically said. Ellen and he were gone before I could even turn around to look at Samuel. Samuel was so fragile. I ran to Samuel's room. He was playing with his matchbox cars. "I'm sorry. I love you", I said. "Do you want to talk about anything? Should we go somewhere together?" I asked. "Vroom, Vroom," was the only sound Samuel made as he pushed his cars around his imaginary city. I kissed the top of his head and went into the other room. I had absolutely no idea what I should do.

Eventually their father didn't call or come over at all. I had the children call him on his birthday and Fathers' day a few times when I had a phone number for him. Once in a while he would send one of the children a birthday card or a Christmas card. It usually wasn't Samuel. This was Samuel's male role model I used to say to myself in despair. I felt so guilty for giving him such a father.

I was left to pick up the pieces of this shattered child and he was shattered. Samuel was, and probably still is, the most sensitive of my children. All of the children reminded me of a glass vase that has been dropped on a hard surface. They were broken into pieces not necessarily by the divorce but by the fallout of the divorce. I am referring to how we adults handled it or I should say failed to handle it in any even remotely mature fashion. Like the glass vase the pieces would never quite fit back together again. There were chips, cracks, gaps and uneven spaces and there always would be. Samuel was perhaps the most shattered.

It seemed like all of this hurt, angst and disappointment just faded away when Brian came into our lives. After an initial period of skepticism, Samuel came to idolize Brian. The girls were not quite as accepting of Brian as Samuel but they grew to love him in their own way. Brian was to Samuel everything his father had not been. Brian was involved in Boy Scouts with him. Brian encouraged and attended all of Samuel's athletic events. Brian and Samuel did projects together. In three short years Brian easily filled the void left by Samuel's father and their relationship seemed to heal those old wounds. It was a blessing that their father disappeared from our lives because it made it much easier for us to form a family with Brian.

Their father saw them for the last time when Samuel was about 10 years old. He asked to have them for a visit during their Spring break. Brian and I were married by that time. The children didn't argue with me much when I said they were going to visit their father. I wasn't sure if I should let them go. I felt somewhat comforted in that Jessica was old enough that she would call if there was a problem. I had his address and phone number. He and the kids were going to spend the week at his sister's house. She is just a wonderful person. I put them on the airplane with a feeling of trepidation. "I hope I am doing the right thing," I said to myself the entire trip to and home from the airport. Jessica called and complained from his sister's house. Ellen had a good time. Samuel was silent and never said a word about the trip or his father. They never went to visit him again.

"Dad's wife called me, "Jessica informed me. She was by this time a young adult. "He is very sick in the hospital. I'm going to go see him. It feels weird to call him Dad. I am going to see him because I am afraid I will regret it if something happens to him and I haven't had any contact with him since I was a kid. Ellen and Samuel don't want to go," she said. Jessica still talks to him occasionally. She has met his new wife and children. Ellen spoke to him a few times but stopped communicating with him many years ago. Samuel forbids you to speak of him in his presence and we can never refer to him as Samuel's dad or father.

"I quit," the babysitter said as soon as I walked in the door from the office. "Samuel is impossible. He refuses to do anything I say. He doesn't follow any of the rules. I can't deal with him anymore," she said as she stormed out the door. I knew there was no reasoning with her. By the time she quit Samuel's toys, all of them, and TV privileges had already been taken away. "Samuel you have to do what the babysitter says," I had told him the night before. "If you don't I will take your bicycle away". He loved his bicycle more than anything. Samuel didn't say anything. And he didn't care or at least he didn't let on that he cared as I took his bicycle with me the next day to store it at the office. It sat there for months and he never once asked about it. There was nothing left to take away.

"Hey why don't you call one of your friends to see if they want to do something?" I suggested to Samuel as he was milling aimlessly around the house. At age 14 he was usually spending time with his buddies. "OK," he said hanging his head. I watched as he called a friend from the phone in the family room. "Hey Ryan do you want to do something today?" I heard Samuel say into to the phone. Then Samuel was quiet. I was holding my breath hoping that his friend could come over to the house. There were a few moments of silence with Samuel peering at the floor while his friend must have been talking or asking his parents about going out. "He's dead. Ok. Later then," Samuel said and then he hung up the phone. "What happened?" I couldn't keep from asking as if I didn't already know from the look on Samuel's face. "It's Father's Day and he is going to do something with his dad," Samuel responded. "Oh," was all I could say. Samuel slunk away to his bedroom to play videogames. I tried to coax him out a couple of times that day to go and do something with Gary and I but he simply didn't respond. He stayed alone in his room playing videogames all day.

This was one more event in what seemed an endless parade of events that made me feel totally helpless, powerless and angry.

Words were so meaningless. Hugs helped but only temporarily. Would Samuel ever get a break? Would he ever heal? What could I do to help him? You see this was our first Father's Day without Brian. He died in April of that year.

Samuel descended into a world of drugs, alcohol, association with, to put it mildly, unsavory "friends", run ins with police, idleness and lethargy. A description of the whole litany of events would be too monotonous and painful. It had begun while Brian was sick but I had been too busy to notice. That is when I really lost Samuel. I had missed the warning signs.

The phone rang. I picked it up in the family room. Brian was sitting in his chair right next to the phone. "This is Officer so and so of the police department. Can you bring your son, Samuel, to the police department, tomorrow at 10:00 am? We want to talk to him." "OK", I said and hung up the phone. "Who was that?" Brian mouthed to me. "It was nothing," I responded. Brian looked at me like he knew I was lying.

Samuel had lost both parents – Brian to Lou Gehrig's disease and me to being a full time caregiver to Brian and Gary. Why did I think a 13 year old could understand and cope with what was going on? How could I have let Samuel down when he needed me so desperately? Would anything have been different if I had paid attention? Should I have put Brian in a nursing home? I didn't want to do that. I promised Brian I wouldn't do that, but at what price? Brian was going to be gone soon. Samuel had a lot of years in front of him. Did I make the wrong choice? Wasn't Brian's suffering enough? Why did the children have to suffer as well?

"I started smoking marijuana because I just couldn't handle coming home and seeing Brian sitting in that chair in the corner of the room," Samuel told me years later. Brian had been a man of infinite energy and vitality. I never saw him sit and watch television unless it was a particular football game. He was always doing something around the house or with the children when he wasn't at the office. He often took Samuel to the construction sites with him on the weekends. When Samuel would come home from school after Brian was ill, Brian would be sitting in his handicapped chair in the corner of the family room watching TV. He would have been there all day. He couldn't speak or move. I realize now that Samuel avoided being in the same room with Brian. Later on Samuel avoided even being home except to sleep.

Why did Brain suffer for so long? I often wondered if the suffering would ever end. I hated myself for thinking that, but we were all well beyond our limits when died. Samuel had obviously reached his limit long before Brian took his last breath. He escaped into the world of drugs. I was too preoccupied or naive to notice.

"Mom I am leaving military school right now," Samuel said to me over the phone. It was the day after he had turned 18. It was the middle of the school semester. "You can't do that! " I exclaimed in panic. I tried to persuade Samuel to change his mind by logically explaining what the consequence of this would be for his life and his future. That kind of reasoning never worked with Samuel. "You don't have any money and I am not going to send you any. You have to stay at school. We can talk about this at the end of the semester," I said firmly. "I don't care. I am leaving right now," he said as he hung up the phone. I called the headmaster of the military school. "Legally we can't keep him here after he is 18. If he wants to go we can't stop him," the headmaster told me. I spent a sleepless night wondering what would happen and what to do. As it turns out one of Samuel's teachers was able to talk some sense into him. A phone call from my Father helped as well. Samuel stayed at school through the end of that semester. It was a sleepless week for me.

"Mom I don't want to go back to military school. I want to stay at home and get a job," Samuel said a month or so after he arrived home for the summer. "If you get your GED and enroll in community college I will agree," I said. Samuel was 18 now. We had moved to another state so he wasn't hanging out with his old druggie friends. I hadn't detected drugs at all since we had moved. But in the end it boiled down to the fact that I knew I couldn't make Samuel go to school or really do much of anything he didn't want to do. I'm not sure I ever really could. I hoped that if he made the decision for himself he would follow through on his commitment. I was wrong.

Samuel was always the type of kid that routinely did things without thinking of the consequences. I used to describe him to people by saying he would have to hit the brick wall a dozen or so times before he would change course to avoid it. He was determined to do it his way. Maybe some people just have to figure out everything for themselves in their own way and in their own time. Samuel is one of those.

"Mom, I am at the county jail. I was arrested last night for DUI. I was driving around alone in my car drinking a beer," Samuel said. "I'm not coming to get you," I responded. Great I thought as I hung up. Now he will have no high school diploma and no driver's license. He arrived home a few hours later by taxi.

"Samuel, Samuel wake up! Your boss just called asking where you were. Aren't you supposed to be at work this morning?" I asked.

"Samuel, Samuel wake up!" Don't you have a class this morning? Aren't you supposed to be at school right now?" I asked.

"Samuel you can't continue to live with me if you don't work and/or don't go to school! You know that is what we agreed to when you asked not to return to military school," I said one morning after he lost his job and didn't get any credits that semester at the community college. Samuel was silent. He was never one to argue. He would simply ignore me. He got up and went to his room. Many, many more months passed with Samuel doing nothing but staying in his room or watching TV. He simply ignored my pleas and demands to do something.

"I can get him to get a job and go to school," my sister said one day as I was discussing Samuel's situation with her. "You are going to go stay with your Aunt for a while," I said to Samuel. "Please pack a bag. I have made arrangements for you to fly out tomorrow morning."

The next morning Samuel wasn't packed and he wouldn't get in the car. After a few more days of arguing I managed to get him into the car. I packed a bag for him. I left him at the airport that afternoon. His flight left the next morning. I was fresh out of ideas and patience. My sister can be pretty tough when she wants to be. I had no idea if that is what Samuel needed.

How can you motivate someone who has absolutely no motivation? I think the answer is that you can't. They have to motivate themselves. Nothing I suggested seemed to motivate Samuel. No consequence I meted out seemed to motivate Samuel. He didn't want to do anything. He "wanted" to stay in his room, play video games and watch TV.

How does a parent know what to do? I wanted to simply give up. I was angry at him for making my life so miserable. I also understood that he was not doing this intentionally although it felt like it at times. He was miserable himself. He was lost and I didn't know how to help him. I also felt responsible for his problems. I had given him a pretty lousy life. He was my son and I loved him in spite of all of this although I didn't feel like I loved him most days. Still, there was no way I couldn't abandon him. How do you know what will work? I often wondered if it mattered at all what I did or didn't do. Samuel seemed hell bent on doing nothing. At least he wasn't self destructing with drugs and alcohol like before. Maybe he was improving I thought.

"I am putting him on a plane and sending him back to you," my sister said a few weeks after Samuel had arrived at her house. "He refuses to get a job or enroll in school. He sleeps and sits around all day playing video games and watching TV. He will be arriving tomorrow," she said in frustration.

"You can't live here if you don't go to school or get a job," I said to Samuel. I felt like I was a broken record – the vinyls they call them now that have a scratch and get stuck repeating the same small part of the music over and over again. You love the record so you pick up the needle and move it each time it gets to the scratched part until you get so tired of doing that you throw it away. I don't recall how many times I said that to Samuel or over how long a period of time. I can't remember how it finally came about but he eventually went to live with a new friend in a sketchy part of the city. Maybe he finally got tired of being yelled at every day. I know I was tired of yelling.

I tried not to worry. I had no idea what Samuel was doing. I didn't really know where he was living. He didn't have a phone so I didn't hear from him for a few months. Maybe no communication is best I thought to myself. Samuel had and maybe still has a way of manipulating me. My parents came for the holidays and my Dad wanted to visit Samuel. I'm not sure how he got in touch with him but he went to pick him up to come stay with us for Christmas. Samuel wouldn't look at me or speak to me. He spent most of the time in his room coming out only to chat with my Dad.

Samuel had been home for about a week. I was wondering how he was able to get so much time off from work. It was time for him to go back. My Dad couldn't bring himself to talk to Samuel about going back so I went into his room or at least into the doorway to talk to him. "Samuel when do you need Grandpa to drive you back to Adam's place?" I asked. I was trying hard to avoid the past and not to show any disappointment or anger. I can remember him sitting at the desk in his room. Funny how some memories are so clear. He was sitting at this desk with his head bowed when I entered the room. He still wouldn't look at me. I had to address my comments to his back. He never looked up from the desk. He was silent. I was getting frustrated. Then I saw that his shoulders were shaking. He was sobbing. "I can't go back there!" he cried. He kept shaking his head and repeating, "I can't go back there." I continued to stand in the doorway without saying anything. "I don't have a job. I tried but I couldn't find one. I sit on the couch and watch TV all day. I sleep on the couch at night," Samuel said between sobs. Now he had his hands pressed on either side of his head like he was trying to squeeze something out of it. "I am going crazy," he shrieked. I think I said calmly "What do you want to do?" "I want to go back to school," he said. "Please don't make me go back there". The next day my Dad took Samuel to pick up the few things he had at Adam's place.

I was able to find a junior college where the classes hadn't yet started for the semester. A week or so later, I drove him to another part of the state where he didn't know anyone. It was a good thing the school was far away. I knew this would never work if he lived at home. He found a place to live by answering an ad for a roommate. He enrolled in the local junior college. He was talking to me a little bit by then. He still didn't have a driver's license but the school was in a small town so he could ride his bike or take the bus. It was a cold, gray day when I said goodbye to him at the door to his new place. He looked totally forlorn – like I was abandoning him. I had no idea if he would make it up there. I wanted so much to go back and get him but I knew I couldn't do that. It was a long drive home.

I can't remember many particulars about his first semester. I know that he completed all the classes he took although I don't think his grades were good. I was just happy that he was doing something productive. He made some friends and established a life for himself there. I went up and visited. We talked on the phone. He joined the basketball team. He got a used car when he got his license back. He came home for holidays but he went to school over the summer.

"How were your grades this semester," I asked. "Well I got a B and a C". "What about your other two classes?" I asked. "Oh I had to drop those because I was going to get an "F" and I didn't want an "F" on my transcript," Samuel replied. Somehow this turned into a pattern. Samuel usually started out the semester with a full schedule. Somewhere along the way he would drop a few classes that he was failing so the F would not appear on his transcript. This went on for a few years but he still was acquiring some credits. I often wondered if I should I cut his funding because he was dropping classes. I think I was just happy that he was not immersed in drugs and alcohol. I was happy for any sign of improvement no matter how slight. I knew it would be a long, slow process for Samuel to find his way. At the time I didn't know how long. I had to remember to be patient. Still I agonized over whether I was doing too much for him.

How much tough love is too much? I don't think tough love alone works, not with someone like Samuel. Yes I had people tell me I just wasn't tough enough on him. I just needed to let him fall on his face. I think he had already done that and I didn't see him improve afterwards. He felt abandoned already. Did I really want to abandon him as well? I was afraid Samuel would just disintegrate into nothingness again if I put too much pressure on him. If I stopped paying for school he might go back to sitting in his room playing video games. I hoped that he was starting to care about some things again. If he started to care about things, like basketball, maybe he would start to care about other things. If I took it all away by refusing to pay for school, any progress would be lost or so I thought.

"Mom my friend Alex was just accepted to a great school in Los Angeles. He wants me to move there with him. I could go to community college there," Samuel said excitedly. Samuel had been out of high school for about 4 years by this time. "Will you be a sophomore?" I asked. Samuel didn't respond. I remember thinking that he had a friend that was accepted to a great four year university. That was definitely an improvement in his choice of friends. I agreed.

Samuel came home for the summer before the move to Los Angeles. "Where are you going to work this summer?" I asked Samuel one morning after he arrived home. "Starbucks is hiring. I saw a hiring sign when I was in there the other day," I continued. I sensed that if Samuel just got out there he would start feeling better about himself. I knew I couldn't do it all for him but I also knew he wasn't going to do it by himself. It was a constant struggle trying to figure out when to push and when to back off. I thought this was a time I really need to push. So I got the information regarding the hiring location and gave it to him.

"Samuel did you go to the hiring fair today?" I asked. Dead silence. This went on for a couple of weeks. Was he just innately lazy? Was he afraid to fail? I was afraid of undoing the little progress he had made by pushing too hard. Finally I got the information for the next hiring fair. I took Samuel there myself and waited for him. "I was hired," Samuel told me a few days later. He seemed relieved, happy and anxious all at the same time. Now I hoped he would actually show up for work.

With Samuel I learned to set an imaginary line – like a 50 yard line in football. I would push up to that point but I wouldn't let myself cross that line no matter how much I wanted to. I decided, in advance, how far I would go to help him but I would not go past that point. I knew I had to set limits on how much I would do for him. The amount varied with the situation. I tend to do too much for people that I love. I had to fight against that urge.

"My nephew, Brandon, is spending the summer with us. His mother died a number of years ago. His father remarried. For some reason I can't understand Brandon's father refused to attend his college graduation. My nephew is scheduled to take a job teaching English in Japan. For now he sleeps most of the day. He leaves a huge mess in the kitchen. Oh and he bought a puppy. He has no money and he is leaving for Japan supposedly in a few months but he bought this puppy which is peeing all over my carpet. I don't want to kick him out. I don't know what to do with him. He is not a bad kid. He is smart. He is not mean. Oh but this is the piece de resistance. My husband, daughter and I were having breakfast Saturday morning when my husband's emergency work phone rang. He is on call all hours of the day or night as he works for a huge international company. It is never good news when that phone rings. My husband jumped up leaving his breakfast uneaten and ran to the study to take the call. "Brandon," he yelled as he burst out of the study. I have never heard him so angry. Brandon was still asleep in bed as far as I knew. Brandon did not appear. My husband barged into Brandon's room, "Don't you ever call me on my emergency cell phone again." I talked to Brandon about the puppy and the cell phone incident later. I don't think he had a clue why we were so upset. He is not a bad kid. I can't throw him out of the house. He has nowhere else to go." my friend related to me in a tone of frustration and desperation. As I listened to this story I couldn't help but feel relieved. Samuel was not the only young man acting in this manner.

"I haven't talked to him in weeks. Then he called to tell me that it is my fault he is not going to graduate from college. What did I do? I turned off his cell phone service because he was running up huge charges. I warned him to stop charging so much. We bought him a condo to live in while he went to school. He moved out of the condo because he wanted to live with friends. I think he does not want the responsibility of even doing the minimal things we ask of him at the condo. I don't even know if he is going to enroll in school this semester. Why is he blaming me for his situation? He has become so lazy. He treats me so disrespectfully. Every time I talk to him I feel so guilty like I am such a terrible mom," Louise said. "I have no idea what to do. I want him to graduate from college. I can't understand what he is doing. Doesn't he want to graduate? When I was his age I couldn't wait to get out of school and start making some money. I knew exactly what I wanted to do. Steve and I don't know what to do with him."

"He sat on my couch for about a year until I finally threw him out. Then he went to live with his dad," she said. "Is he doing better with his Dad?" I asked. "No he is sitting on his couch now and doing nothing," she replied. "How old is he?" I asked. "21", she said with a look of helplessness and resignation. I shook my head in commiseration.

Are we doing too much? Are we not doing enough? Are we doing all the wrong things? What are the right things to do? The guys I grew up with didn't have these issues. What am I doing wrong in raising my son?

"Are his parents divorced?" I asked Gary at the dinner table that night. "No, they are still married and he has a younger sister that goes to my school," Gary replied. "Do you know anything about him or his family?" I continued to probe. "No," Gary responded. Earlier that Monday I received an email from Gary's school advising the parents that one of his classmates had committed suicide the prior weekend. His mother found him hanging in the bathroom of their house. He was a freshman in high school. I didn't know the boy or his parents. I was searching for some reason that I could use to diffuse my own fears for Gary. I didn't find it.

I don't have enough information about these situations or really the training to know if there is a pattern. I do know that some of the parents are still married, some of the parents are single parents and some of the parents have remarried and their sons have stepfathers. But I sense there is more contributing to this lack of direction than just the marital status of their parents. Still young men in our culture receive a subliminal message that they are not quite a man if they have a close relationship with their mother. Somehow as they become adolescents such a relationship emasculates them. After all don't only homosexuals have close relationships with their mothers? Perhaps being raised by a single mother, especially with no father, and/or a "powerful" mother creates a conflict for a son as he forms his male identity. Must he fully reject his mother or at least keep her at arms length in order to become welcomed into the brotherhood of "real" American men? It appears that way to me.

"I attended the Anglo male discussion group at diversity day today," Gary announced at dinner that night. I was silent as I had no idea how to respond. "We talked about how we are embarrassed to be white males or feel guilty for being born an Anglo male. We just kind of vented..." Gary said. He seemed relieved rather than angry. He continued, for a while, to relate what happened at the discussion group.

Wow, I thought, the school held a diversity day that separated everyone into their own ethnic group. I was hopeful when I heard about "diversity day" that it would bring the students together by engendering respect for their uniqueness which makes up the whole. After listening to Gary I would say it backfired. I think somehow the message that these various groups can come together to make up a "whole" got lost. Gary was resentful although I really couldn't pinpoint the source of the resentment. This is a kid who has grown up in an ethnically and racially mixed family. "Diversity Day" seemed to be more a celebration of our differences and less recognition of connections and commonalities. "I hope the school reevaluates holding another "Diversity Day" next year," I said to Gary. They may be sending the wrong message I thought to myself. I wondered if this event helped or hindered Gary's quest for an identity. Does the "lost generation" consist of members of all ethnic, racial and socio economic groups? Maybe it only affects the sons of those families that have the financial means to do too much for their sons.

I, for one, am concerned that we may celebrate the act of overcoming adversity too much in our society. By implication if you don't have ethnic, racial or socioeconomic disadvantages to overcome you don't have anything to be proud of or worse you should feel inadequate and guilty. That is a part of the message I think Gary is getting at school and elsewhere. I sensed that Gary feels, among other things, a bit alienated and guilty about his comfortable circumstances.

I wanted to assuage Gary's feelings of guilt and resentment with more than dishonest platitudes. So I started thinking. Anglo males have been bashed a lot in the media and our culture in recent years. We have portrayed the Anglo male recently as "doer of all evil". They engage in behaviors designed to wrest everything - power and money – only for themselves. They are guided only by their own self interest and their greed. I have personally experienced extreme prejudice by Anglo males in the business world. I know much of the criticism is well deserved. Yet I couldn't help but think this is not just an Anglo male issue. Some of the worst treatment I received in the work place was from other women. Isn't it really about the nature of all humans to get and keep power? The persons who want to get and keep power cut across all racial and ethnic lines. It is just that the Anglo males have the power and have had the power for quite some time.

"Gary, it may be, that any group that comes to power is going to engage in the same types of conduct as the Anglo males because they will want to maintain their power. It may be that the people who engage in predatory behavior are the ones who rise to the top. I am not condoning that type of behavior but I do believe it is human nature, not just Anglo male nature. Anglo males are not innately evil or bad," I said. Gary smiled and seemed relieved. He quietly went back to doing his homework. As I said earlier Gary is part of a racially and ethnically mixed family. I believe he knows to respect everyone no matter what their background. I want him to know he can respect himself as well. Maybe I forgot to tell him that in my zeal to get him to respect everyone else. Maybe we are making that same mistake in our society as a whole.

"Let's watch a movie together," I suggested to Gary one evening. "As long as it is not one of those girl power movies, I am OK with it. We've talk about those at school too much," he responded. I didn't explore that issue with him. It seemed best to leave it alone. I had to admit that I haven't seen any of them. I am referring to the movies or TV shows where a woman is simply substituted for a male in the film. I can't think of any names off the top of my head. The woman is a "superwoman."

Lest you be tempted to bash Gary he has been raised his entire life by a single, working mother. I don't think he lacks respect for women. He has two very strong, independent sisters as well. That is precisely why I am concerned. Here is a young man who has good personal experiences regarding other ethnic and racial groups and women and yet is being turned off by the messages of our culture. I am all for women and minorities being treated equally but are we going overboard? After all we don't want young men to feel inadequate or guilty like we women (and I assume also minorities) did for years just for being who we are.

This is one of the reasons I am against what I perceive to be the "male bashing" TV shows. I am referring to "Married with Children" and maybe now "Family Guy." I haven't watched a full episode of Family Guy and only a few of Married with Children. I couldn't handle the portrayal of the father as a bumbling idiot or a buffoon. Maybe it is entertaining to adults but, I think, it can be damaging to children. It almost seems as bad as the stereotypical way women used to be portrayed as "model housewives" along the lines that the "Stepford Wives" movie addressed.

"Could you talk to Gary about running for Student Senate?" Jim asked me when he saw me on campus one day. "Well he has never mentioned to me he has any interest. He is awfully busy with school and sports already. I don't know how he could fit another thing into his schedule," I responded. "We have no male leaders at our school. We need male leaders," Jim responded. I have heard the same complaint from other institutions as well, for example, the churches.

What is happening? Are we inadvertently pushing the men out? It seems as if an identity crisis of almost epic proportions is occurring among young males. Is this why many of them are sitting on couches doing nothing, dropping out of or not enrolling in college, committing suicide? Samuel is 12 years older than Gary. But is this lack of direction something that is continuing?

My parents generation and even to some extent my generation grew up with the male role model as the sole or at least primary breadwinner who made the critical decisions in the family. He was the leader or head of the family. When I say this I think of TV shows like "Father Knows Best", "Leave it to Beaver" and "The Nelson Family". Those role models are definitely passé. But what has replaced it? I hear women comparing notes about the perfect husband. They brag about whose husband does more. In the media we seem to be bombarded with images of the perfect husband and father. The perfect husband works at a pretty demanding job, makes enough money to support the family, shops, cooks , takes the kids to daycare, helps with homework, coaches their kids teams, does housework , is emotionally available and supportive , always patient, a tower of strength and can manage everything unassisted if his wife has career needs of her own. Can anyone even come close to that image?

"I want to be a teacher," Samuel said to me a few years ago. "Great," I responded. Samuel had finally found something he wanted to do. This should motivate him. "Yeah but I will never even be able to afford to support a family, buy a house or go on a vacation. No one wants to marry someone poor. I can't do it," Samuel continued. Do we define maleness still by the amount of money a man makes? Is it still true that the more money he makes the more respected he is and the manlier he is. Where does that leave men in a world where women can often earn as much or more than men? Do we need to take that part of the equation about "making really good money" out of the male image? That was certainly one of Samuel's issues in forming his identity and in finding motivation.

Are we expecting men to be "super men" like they used to expect my generation to be super women? Should we rethink that? Are they checking out because they know they can never meet those expectations and the pressure is too much? There was a difference with us "super moms". We could opt out while still doing something socially redeeming. We could stay home with the children. Do they have that option? Are we doing to them what was done to us? Do they think they have to fit into this box marked "perfect male" in order to be loved and accepted? Is there any wiggle room? If they want something different do they have to engage in a huge negotiation process that exhausts them and antagonizes their family?

Women seem more empowered than ever right now. To my observation, as the power and success of young women has increased that of the young males has, at least in their own minds and actions, decreased. It reminds me of a see saw with a man and a woman sitting on opposite sides. When the women pushes herself up the man's side automatically goes down.

How can we prepare our sons for this world? The suicides, drugs, alcohol and lack of motivation indicate to me that perhaps we are not doing a very good job. I want to help my sons navigate this world we live in. I don't want to walk into a room someday and see either of them hanging from a rope. We talk so much about young women these days and rightly so. But have we inadvertently forgotten about and neglected the young men in the process? I talk to my sons about all this stuff. They complain that I am being ridiculous. But I sense that they need to hear it and even like it although they won't admit it.

Maybe diversity day wasn't all that bad because it gave me some new insights into Gary. It opened the door to this discussion. Hopefully I won't miss the signals and we can continue to discuss these types of issues. His self esteem and identity are in the formation stage and very fragile. I want him to respect others but also himself.

"Mom, Mom they have promoted me to supervisor at work!" Samuel said excitedly. It was a slow start but I think Samuel enjoyed being good at his job and fortunately he was recognized for it. He became a valuable employee. He has been with the company six years now.

"Mom I am going to graduate with my teaching degree next year! I am thinking of entering a teacher exchange program to go to a foreign country to teach if I can't find a job here or maybe I'll go after working here a year or two," Samuel said.

You can't motivate another person. You can plead, cajole, mete out consequences for certain behaviors but in the end it boils down to their motivation or lack thereof. Nothing seemed to motivate Samuel. What finally happened? Maybe he just matured. I can say that with the passage of time I have seen his self confidence and self esteem grow. He is no longer the lethargic, unmotivated young adult sitting on the couch playing video games. Oh he still does that too much in my opinion. Now he has something he wants to do – teach school. He has a goal and he is working very hard to get there. He continues to work at Starbucks. He seems better able to cope with the ups and downs of life. He wasn't going to make hundreds of thousands of dollars a year like the people our culture celebrates and so in his mind he couldn't be successful. But when he decided it was OK to be a teacher like he wanted to be- that he wouldn't be a failure - things started to change. He loves kids and loves sports. He can combine those loves with a career. Hopefully he can get some respect for it as well. Somehow, at some point in time, he just started to care about things again including himself.

"Mom I just found out that I don't have the right classes to be able to graduate as I planned. I will have to go to school another year and a half," Samuel said. I was terrified. I could hear the frustration and disappointment in his voice. How would he handle this I wondered. Will he simply give up like he did in the past?

In the end they have to want it - something. They have to set a goal for themselves. If we do too much for them or make it too easy for them then they don't feel good about themselves. Samuel insists on supporting himself by working full time and going to school full time. He is still somewhat fragile but he continues to grow stronger with each milestone he passes. Samuel has been able to take some huge adversities in stride. Those adversities would have derailed him a few years ago. It has been a long, slow and at times very painful process.

Did Samuel struggle because he was raised by a single mom? Was it because he suffered the loss of two fathers before the age of 15? Is it just because I was a bad mother? Was it because he was so good at manipulating me? Was it because I did too much for him? Was it because he didn't have a male role model? I don't know the answer. Time has been Samuels' friend. Has he just finally matured? Has he healed? Has he just realized time is running out to accomplish what he wants? Does he realize he can't have a satisfying life and a family unless he feels good about himself which means, to him, accomplishing something? Did he finally set some realistic goals for himself? Has he finally found something he would like to do? Is it one or all of the above that has motivated Samuel?

For long periods of time in my life I have felt weighed down by failure. I even looked in the mirror, at times, expecting to see my shoulders stooped by the weight of failure. Should I feel like I am a failure because Samuel did not follow the script set out by our culture? Certainly some of my relatives have voiced that opinion to me. That can be hard for some of us. You are not a failure as a parent and your child is not a failure if they don't follow the script or normal pattern. Not everyone graduates from high school, immediately attends a four year university from which they graduate and then finds a good job. Our children must work it out for themselves in their own way and in their own time. We can help. We can give them unconditional love but we can't do it for them.

Children are such individuals. I think I have learned you need to tailor your parenting to fit the child. My parent's generation thought you treated every child exactly the same otherwise their notion of fairness would be violated. I found that didn't work. Now when my children complain that I am doing something different for one of their siblings I respond, "They are a different person than you are and that means a different way of handling certain matters." There are limits to the variations of course.

As parents we can try too hard and do too much. That goes against everything I was raised to believe. It is a lesson I have resisted for years. On this issue I am definitely a slow learner. I kept hitting the same brick wall but the light wasn't going on. I'm still not sure I can control the urge to try harder and harder. What is that stupid saying? Oh yeah "when things get tough the tough get going". Somewhere I got the idea if things aren't working out the answer is to work harder. That is the way school works isn't it? If you don't do well at a subject then you need to work harder –study more, etc. Jobs can be that way as well. Problem is that doesn't work too well with relationships. In fact with kids and in marriages sometimes it seems the more you try the less they try. If you keep it up long enough you will be doing it all by yourself. I found myself in that situation with Samuel.

I know Samuel's situation is, in some ways, unique. Samuel has never spoken about it but I know he bears a huge sense of guilt over how he handled Brian's illness. He felt he should have been a better son. He feels he should have spent time with Brian and helped care for him instead of escaping into a world of drugs and alcohol. But Samuel was a child. I hope Samuel can forgive himself for not meeting his idealized standard as to how he should have acted during the dark time that Brian was ill and dying. I hope he can also forgive God.

This is Samuel's journey. I hope I can be a part of his journey and even help him in some way. He is still so fragile and will probably always be that way. The cracks and gaps will never fully mend. All I can offer to my sons (and my daughters) is a mother's unconditional love. Apparently sometimes that is not enough. I try to keep my finger on the pulse of Samuel's emotional health so I can step in when needed. I have tried to apply lessons learned raising Samuel to Gary. I hope to help prevent Samuel from falling into the abyss of lethargy and despair ever again. Just because Samuel is a young adult male does not mean he doesn't need the support, love and connection with his family. I am proud that he can accept that without feeling he has been robbed of some of his manhood. He is sometimes still ridiculed for it but he handles it well. After all he only has a mother and sisters to turn to for support.

Too many choices are as bad as too few choices. Often we define ourselves or discover what who we are and what we want by rebelling against the expectations of our parents, our society, etc. In the absence of firm expectations young people can become overwhelmed and wander aimlessly hoping by some miracle to find what it is they want to do with their life.

As with women, men now have more choices but with choices come dilemmas. Our challenge is to foster an image of male identity that is not one of "super man" and that allows for variations while still providing some parameters or guidelines. With too many expectations or two little expectations they check out or drift aimlessly. We can't afford to let this generation of men drift without any purpose. The result of that seems to be low self esteem and a proliferation of suicides, drugs, video game addictions, alcohol and finally a lack of meaningful male participation in the family, community and society. I don't think any of us want that.

Chapter Thirteen

True Friendship – Does It Still Exist?

I hadn't been back since it all happened. It happened quite a long time ago – almost 16 years ago now. As I prepared for this business trip I promised myself I wouldn't do it. In fact I swore I would resist any and all such urges. As soon as I disembarked the plane I am afraid it started.

Why do I insist on revisiting the past? Do I just like to torture myself or is there some positive purpose to this exercise? I was on a mission to revisit my past even if I didn't want to. I was inexorably drawn back there.

It is this past – the events that happened in this desert city - which I sought to escape by marrying Warren. When I met Warren in Italy, I hadn't resolved or come to terms with this past. I was still mired in the past. I wanted an easy escape and I found it in my new relationship with Warren. Oh I didn't realize that at the time. I only see that now.

New relationships are so full of possibilities. They can be the catalyst for new beginnings in every aspect of our lives. Romantic relationships, when they are new, have the euphoric effect of a drug. At first, new relationships seem like an escape from the past. But in fact the past, if left unresolved, will haunt and destroy any new beginnings as it did with my relationship with Warren. The seeds of our divorce were sown in the very beginning by the unresolved issues of our past lives.

The first encounter with my past, on this business trip, did not occur of my own volition. I passed by it on my walk from the gate where I disembarked the airplane to the baggage claim. I was struck by the starkness of the scene. The last time I was there it was teeming with life. Back then these were the United Airline gates my young children used to fly out of to visit my sister or parents. Now even the chairs had been removed. It was a big empty room. The emptiness served as an even stronger reminder of how much time had passed and how much had happened since the last time I waved goodbye to the children as they disappeared down the ramp. I continued to follow the signs to the baggage claim and then to the car rental shuttle. As I crossed the street to the island to catch the shuttle I remembered that this is where I used to drop my parents off to catch the plane back to my hometown. I see myself hugging them and saying good bye with tears in my eyes. It all seems so real! My children grew up here but they don't think of this place as their hometown. Sadly, my children don't have a hometown. I catch the rental car shuttle bus and silently celebrate that there are no memories here.

This is why I left. Memories were everywhere. They surrounded me and, for a while, they suffocated me. The memories were painful back then. The memories are still painful. I was surprised by the strength of those memories after so many years. I felt tears welling up in my eyes. Some memories are merely poignant as so much of my life is behind me now. Some memories evoke regrets for my choices and failures and for the roads not travelled. Then there are memories of the unhappy events over which I had little or no control. These are the most powerful memories. I felt paralyzed by the intensity of the pain those memories evoked.

Oh there is much to regret and there is much to celebrate about my life here. I do feel sad that so much of my life has gone by. I feel like I failed to enjoy so much of it. I do regret getting caught up in the treadmill of life. I imagine myself as a hamster running inside the wheel in its cage. In my drive to get to the next task I missed out on the joys of the moment. I remind myself that I did gain valuable insight and wisdom during those years which has helped me to avoid this pitfall in my later years. If I allow my thoughts to dwell here too long I will be overcome with sadness for what is past.

But there are other memories as well here in this city. A real tragedy happened in my life when I lived here. In many ways that tragedy has defined my life. I calculate events as prior to or subsequent to the tragedy. I calculate my personal growth before and after that event. I mark the emotional growth of my children based on that event. That event marks my life and the lives of my children in so many ways.

If I ignore my memories I feel like I am acting outside of myself. If I indulge myself and go back in time I feel overcome with grief and regrets.

I found myself driving, without any conscious thought, around this city in the desert where I spent so many years of my life. It was here I spent my life as a young adult, wife and mother. It was almost as if someone else was in control of the vehicle. I drove past the last place I worked. I drove past the first place I worked right after I moved here. I drove past the historic district where so many events in my life took place. I stopped in front of the beautiful historic home that houses a restaurant and is a venue for private parties. The wedding reception for my last marriage took place in that house. Many years before that I threw a 40th birthday party for Eloise there. She was one of my closest friends. I tried to recall the last time I saw her.

"Eloise, Eloise!" I called as she walked past me in the cavernous hallway of the sports arena. She finally turned and said hello. We hadn't seen or spoken to each other in months. She didn't ask me how I had been. "Can you and Brian come over for dinner with some friends next weekend?" is all she said. "We are going to be out of town that weekend," I responded. "Another time then," she said. I never heard from her again.

I can't help but wish that I were staying with Eloise and her husband while I am here on this business trip. We could be reminiscing now about when our children, who are now young adults, were toddlers. We spent that part of our lives as friends. We had met quite by accident. We instantly connected. We did so much together with the children and with our spouses. We spent all our holidays together. In fact we saw each other almost every weekend when the children were young. Our spouses even became good friends. Then one day our friendship ended just as suddenly and mysteriously as it had begun.

Eloise and her husband didn't come to the funeral. They didn't send flowers or even a sympathy card. Maybe they didn't know that Brian had died. They knew he was sick with Lou Gehrig's disease.

I ran into Eloise at a restaurant a few months after the funeral. She was waiting in line in front of me. I recognized her immediately. I hoped she wouldn't notice me. When she turned to go to her table she saw me. After I placed my order at the counter I sat at a table at the opposite end of the restaurant from where Eloise was. I deliberately sat with my back to her. A short time later, I looked up from my food to see here standing next to my table.

"Don't you want to talk to me?" she asked. I wanted to scream some things at her but I didn't. Did she even know what had happened in my life since I last saw her? Did she even know Brian was dead? Did she care? "I have nothing to say to you," is all I said. She looked hurt, turned and left the restaurant. What would I have accomplished if I said those things to her? We could never be friends again not after what she had done. She was my closest friend. Right after Brian was diagnosed she and her husband disappeared from our lives.

Still for some mysterious reason I called her many, many years later. I lived in another state by then. We chatted. We brought each other up to date regarding our children. We exchanged contact information. Neither of us ever contacted the other again.

It feels so incredibly empty to return to a city where I spent so much of my life – 14 years- and so many important events in my life occurred and yet I am seeing no one from that time in my life. It feels like a huge void. My thoughts returned to Eloise. What if I had said those things to her in the restaurant? What if I had told her how much she hurt me? Would we have rekindled our friendship? Do I really want to be friends with a person who deserted me at one of the most difficult periods of my life? Maybe, while I am here on business, I should pick up the phone and call her to see if she can get together for a cup of coffee. I was tempted to call her but I never did.

I continued to drive around the city. I drove past the last home I lived in, past the school Gary attended for kindergarten, past the high school my oldest daughter graduated from, past the elementary school my children attended and past the church we all attended. But I never did drive there. I couldn't. I had stopped going there long before I moved from this desert city. I felt guilty about that even when I still lived here. Now I felt as if I should go there but I can't seem to direct the car there. I am not exactly sure what will happen if I go there but whatever it is I am afraid of it. There is something about seeing that name etched for all eternity into a stone in the ground that unnerves me. In the past I would start sobbing uncontrollably when I saw it. I have no reason to doubt that would happen now and I don't want to be so unnerved while on a business trip.

It was 24 years ago when I first saw this city in the desert. I had already decided we were going to move there – the whole family. I had never been here when I made that decision but sadly anything was better than where I was living at the time. I was living in my hometown which was located in the "Rust Belt". It was 1985.

I always smell the desert before I see it. It is a peaceful smell or I feel peaceful when I smell it. That was the first thing I experienced and came to love was the smell of the desert. It may be what I miss most about the desert. Smells are so much more evocative and memorable than any other sensory experiences. Sometimes the only thing I can remember is the smell. You can't really describe a smell in words. It is one of those things you have to experience. You just know it when you smell it. Like the smell of the perfume or cologne of a loved one long after they have gone. The smell of the desert is best experienced at night or very early in the morning. I remember smelling it on my very first visit as I explored the city in my rental car at night. In spite of the painful memories I feel peaceful as I drive though the desert at night with the windows of the car rolled down. I feel enveloped in the comforting arms of the desert.

The desert is a beautiful and fascinating place. As you drive you see lights everywhere and then suddenly you see total darkness. This city is huge now. It is ever so much bigger than when I moved here. Then it was a sleepy, little desert town. But in spite of its growth there are still mountains in this desert that defy development. And so I sat on the balcony of my hotel room and looked out over the lights and blackness. I closed my eyes and soaked up the rich smell of the desert.

This desert town is full of beautiful resorts. For some reason I chose to stay at the resort that I had frequented when I lived there. I thought it would have changed so much over the years that it wouldn't matter. At least I didn't recognize it in the photos posted on its webpage when I made the reservation. They have excellent amenities and great rates so I booked a room there. After I settled into my room I went to the restaurant to have dinner. I was amazed to discover that it still bears the same name it did 20 years ago. The only thing that has changed is the color scheme. I waited in the lobby for the hostess to seat me. I remembered the last time I was here.

"Can you meet me for lunch at the Pointe," Brian asked me. "It is too far from the office. I don't want to take a long lunch today," I protested. "I really want us to have lunch with my parents today," Brian pleaded. As usual he persuaded me to do what he wanted. He had a real knack for doing that. When I arrived Brian and his parents were already seated in a booth. It was that one in the corner over there. I saw it when I entered the restaurant this night. His mom and dad were seated in the middle of the booth. I slid into the side across from Brian. We chatted quietly and then I left to go back to the office. It was the last time I saw his mother. She died of heart failure a few days later.

I decided just to eat at the bar. As I sat down on one of the bar stools I remembered that this is where Bill had first introduced Brian and I to his wife. Bill's company did business with Brian's company. They had become friends long before I met Brian. Bill called us a lot right after the diagnosis but he too, like Eloise, simply disappeared from our lives when Brian was in the early throes of the illness. Oh he came to the funeral and even to the event at the house after the funeral. I was amazed that he could do that. I forced myself to stop remembering while I ate my dinner. I returned to my room and thankfully fell into a deep, dreamless sleep.

I never really had a plan for my life, at least not consciously. I wanted to be open to all of the possibilities. I didn't want to be so focused on where I was going that I missed an unexpected opportunity. That was a rather naïve view, to say the least. Without any plan I was buffeted around like a jellyfish in the ocean. You need some sense of direction or purpose I think now. My stubbornness, my obsession to be independent, my craving for affection and my passive rebellion caused me to make choices that I see now were wrong for me. My life, intentionally, did not follow the script set out for women with my background and education. Sometimes I think I just sabotaged myself. Other times I think I just wanted to do the unexpected – to be different and adventurous as much as possible for me.

As I look around I wonder if the people who followed the "script" are really happier than I am. They are in long marriages with grown children living in the same house in the suburbs in which they raised their families. I was, for the most part, following that script in my life with Brian in this desert city. We had a traditional marriage, lived in the suburbs and raised our children there. I remember feeling stifled by all of that at times.

Do the people who followed the script have regrets like I do? From the outside looking in I imagine them to be very content. I will probably never know because for some reason we don't talk about those things or won't talk about them honestly. Often I wonder if I am the only person who even thinks about all this stuff.

I spent three days in that desert town on this business trip. So much had changed sometimes it was easy to forget where I was. At times I was overcome by a constant barrage of "what ifs". What if ……??? How different would my life have been if I hadn't married

Brian? I would probably still live here. I wouldn't have those memories that drove me away.

What happened to the connections I thought I had forged there? When I moved there I thought I would put down roots and that this would be my new "hometown". For a time it seemed like that had happened and then with the death of Brian it all abruptly ended. Perhaps our connections to places are only as good as our connections to the people who live there. The connections to our memories, our personal history and the culture and identity of the place can evaporate slowly or they can quickly dissolve as they did with me.

Perhaps connections with people are best left untested by the trials of life. If Brian had not gotten sick I am sure I would be visiting and reminiscing with Eloise on that business trip. Perhaps I am just too hard and unforgiving when it comes to others. Maybe I should have spoken to Eloise in the restaurant that day. I couldn't at that time. The wound was much too raw. Maybe Eloise would have told me why she acted like she did – why she stopped being my friend when I needed her friendship the most. Would any explanation have been able to change us back from strangers to friends again?

I have come to understand, although it has taken much time, that there are many different types of friendships. A therapist once told me I had an adolescent notion of friendship because I expected too much from people. In retrospect I think she was right. As we mature we have so many competing demands for our time – careers, spouses, and children that there is much less energy and time for friendships. Could I have relegated Eloise to a casual friend? I have learned to enjoy casual friendships but I don't think I could accept a casual friendship from someone who was once so close to me. I think it is OK to expect close friends to be there during the crises in life if not physically at least with some emotional support. No it was better not to talk to Eloise in the restaurant that day. There was nothing to gain. As it is now I have good memories of our close friendship. It is better left that way. I don't need to travel down the road of "what if" I had rekindled my friendship with Eloise. This trip to the desert has made it possible for me to stop making that journey. That is a relief!

Unfortunately everyone acted like Eloise during the time Brian was ill and dying. I lost all my friends. Everyone abandoned us. I was bitter about that for many, many years. I made no effort to form any close friendships. Should I trust again? We have no idea how our friends, spouse or children will act in difficult times. We have to have faith they will rise to the occasion and support us. Everything in life is a risk especially relationships. I can't hide from that forever. I was too lonely. I was going to have to trust again. I hoped to make better choices in friends this time around.

An envelope arrived in the mail the other day – just before I left on my business trip. It had a return address indicating it was mailed from my hometown. I anxiously ripped it open. Funny but I still get excited regarding news about my hometown even though I haven't lived there in 30 years. I guess for my generation that connection runs deep. I am sad and relieved that my children will never have that connection. I opened it to find an obituary. On top of the obituary was a handwritten note. It was from a friend of my parents. She was a neighbor of ours and had been their friend since I was about five years old. My siblings and I had grown up with her three sons. I always think of her with such fondness. Just seeing the note from her brings back good memories of spending time with her family.

"I thought you might be interested in this. I know you babysat for her for many years," she said in the note. I knew from my Mother that my friend had been battling cancer for a number of years. It had been in remission for a quite a while but apparently it had recently returned with a vengeance. She was only 61 years old. We had a deep connection when I was in high school. After I moved away, I would visit her when I came home to visit my parents. She always seemed glad to see me. But our visits had definitely tapered off over the years. I would contact her but she rarely had the time to see me. I was hurt that she didn't want to get together. She had been someone I could confide in as a teenager and young adult. We seemed to understand each other even though we were from totally different worlds. Those talks helped me escape the provincial attitudes of the city in which I grew up.

Why didn't we maintain that connection? I wanted to stay connected. Do friendships have limited life spans? Do I just care more about other people than they care about me? Do I value friendships more than other people do? Am I wrong or weird for feeling that way? Am I the only one who feels so intensely lonely in 21st century America? These aren't new feelings for me. I have felt lonely and alienated since I was a child.

I often wonder if our ability to connect is damaged early on in our life whether we can ever completely heal from that injury. I was driven by fear to seek and also to run away from relationships. Fear has been my constant companion since childhood. Anxiety may be a more accurate term but for me the feeling is definitely one of fear. When I was young I would sabotaged close friendships when I revealed too much of myself to the other person. Was I was afraid they would reject me so I rushed to do it first?

Is loneliness just part of the "human condition"? Why don't I have satisfying connections with friends in my life? I know I have chosen poorly. I have rebuffed people who wanted to be my friend because I was courting the friendship of a more" desirable" sort of friend. There is a certain status in being friends with certain people and this was not true just in high school or college. Some of this behavior is born of desire to be part of the "successful crowd". Some is born of the assumption that all good things can only be achieved through hard work, including friendship. If a friendship was too easy it couldn't be good. Sometimes my rejection was born of my need to pick people who really couldn't connect with me because in reality I didn't want to or couldn't connect with them or anyone else for that matter. I have been deluding myself about my desire to find others with whom I can feel connected. I really didn't want to or couldn't. In the last few years, I have made a conscious effort to change that part of myself and my life.

"Mom have you heard from or talked to any of your friends from Pittsburgh this week?" I asked. "Well I got a letter from Martha Harris. Roy Hillman called and we talked for a while. You remember Roy don't you?" my Mother said and then she continued to relate to me some of the events back in my hometown.

My Mother left a huge number of friends when she recently moved to the city where I live. These were relationships that she had forged over a period of 40 years through her church, school and community activities. I couldn't imagine the loss. Although it did strike me as odd that my Mother never talked about feelings –either hers or theirs. Her conversations were always about physical events –a trip, a birth, a death. Still her connections run deep because she has shared so much with these women even if much of it was unspoken. She has shared her life with them through the experience of raising families together and living in and being a part of the same community.

We, as young women, had so many more important things to do than our mothers. We weren't going to waste our time going to circle meetings, bridge club, community activities, church organizations and the like. Those activities were stupid. After all you weren't even paid for doing any of that stuff! How could there be any value in it? If only we hadn't been so arrogant. There is such tremendous value in those activities but not the type that can be measured by the size of the paycheck.

The women of my childhood community did a lot of good things for each other and for others who were not as fortunate as we were. In doing so they also forged friendships and connections with each other. I see now that our deepest connections and friendships are formed when we engage together in activities that have a worthwhile common purpose.

These types of relationships can't be forged in the business community. Relationships in the business community are utilitarian in nature. We are naive if we expect business associates to be our friends. I learned that lesson well in the aftermath of Brian's illness and death. I want to try to create some relationships like those of my

Mother's generation. After trying to distance myself so much from my Mother and her generation it strikes me as such an irony that I now seek to create what she had in terms of friendships and community connections.

"Hey what do you say that we schedule one day a month when we go to the area food bank and volunteer together," I asked my new group of friends at lunch one day. Everyone looked down at the table. There was total silence. Was it that they didn't want to do anything with me or was it they just didn't want to commit to this regular activity? I tried to explore the idea a few more times and then I gave up. We continue to have lunch together regularly so I don't think it is an issue about spending time with me. What is it then?

My generation goes out to eat or goes to happy hours where we talk about our lives, our work, and our families. Yet I don't feel connected to these people when I engage in those activities. Our parents didn't go out to restaurants and engage in such conversations yet they formed strong bonds. I realize now that conversation alone, even if we are sharing our innermost feelings and thoughts, doesn't create enduring connections. I often leave such happy hours feeling very empty and alone. We need to share experiences – do things together for a common purpose and often for the common good. We think things like bridge clubs and community events are a waste of time. But are they?

Friendships and relationships develop through a combination of sharing experiences by engaging in activities together and through sharing our thoughts and feelings. For some reason my generation has an aversion to any type of group activity. I think part of it is that most of the women of my generation work but that is not all of it. I find even stay at home moms, who no longer have young children to care for, don't join community or volunteer organizations.

Why is that? What are we afraid of? Is that our way of avoiding friendships and connections? Do we want to avoid dealing with people we may not like? After all if we go to a meeting there will be people there that we disagree with or who have different ideas about how things should be done. This can lead to conflict and conflict can be exhausting and time consuming. We may even have to compromise a little. It seems that my parent's generation used to first ask what they could do for the organization. I am reminded of that famous line of JFK, "Ask not what your country can do for you. Ask what you can do for your country." It seems that my generation first asks what the organization can do for them. Maybe we have it backwards. If we don't see a benefit to us or we don't get immediate gratification we simply stop participating. It reminds me of a toddler who, faced with the specter of sharing with a friend, merely picks up his toys and goes home.

For so long I yearned to belong to someplace or something, maybe in my youth even someone. I married. I had children. I moved to different cities. I returned to my hometown. Yet I still could not recreate or find that feeling of belonging I felt as a child. It is just a figment of a child's imagination or some bourgeois notion? How does one lose that feeling? How does one acquire it again? Is there really some mysterious force that draws us to and holds us in one place or to one person? Am I the only one who craves closeness and intimacy? Am I the only one who thinks it is missing from my life?

I have never had many friends. Secrets stand in the way of making and keeping friends I think. The secrets of my childhood separated me from others. The reality of our family life was so different from the community perception that I felt I was living a lie. If people knew the truth about my family they wouldn't like us or so I thought. If they knew the truth about me they wouldn't like me or so I thought. I couldn't tell anyone that the outward reality was all a deception. I was terrified of doing that. Thus began a lifelong pattern of separating myself from others. Even as a young adult, I couldn't let anyone see who I really was. I had to maintain the image that I was perfect. Oh silly I know but for a long time I was naïve enough to think that people couldn't see through the perfect image that I tried to portray to the world.

In striving for this unattainable goal of perfection I certainly couldn't share my faults, fears or failures with anyone. I couldn't be honest with myself so I couldn't be honest with anyone else. When I speak of honesty I am not referring to the chest beating and bad behavior I see exhibited on TV, in movies and unfortunately in real life. I think of that as pseudo honesty. Showing people behaving abominably is not the same thing as being honest about our behavior. Bad behavior is just bad behavior and often seeks to be seen. Honesty about our poor behavior involves some intense soul searching. We try to avoid that at all costs. Being constantly busy serves the purpose.

"Well I have to take Tom to school and pick him up every day. I have to take him to his after school activities"... blah blah blah. I get tired just listening to the list of everyone's everyday activities and commitments. Those activities don't include involvement in community activities with other women or men except for an occasional activity at our children's school. That activity confers a direct benefit on us so we will make time for that type of activity.

When did mothers stop being a whole person and evolve into a one dimensional being with no interests outside the family, home or office? When did we start to forget that community service benefits us as much as the recipient? Do we "wear" our laundry list of activities like a badge of honor? We try to one up the other person to show them we are busier than they are. After all the woman who is the busiest wins the gold medal. Could it be partly a result of our obsession with making our kids "happy" instead of raising them to be responsible, successful adults?

In this competitive world we have to be "successful". In order to do that we have to be able to measure our success and consequently our worth in something concrete. For stay at home moms they measure their success by the accomplishments of their children and husband. In the business world we measure our success by the client we retained, the successful project completed, the profits earned, the raise we received, etc. But how do we achieve and measure "success" in our relationships to our friends and community?

We, as a society, value hard work. That is an admirable quality. But does that same quality work against us in eradicating loneliness and forging meaningful relationships? It seems that the hard work of the business world and academic world is not the hard work of relationships. Relationships require a totally different set of skills and a different view of results. We often fail to see or make that distinction. In fact the skills that make us successful in the business world may actually be detrimental to the building of relationships. In the business world, especially for those people at the top, are accustomed to having their orders carried out without the necessity sometimes even of politeness. They bark orders and they get carried out. It is often a matter of expediency. Often people want to curry favor with their boss or supervisor and the boss can become accustomed to obsequious behavior. In any event that is not the way a marriage, monogamous relationship or any relationship among equals perhaps works best. Don't we need to suggest, compromise, listen and adapt in our family and community relationships? It takes time to establish and build such relationships. In the business world there is often a defined and even rigid set of expectations and behaviors. That is not necessarily true outside the business community.

Do we avoid personal relationships because the hard work is not subject to a specific formula? Personal relationships require so much of more of each of us and on a much deeper level than the hard work of the business/academic world. It ultimately requires that we give of ourselves sometimes even without expecting or getting something in return.

"My husband, Manny, can fix your car," the receptionist at the office said to me one day. I had been discussing with her that my car needed repairs but I didn't have the money to pay for it. "He is an auto mechanic," she continued. Margaret, the receptionist, and I had just started to work at the same office. "What does he charge?" I asked. "You will have to talk to him about that. Why don't you come over on Saturday and you can talk to him about everything," Margaret replied.

The children and I arrived at Margaret and Manny's house Saturday morning. Manny agreed to fix my car for the cost of the parts and a six pack of beer. While Manny was working on the car Margaret insisted we stay and eat with them. I tried to decline. They had been far too generous already but Margaret insisted. After all they had seven children of their own to house and feed.

This was the beginning of a long and wonderful friendship. We helped each other out although Manny and Margaret did much more for me than I ever did for them. I watched their children. They watched my children. I helped Margaret with some legal issues. We gave of our talents and abilities to each other without any expectation of repayment. We gave because we genuinely cared about each other. We forged a close connection to each other and we grew to love each other very dearly. It has been 25 years since we spent a great deal of time together yet I still feel a surge of love when I think of Margaret and Manny. An irrevocable bond was forged.

"Can you help me in the yard for a little bit?" I asked Warren, my husband. To my surprise he actually got off the couch and came out for a few minutes to help me. I felt something wonderful feeling at that moment. We were doing something productive together even if it was as simple as working on the lawn. It is the simple things that count I reminded myself. The good feeling went away when Warren left abruptly to return to his TV watching. Somehow watching TV together does not engender that same connection. I realized this was part of what was missing in our relationship. We had stopped doing anything together.

What do we need to do to create satisfying friendships and community connections? This is one thing we can't achieve or accomplish alone. Relationships take time to build. We must be patient. We don't get immediate results. Sometimes we don't get any results at all. Some relationships just don't form.

Recently I lost another friend - just a month or so ago. She had been battling cancer for a little over a year. Until about 6 months ago it looked like she might be winning. But suddenly her body gave out. Apparently it happened right after I had my last visit with her. When I was there you literally would never know she was sick except for the loss of her hair. She said she looked like, "Heather Locklear on crack" when she wore her blond wig. During that last visit everything was just as it had been on my previous visit.

She and I were very new friends. We had lived in the same city for 8 years but we never knew each other. Our paths finally crossed and we became instant friends. We stayed in touch after I moved. We had such plans the two of us! We never got to do any of it. Shortly after I moved to a new city she was diagnosed with cancer. Her life revolved around the next round of chemotherapy or doctor visits. Our travel plans were put on hold.

We formed a friendship under the most unlikely circumstances. I hugged her the first time I met her. We shared a time together that was unique to the two of us. That shared experience brought us together. But there had to be more to our friendship. Everyone who shares a common experience does not become close friends. The time we shared together was a very difficult time for me. She was my divorce lawyer.

We were from similar backgrounds. She shared my world view. But there was more to it than that. We were an unusual commodity. We were two middle aged women who were very happy being single. She had never married. I had been married more times than anyone should be in one lifetime. We were enjoying our lives. We weren't waiting for a relationship to materialize so we could start living or being happy. For me it was a long, difficult journey to arrive at this place. We were going to be companions on some great adventures. That will never happen now.

"We can't stay very long. We are going to go to this party. We hope to meet some men there," Susan said to my hostess. We had gathered at my friends' house for a glass of wine. Susan and her friend lived in the neighborhood. I am surprised that I still meet so many women who are simply waiting or treading water in their life as they wait to meet some guy. These women plan their lives around finding places to meet men. Their days are filled with lonely activities. I used to be one of them although I pretended to myself and others that I wasn't. That, after all, is how I ended up in a relationship with Warren after Brian's death. I thought we were, as a society, getting past that. Why do we do that? Wasn't part of our "liberation" as women to be able to live a fulfilling life without a man? Maybe if we could find fulfilling connections elsewhere in our lives we wouldn't be waiting for "Prince Charming." Maybe we need to discover how rich our lives can be in relationships other than a monogamous relationship? Admittedly the way our lives are structured makes that very difficult. The 40+ hour work week does not leave a lot of time, energy or opportunity to develop other connections. That is a huge obstacle and a huge challenge.

Sometimes we feel a connection and it doesn't develop into anything more and sometimes it does. Sometimes there is no connection. Sometimes the connection is very limited and sometimes it is broken by the other person for reasons never shared with us. I have come to accept that there are all different types of connections. I so wanted every connection to satisfy my deepest longings. Of course no one can do that. I have learned to enjoy connections on many levels now. I have a rich variety of friendships and connections. I have neighbors, professional friends, friends that like to go to the theatre, friends that like to eat in good restaurants, and on and on. I enjoy each friendship without trying to force more out of it. Sometimes a deeper connection happens but it can't be forced. I reserve my deepest connections, love and trust for my family and a few friends. My life is filled with a variety of interesting and satisfying relationships.

We buried him today. We didn't really have a memorial service. We just buried him in a grave under a beautiful tree. For the most part I was responsible for the loss. Samuel was out of town on a trip and I was taking care of him for a couple of weeks. Thankfully he didn't suffer much. He died quickly. Samuel adored him. It was a fitting spot for his final resting place in Samuel's backyard under a tree. We shed tears. Most of our tears were for Samuel because we understood how much Rocky meant to him and how much he would miss him. Samuel's tears were probably for himself because really any tears of grief are tears for the survivors - ourselves. Tears couldn't help Rocky now. Samuel removed the lifeless body from the blanket and gently placed it in the hole he had dug. He placed Rocky's sweater over him - the one that had always kept him warm on cold days. I started to cry as I went over the events of the last few days in my mind.

Are we too attached to our pets? Is it emotionally healthy to be that attached to an animal? I hear people at the dog park refer to themselves as the "doggy mom" or "doggy dad". That is a recent phenomenon at least in my experience. Has our connection to our pets increased as we feel more disconnected from each other? Have we allowed them to become a substitute for human companionship instead of a supplement to those human connections? Dogs love us whether we have failed at work, are fat, ugly, and love us even if no one else does. A pet's love is immediate and unconditional.

There is a risk in seeking a connection with another human being. We have to let our guard down. We have to invest in those relationships by spending time and revealing ourselves in order to develop that connection. We have to let them see who we really are without all the facades we put up in the professional world. We have to be able to risk being hurt or rejected. With dogs we don't have to do that. The love and affection of dogs is a given if we just feed and love them. If only it were so easy with humans!

Our connection to other people grows in proportion to the amount of mutual effort we put in and the level of vulnerability. In the process of forming connections we grow and learn about ourselves, the world and others. If we chose to love only pets then we are living in a cocoon because the connection to our pet can only grow in our own minds. Relationships with pets have a place in our lives but we should be careful they don't become replacements for human connections. Keep the relationship in perspective I say to myself. Still my heart aches for Samuel. My heart aches for me. My heart aches for Rocky and for my dogs who lost their best buddy.

Maybe it just boils down to the fact that we just don't value them – friendships, relationships. If we don't value them we won't spend time on them. And if we don't spend time developing them we end up without them.

If we continue to measure success by how much we earn, what we have acquired or how successful our spouse and children are then there will always be barriers to friendship because there will always be competition and jealousy. I learned long ago not to compare myself to others. That is not to say that I can always do it but that I try to live that way. There will always be someone prettier, smarter, wealthier, a better mother, better business woman and so on. I strive to be better than I am. In setting that as a goal I am competing with only myself. I believe when we do that it is easier to share our struggles, our achievements and our failures with others and to truly share and connect. If under the guise of sharing you really want to show off then the barrier will not be broken down. I want to tear the barrier down.   Life is so much richer when it is genuinely and intimately shared – when we expose our vulnerabilities.

"What do you do for a living? Are you married? Do you have any children? How old are they? What do they do? Where are you from?" I approach friendship differently now. You see with the start of my new life in my new city I had promised myself that I would abandon my habit of interrogating people about their background, profession, education, etc. I used to have a list of questions in my head that I would go through in deciding whether this person was someone I would want to get to know better.   It was a very judgmental way of selecting "friends." I abandoned that checklist for a variety of reasons but primarily because it isn't a reliable indicator of who will be a good friend and who will not.

Sadly, after the questions were answered I would form judgments and put people into a box —make assumptions about them - based on those criteria. Now I want things to unfold in the present. I don't want to set limitations on friendships based on a person's past. I certainly do not want to be judged on the basis of my past life and mistakes. Who would want to be friends with someone who has been divorced twice and married three times? I don't want to be defined or limited by my past in her eyes or in mine. So I decided to abandon my checklist. I don't ask questions and I don't have to answer any.

When I was younger I would have thought that was so dishonest. How could I think it was right to hide my past from potential friends? I don't see it that way now. I am more than a compilation of my past experiences. I am not hiding something as much as I am avoiding having limitations and expectations placed on me based on my past.

I don't want to form friendships with only those who share my world view. Life becomes so stale when you interact only with people who think like you do. We middle agers tend to do that –stay within that narrow range we call our comfort zone. I think long term relationships aid in that process. They can make us lazy about seeking new friends and interests. We have our mate to meet our basic requirements and it is comfortable. I want to get out of my comfort zone and spend time with persons who have different interests, backgrounds and world views. It makes life so much richer. I love the diversity.

As I look over my life I often wonder "what if" I had pursued a certain close friendship or not pursued a certain close friendship. Would my life look any different now? What makes a friend? Are we inexorably drawn to other persons by unknown forces – spiritual forces we can't see or understand? Or can it simply be boiled down to science – we are compatible with certain persons for reasons that can be quantitatively and qualitatively enumerated. Can friendship grow where there is no instant connection? I can remember callously telling someone when I was much younger that friends are replaceable. I don't think that anymore at least not for certain types of friends. There is a mystery to friendships like all things in life. Oh sure there is a list of qualities we seek in a friend but in the end there is something more to it than meeting a list of qualifications.

"She is kind of bossy and she talks about herself all the time. She doesn't seem interested in hearing what is going on in anyone else's life. I don't want to spend any more time with her," I said to myself shortly after having lunch with a few new acquaintances.

Even with my resolve in my new life, I still almost let that initial impression close me off from a wonderful friendship. I have to constantly remind myself to recognize an initial impression as just that - nothing more. It takes time and patience to find new friends. We have so many layers to peel away.

"Welcome to the group. Please have a seat. We would like you to introduce yourself to the group after everyone arrives," the hostess said. But her eyes and tone of voice were not very welcoming. She kept looking at my clothing. I had worn a low V neck dress. The dress didn't reveal anything but it definitely gives the appearance that it does. I didn't intentionally wear that dress. It was very hot and it was a cool summer dress. I was looking for a group of people with whom I would want to spend time. My V neck dress was the perfect attire for that quest but I didn't know it at the time. I, with my V neck dress, was subjected to incredible looks of disdain and even disgust.

I returned for a few more meetings but I got the same reaction. I have found that the least friendly and most judgmental people are often found in churches. I never went back. I knew I wasn't wanted and I knew I didn't want to be with a group of people who judged me by what I wore. Just imagine if they knew my history! The group seemed genuinely concerned about the homeless, the rights of gays in the community but not concerned about welcoming a new individual into their group whose dress code they disagreed with. Sometimes it is harder to see our prejudices on an individual level.

Americans have such hangs up about sexuality! Apparently the puritan spirit still lives on. If you don't believe me try your own experiment. I will continue, occasionally, to wear a V neck dress to church and other functions!

Being connected to my adult children has made all the difference in my life. Those connections have been forged by time, patience, love, forgiveness, understanding, honesty and sharing. Because of those connections I can risk myself and put myself out there in hopes of developing other satisfying connections. Without my home base of unconditional love I couldn't do that. I need a safe place where I know I am loved. I have found my "home". I no longer feel lonely or alone. Oh I do on occasion but that is rare. I find myself feeling that way out of old habit and old fear. Being alone is not the same as being lonely although we tend to confuse the two in our society. We find our home in our connections to our family and our community. It can be a difficult pursuit but one that makes all the difference as to how fulfilling our lives will be. I hope you, the reader, have or can build such connections in your own life as I have in mine. It is a process and a journey but one in which the rewards far exceed any effort expended.

CHAPTER FOURTEEN

Where Do I Go From Here?

I am 55 years old. Most of my life is behind me now. I have spent the past 30 years working, raising children and at times, being married. My children are now all adults. They are settled into their lives and careers. I have been married more times than I care to remember. My "career" has been supremely unsatisfying and I have achieved whatever I am going to achieve in that "career". If I sound bitter I don't mean too. That can happen if I dwell too much on the events of the past. I don't want to do that. I want to focus on the present and to a smaller extent what lies ahead.

For the past few years the question has been haunting me "Where Do I Go From Here?" In finding an "answer" I felt compelled – driven -to look down every road not taken – lost loves, lost careers, lost jobs, lost friendships, lost opportunities, lost adventures. I guess I thought that reviewing my past choices and mistakes would help me chart a better path for the future – what little there is left. In fact, I started on a journey down some of those roads – only in my mind of course. I discovered there was some value in looking back and trying to find out why I made a particular choice. But, once I passed that point in my travels on "the road not taken" the journey was of little or no value. The journey became a total fabrication. It wasn't based on any facts but only on my speculations and fantasies. It went something like this: If I had married this person I would have been happy because… Fill in the blanks. I have absolutely no way of knowing if that conclusion is even remotely true. I didn't want to create a fictional journey or journey's end. That can't form a solid foundation on which to find the answer to the burning question "where do I go from here?" On this next part of the journey I want to travel on solid ground. So I stopped my journey down the roads not taken.

Instead I began a journey down the roads I have taken. They are lined with real events and real outcomes. I came to realize that dwelling on the roads not taken was just a diversion or distraction from the real task at hand –coming to terms with the roads I have taken in all their glory, all their pain and all their disappointment. I am grateful for the roads that brought me here no matter how impassable they might have seemed at times. This has been a difficult journey because of the outward events and my inner response to those events. The road(s) not travelled may not have brought me here and so I forever abandon my former obsession with imaging a journey down those roads of lost loves, lost friendships, lost opportunities, lost careers, lost adventures.

I imagine life as a huge ball of string rolling down the roads we have taken. We start out very small. As we roll along on our journey we pick up and discard pieces of string. The further and longer we roll along the more pieces of string we pick up. Eventually we have created this huge ball of string. Some pieces of the ball of string fit tightly together. Those are located more at the center of the ball of string. They form the core. As we move out from the center, pieces are less strongly attached until we reach the pieces on the periphery of the ball of string that are flying around only loosely attached. The strings on the outermost edge of the ball can become more solidly attached or they can be discarded. As I examine the entire ball of string created on my journey, I realize that I would definitely like to throw away certain pieces. But I recognize that the whole is a compilation of the individual strings. Each piece or string makes up the whole and the whole would not be the same without each piece. So I keep them all. And for those pieces that I am still not quite comfortable with there is always time to change and grow and therein lies the excitement of life. So much more lies ahead and now I have the solid core to ground me.

Through most of the years of my life I persevered believing that things would get better and they have. I made the best of challenging situations in my life, at times, but in the end that was not enough. I have learned that making it through is not the same as overcoming it. Overcoming something means coming to terms with it. That requires serious, thoughtful reflection and the willingness to see things and change them especially yourself. Getting through simply means gritting your teeth, putting your head down and persevering to the end. That may develop some character but it rarely leads to genuine growth. I spent too much of my life persevering and too little in "overcoming." For many years I confused the two. Now I understand the difference.

I feel as if I have arrived finally at a place that I love – physically, spiritually, emotionally and intellectually. (It is still a challenge to maintain that balance.) How do I want to spend the remainder of my years? They are very limited in number and I do not want to squander them. What have I acquired along this journey? I have acquired courage and freedom. The freedom was always there I am sure but I lacked the courage to exercise it until I reached this point in my life.

- Freedom from other's expectations of me;
- Freedom from concern with what others think of me;
- Freedom from the burden of pleasing others all the time;
- Freedom to please myself at least some of the time;
- Freedom from the limiting messages of my childhood;
- Freedom from my own confining self image;
- Freedom from having to act in conformity with that self image all the time;
- Freedom from defining myself as being a "good person";
- Freedom not to seek approval from everyone or to stop myself when I start;
- Freedom from the pain of the past;
- Freedom to believe in myself;
- Freedom to enjoy life in the absence of a monogamous relationship;
- Freedom from the negative messages that I am unlovable, that I don't deserve to be happy, that I have to earn love, that I have to suffer to be happy;
- Freedom to believe the good messages about myself;
- Freedom to not be dependable and responsible all the time;

- Freedom from always setting goals and working to get a result;
- Freedom to be present without any personal agenda but just to enjoy what is unfolding and to help others with what they might need from me;
- Freedom from the illusions of love and life;
- Freedom to set limits on others;
- Freedom to stop always putting others' feelings and needs before mine;
- Freedom to act as I want to even if others see it as silly or inappropriate for my age;
- Freedom to believe anything is possible;
- Freedom to trust and enjoy the intuitive and spiritual side of life;
- Freedom from defining myself by where I live, what I own, what I do for a living or what I have or have not accomplished;
- Freedom from judging others and myself all the time;
- Freedom to believe in myself;
- Freedom to show kindness and compassion without feeling like I am weak;
- Freedom to show kindness and compassion without feeling embarrassed;
- Freedom from the burden of being engaged in a productive activity all the time and feeling worthless if I am not;
- Freedom to enjoy the richness and diversity of human relationships rather than always seeking a "prescribed" attachment;
- Freedom from waiting for "it" to happen in the future so I can begin my life;
- Freedom from seeing life as an unending series of "have tos";
- Freedom to move through and enjoy different groups of people without losing myself;
- Freedom to forgive myself and others;
- Freedom to experience relationships unfettered by the constraints and limitations of too many expectations, especially old ones;
- Freedom from wishing things are other than they are;
- Freedom to be alone without being lonely;
- Freedom not to tone myself done so as to avoid offending others' notion of how a woman should act and/or be;
- Freedom to enjoy things as they are;

- Freedom to be more than the sum of all the parts;
- Freedom from the haunting imaginings and regrets of the road(s) not traveled.

I am, in the end, finally connected. I am connected to my family, my community, the world, my past, my future, my God. I am part of a whole. All of these connections are imperfect because I am imperfect. But I see in the good parts of these connections something that I want to and can build on. These are the stepping stones of my future journey.

When I find myself getting incredibly anxious, fearful or discouraged I close my eyes, stop all the noise and chatter in my head, and imagine I am in the presence of God. I know there are as many definitions of God as there are people who believe in Him. For me God has remained the deity of my childhood - the Christian God because I can find no fault with the teachings of Jesus Christ. His message of unconditional love, acceptance, forgiveness, mercy and on and resonates with me. I have discovered that true "safety" and peace lie only within me.

I have been sustained on this journey by my faith in God although I didn't always know it. He is my center – my touchstone. I have felt His presence, strength and love in my darkest hours. It is so very difficult to find words to explain spiritual matters. They are best experienced. I do believe there is something greater or more than just the world we see and our individual lives. I was able to tap into the connection to those things including God to give me the strength to get through Brian's illness and death. I have felt those things. We are part of something other than what we physically see and experience. There are things we simply can't understand or explain.

We are on a journey and each experience, good and bad, is part of that journey that propels us toward greater personal growth and hopefully spirituality. I don't believe in fate because that, to me, implies a lack of choice. I don't believe everything is decided for us or mapped out for us. We are presented with certain circumstances and we choose how to respond. There will be a price to pay for avoiding growth. It may only be in the inferior or unsatisfying quality of our lives and our connections.

My life has also been enriched by my faith. My faith has opened the door for me to see that everything – all that I have- is a gift. That allows me to enjoy and treasure those gifts like a young child treasures and enjoys a new toy at Christmas. Before I believed that I was entitled to certain things or I had earned certain things. Then when the thing was taken away or didn't materialize I would become angry, bitter, resentful or arrogant. I wanted things to be different than they were- the way I wanted them to be. Those attitudes poisoned my life. The poison spread through my life like the movement of the water when a small pebble is dropped into it.

I am acutely aware that we cannot control our outward circumstances. But we can control our responses to those circumstances. We can triumph over the adversity by not becoming bitter and angry. We don't celebrate that such adversity has happened. I certainly would not have chosen for Brian to die or my children to turn to drugs and alcohol. But I can choose to see my time with and love for him as a gift to be celebrated. I choose to focus on that part of the experience rather than the excruciatingly painful parts.

I don't believe God has created some great plan for my life. To believe that would make things easy for me. I believe that I have the freedom to make choices. To believe otherwise would absolve me of any responsibility for my mistakes and transgressions. It is in coming to terms with our mistakes and transgressions that we grow to become mature human beings. When we make the choices and control our actions we are forced to deal with the consequences of our actions including regrets, hurts, pain, the need for forgiveness of others and forgiveness of ourselves. That is the human experience. It is in those experiences that we feel most alive and it is those experiences that cause us to grow and mature.

I believe that something positive can come out of great suffering and tragedy if we arrive at the right attitude about it. That is not to say I seek out or wish for suffering or tragedy for myself or others. And certainly great tragedy exists that exceeds all reason like the type we see in places like Africa. (I can't speak to that level of suffering and tragedy.) We can acquire a new perspective on life through suffering and tragedy wherein we really learn to appreciate and enjoy all that we do have. We stop wanting something more or something different. Isn't one of the greatest sources of our unhappiness wishing things were different than they are?

It will be a challenge to maintain these ideals and principles and to be true to myself as I deal with the often pressing responsibilities of life. My old behaviors and attitudes have not disappeared. They never will. The difference is that, at this point in my life, I can usually catch myself engaging in these old behaviors or believing the old messages, very quickly and I can stop myself. I usually can forgive myself when I do so and I can usually apologize to others when I do so. Sadly, I find that those closest to me suffer through the worst parts of my personality. But precisely because they are close to me and I do love them I am forced to deal with those parts of myself. If I lived in a community where I was anonymous then I could persist in my resistance to change myself.

I feel that I have reclaimed the young girl that I was - the idealist and the romantic. She has been tempered by life. I have injected her with some pragmatism and realism. All the various parts of my personality that have been at war for years have finally come together and formed a cohesive whole. I no longer feel splintered. I have found balance within myself and learned to seek a balance in all things. I have found the love of and joy in life.

I have a solid foundation – my family. I am deeply connected to my children. We forged our connections on our journey together through the experiences we shared. Connections are so very difficult. They require so much of us! But they are so rewarding! When we share with each other we connect to each other. During the most difficult parts of the journey we couldn't connect. We had much to forgive each other for at the end of certain parts of the journey. In living through good and difficult experiences together, healing together and forgiving each other we formed a bond. We have shared our thoughts, our feelings and our lives. As we go forward, our individuality enriches the whole but we keep our focus on what we have in common, not what separates us? We share a special and unique bond. That bond grounds us. We have been able to build on the strength of that bond to forge other connections.

The love and support of my adult children has given me the courage to grow and exercise these new freedoms. Oh the confidence born of my life's experiences has helped but that alone, in the absence of their love and support, would not have given me the courage I needed. I feel empowered to be who I want to be, not just a reflection of what is expected of me. I can make choices knowing that my family will still love me whether I succeed or fail. Is there a better gift we can give one another than being loved and accepted for who we really rather than what they want us to be or imagine us to be? We can't earn this kind of love. It is a gift. This love of my family is my safety net. It reminds me of the net underneath the high wire trapeze. In our attempts to soar to greater heights we may fall but always to the safety of the love of our family which will then bounce us back to even greater heights.

I hope my children feel the same about what I provide for them. That is not to say we do not challenge each other on inappropriate behavior and other things. It just means we will love each other even if we behave inappropriately on occasion. We help each other to be the best we can be in all areas. We are all a work in progress but in the end we love each other for who were are. We are deeply connected to each other. And I am deeply connected to God.

When we connect to others we think about and care about more than ourselves and our own self-interest. When we connect with others we think and care about the good of our family, our community, our country, our world. We become concerned for the greater good – the good of all mankind. This book is my attempt to connect with you the reader. I hope it may help you to examine your own lives and in some small way to help you to find meaningful and fulfilling connections in your own lives.

I used to think that when I had enough money, enough activities, enough companionship, enough love I would feel secure and safe. That is a myth. Our safety and security lies within each of us. It is comprised of our faith in something greater than ourselves and in the confidence that, with that faith and connection, we can overcome any obstacles and even flourish in spite of them. We can and will triumph. Wallace Stegner's book, "Crossing to Safety" drove this point home to me.

I don't know what lies ahead for me in terms of the events that will happen in my life. I remind myself not to take anything for granted. I remind myself to be grateful for and treasure all that I do have. I will enjoy my new found freedoms. I will enrich the connections I do have. I will seek stronger and new connections to my family, community, country, God and world. I want to show my gratitude for all that I have and all that I have been given by giving to others. I will seek and I hope find ways to, in some small way, make this world a better place for my having been here. I hope this book is the first part of that new journey. It is up to you the reader to decide if, in writing this book, I have started on my new journey.